Chicken Soup for the Soul®

All You Need Is Love

Chicken Soup for the Soul: All You Need Is Love
101 Tales of Romance and Happily Ever After
Amy Newmark

Published by Chicken Soup for the Soul, LLC www.chickensoup.com
Copyright ©2023 by Chicken Soup for the Soul, LLC. All Rights Reserved.

The publisher gratefully acknowledges the many publishers and individuals who granted Chicken Soup for the Soul permission to reprint the cited material.

Front cover photo of heart courtesy of iStockphoto.com (©Studio Light and Shade), photo of beach courtesy of iStockphoto.com (©Oleandra9), photos of blue flip flop courtesy of iStockphoto.com (©DawnPoland), photos of orange flip flop courtesy of iStockphoto.com (©Serhii Tsyhanok)
Back cover and interior photo of couple courtesy of iStockphoto.com (©SHansche)
Photo of Amy Newmark courtesy of Susan Morrow at SwickPix

Cover and Interior by Daniel Zaccari

Publisher's Cataloging-in-Publication data

Names: Newmark, Amy, editor.
Title: Chicken soup for the soul : all you need is love / Amy Newmark.
Description: Cos Cob, CT: Chicken Soup for the Soul, LLC, 2023.
Identifiers: LCCN: 2023932175 | ISBN: 978-1-61159-102-6 (print) | 978-1-61159-339-6 (ebook)
Subjects: LCSH Love--Literary collections. | Love--Anecdotes. | Dating (Social customs) Literary collections. | Dating (Social customs)--Anecdotes. | Marriage--Literary collections. | Marriage--Anecdotes. | BISAC SELF-HELP / Motivational and Inspirational | SELF-HELP / Personal Growth / Happiness
Classification: LCC PN6071.L7 C38 2023 | DDC 810.8/02/03543--dc23

Library of Congress Control Number: 2023932175

PRINTED IN THE UNITED STATES OF AMERICA
on acid∞free paper

30 29 28 27 26 25 24 23   01 02 03 04 05 06 07 08 09

Chicken Soup for the Soul.

All You Need Is Love

101 Tales of Romance and Happily Ever After

Amy Newmark

Chicken Soup for the Soul, LLC
Cos Cob, CT

Changing lives one story at a time®
www.chickensoup.com

Table of Contents

❶

~The Dating Game~

❷

~Man of My Dreams~

❸
~Meant to Be~

❹
~Keeping Love Alive~

❺

~Never Too Late~

❻

~Take the Risk~

❼

~That's Amore~

❽

~Believe in Miracles~

❾

~Love that Doesn't Die~

The Dating Game

Written for Love

When we find someone who is brave, fun, intelligent,
and loving, we have to thank the universe.
~Maya Angelou

On Sunday, October 9, 1994, I was dragged to a Detroit Lions football game by my father. His buddy had bailed on him at the last minute, and my mother had other plans. So, that left me.

I was seventeen years old, and I brought two things with me to the game: my signature brand of teenage sarcasm and an issue of *Seventeen* magazine — because that's how we passed the time in the era that pre-dated smart phones. I could have thought of a million and one places I would rather have been that day.

Only ten years later would I come to realize the significance of this date and how it would change my life forever.

I had always loved to write. When I was eight, I "published" my first lifestyle magazine, a creation comprised of an entire roll of Scotch tape and two steno pads I pilfered from my dad's home office. To this day, the three issues are still in my possession. They, along with several issues of *The Explorer*, the high-school newspaper for which I was editor-in-chief, are tucked inside a box in the basement.

Many years later, in 2000, I found myself living more than 900 miles from home in South Carolina while I worked as an on-air reporter at a CBS affiliate. Often anxiety-ridden and homesick, I grew ever more dependent on the act of writing as a much-needed cathartic release.

I wrote an entire children's book one afternoon in the time it took to down three lattes at my favorite café in Five Points. The next day, I illustrated a makeshift cover and printed a prototype copy at a local Kinko's. It pacified me to hold a hard copy in my hands. In the months that followed, I queried countless literary agents.

I was certain my book would become The Next Big Thing. But when, over time, the ratio of rejection letters to junk mail became 3-to-1, I relinquished hope, and my lone copy took its rightful place in the dark, dusty abyss under my bed with my other past writing ventures.

Fast-forward to the fall of 2004.

I was back home in Michigan and working for my local government-access channel as a content creator, which meant that a typical day could include myriad tasks — including taking photos of a meet-and-greet between the mayor and a local resident at City Hall. She had, ironically, just published her own tome about her tenure as a den mother at my college alma mater. She brought her publisher with her that day, and at the end of the meeting, something occurred to me: I was inhabiting the same airspace as a book publisher.

This chance may never come again, I thought.

I pushed aside my apprehension and literally chased down the publisher in the parking lot. I told her I had written a children's book and asked whether she'd like to read it.

"Sure, I never turn down an opportunity to read new work," Marian said. Then she gave me her business card and invited me to her office the next evening.

On cloud nine, I floated to my car and swore I heard cherubs playing harps in the clouds above.

This could be the turning point, I thought. *This is going to change everything.*

And it did — but not nearly in the way that I had believed.

Twenty-four hours later, with my dusty prototype in hand, I waited nervously for Marian in the cozy lobby of her office. I tried my best to ignore the fact that my stomach was doing flip-flops as I perused the framed book covers that lined the walls. When Marian finally greeted me, I felt in my bones that everything I had written up to this point had led me to this precise moment.

And it had — but, again, not nearly in the way that I had believed.

About five minutes into our chat — before I had even handed over my book — Marian made my head spin with a question straight out of left field.

"Are you single?" she asked.

Flabbergasted, I managed to reply in the affirmative. "But… why?"

Marian scurried off and returned with a photo in hand. There were three people in it: Marian, Football Hall of Famer and former Detroit Lions running back Barry Sanders, and a man I didn't recognize.

"Scott," Marian said as she pointed to the man I didn't know. "His name is Scott Conover. And I think you two would be perfect together. He's a client of mine. He also wrote a children's book — after he retired from the NFL. He played with the Detroit Lions from 1991 until 1996."

I would later realize that Scott was indeed on the field — as a starting offensive lineman — during the game I attended with my father back in 1994.

But I hadn't connected the dots during my sit-down with Marian. All I knew was that I had zero aspirations to date an NFL player. Weren't they all flirtatious partygoers? I mean, I didn't know any personally. But that's what I had come to believe. No, thank you.

When I politely declined, Marian persisted. She told me that Scott was a graduate of Purdue University, had a passion for philanthropy, had never been married and didn't have any children — although he wanted to someday. An avid reader, he'd founded a children's foundation in an effort to promote and encourage literacy among underprivileged youth.

Marian continued, "A fundraiser is planned for his foundation next Saturday. Black tie. You should come. I'll tell him you're my guest."

Well, gee, I thought, *perhaps I should at least meet him.*

And so I did.

On Saturday, October 9, 2004, ten years to the day after I watched him play at the Pontiac Silverdome, I came face-to-face with the man who, after a three-year courtship, would become my husband on July 7, 2007. (Sidebar: We were married by the mayor — who had since become a judge — whom I had met on that fateful day at city hall.)

Was this all just one giant coincidence? I prefer to believe there are none.

I do, however, believe in a higher power who arranges circumstances and happenings in a way that defies logic.

Today, eleven years of marriage and two beautiful children later, Scott and I still regale our friends — and each other — with the grandiose plans we envisioned for our respective books. Scott had once set his sights on a nationwide book tour; I had hoped for soaring book sales and my name on a bestseller list.

In the end, our books produced none of the above.

But they were written to bring us both a love we never knew was possible.

And what could possibly be greater than that?

— Courtney Conover —

The Question

Love is not finding someone to live with.
It's finding someone you can't live without.
~Rafael Ortiz

The year was 1988. My boyfriend and I had known each other more than two years. We'd even met each other's parents. It was the summer after we finished grad school. Chris and I had mentioned marriage a few times, but I had said honestly I wasn't ready. His friends advised him that if I didn't want to marry him that he should move on. But still he waited.

It is odd to realize that a misdialed (or perhaps crank) phone call set our lives down their current path. On a crowded Friday afternoon, I struggled through rush hour to dinner at my parents' house. Before leaving, I had called my parents to tell them I was on my way. This was something I never did. I tried to avoid road rage as traffic crawled along.

Everything turned upside-down when I arrived at the house. Hesitantly, my parents gave me the news. Chris's mother had called them shortly after I had. She had received a call informing her that her son and his girlfriend had been killed in a car crash.

I sat, stunned. Chris was at work, which was why he hadn't come with me. Maybe he'd had to drive somewhere. Maybe a co-worker was with him. It made no sense. I sobbed as I realized that this was the man I wanted to spend the rest of my life with.

Before I could get my own thinking together enough to call him at work just to check, his mother called us. She had finally been in touch with him. It was a false alarm. Relief flooded through me. It didn't matter how upset Chris was that his mother had yelled at him as if it were his fault she'd believed the story of an unknown caller. I was just glad that he was still around.

And then it occurred to me that Chris had tested the waters several times to see if I would accept if he proposed. My answers had not been encouraging, but it meant that he wanted to marry me and was willing to wait around.

I tried bringing it up again to let him know I was ready to say "yes," but I just couldn't figure out how. Tact had never been one of my fortes. He was completely unhelpful in all of this. He didn't understand because all through that fateful afternoon, he'd been hard at work at his office. Nothing earthshattering had happened.

The only way we were ever going to get engaged was if I turned the tables and proposed to him. To make sure he knew I was serious, I decided to get a ring. Trying to figure out what kind of ring to give a guy while I proposed was nearly impossible. There were no guidelines, no tradition. I remembered he liked onyx and ordered a custom ring.

Finally, ring in hand, I had to decide the how and when. Chris was not a romantic. I didn't want to set something up and have him think I was expecting a proposal. Once I had that ring, I was the one who was going to do the proposing. I envisioned returning to the restaurant of our first date, but realized that I didn't want to ask him in public.

Unable to stand the stress and suspense any longer, I nervously pulled out the box with the ring one evening while I was at his place, still unsure of exactly what I was going to say.

"Yes," he said, seeing the box.

"I didn't even ask you anything."

He put on the ring. "Yes, I'll marry you." It was as if he'd been waiting all this time for me to pop the question.

A short time later, he got me an engagement ring—I actually got to pick it out. We set a date, and everything else followed all of those typical wedding traditions. Just because we found our way to the path of engagement and married life a little differently didn't mean that we couldn't hope for a happily ever after, just like everyone else.

— D.B. Zane —

3

5,000 Bachelors and Me

Nothing defines humans better than their willingness
to do irrational things in the pursuit of phenomenally
unlikely payoffs. This is the principle behind
lotteries, dating, and religion.
~Scott Adams

Sixty and single. That wasn't how I'd planned to spend my life. Now I either had to start dating, spend the rest of my life alone, or get a bunch of cats and become the weird cat woman. I decided to start dating.

At sixty, it is nearly impossible to meet eligible bachelors so I tried Internet dating. I saw an ad that promised there were five thousand single men in my age group in my zip code area. This was going to be a piece of cake! I had five thousand lonely men to choose from! I filled out the very long application form online, answering questions about my favorite color, favorite movie and favorite food, etc. When I was finished and submitted my answers, a large banner appeared on the computer screen saying, "We're sorry, but you are incompatible with all of our clients." They refused my membership and didn't want my $29.95 a month dues. I'd been rejected by five thousand lonely, desperate men in five minutes!

Finding someone to date was going to be a little harder than I'd expected.

There was a big community Christmas party coming up. I wanted to go but I didn't want to go alone because there was going to be a dance afterward with music from the 1940s and 1950s and I love to dance.

The only bachelor I knew was Owen. He was a nice man but he was shorter than me and had a very thin, sparse moustache that he filled in with an eyebrow pencil. He also had an artificial knee that sometimes clicked when he walked.

I decided Owen was going to be my date for the Christmas party but I knew he was fairly shy and it would be up to me to ask him to be my date. I hadn't asked a man for a date since I was twenty. It felt awkward when I was twenty, and it felt even more awkward now that I was sixty. At least Owen wouldn't reject me like those other five thousand men had.

But he did.

"Oh, I'd love to take you to the party, but I already have a date," he said.

Owen, with his drawn on moustache and clicking knee had a date. I'd broken a record. In one week I'd been rejected by 5,001 men!

Two days before the party, Owen called and said the woman he'd planned to take to the party had to attend her aunt's funeral in Texas and now he was free to take me. I was sorry the woman's aunt had passed away, and I was sorry someone had to die before I could have a date, but at least I was going to the Christmas party!

I bought a new red dress, new black heels and a black lace shawl to sling over my shoulder in case I had the opportunity to tango. Before the date I put on make-up, sprayed my hair so it would stay in place, and put on my favorite perfume, called Wicked Woman. I looked in the mirror and decided for a woman my age I looked fantastic! Well, if not fantastic, at least pretty good.

Owen picked me up and when I got into the car I noticed two things immediately.

Owen had not only drawn on his moustache, but in honor of the occasion, he'd drawn on heavier eyebrows too, but he'd arched them so much that he looked perpetually surprised. If he'd connected the line over his nose, it would have looked like there was a giant "M" drawn over his eyes.

Hey, I still had a date for the party so I wasn't going to be picky.

Owen was very impressed by how glamorous I looked. He started breathing heavily as soon as I sat next to him in the car. In fact, I looked so fabulous, I took his breath away!

I really did take his breath away.

Owen gasped out, "Your perfume... allergic... asthma… hospital. Can't breathe!"

We traded places and I put the windows down and drove him to the emergency room.

While the staff was working on him, I went to the ladies room and washed off my perfume and make-up and tried to brush the spray out of my hair. I joined him in his room and sat with him. There didn't seem to be much to talk about. I'd nearly killed him and he ruined my chance to go to the Christmas party.

He urged me to take a cab and go to the party without him but it seemed a little tacky to leave him stretched out on a gurney while he was wearing an oxygen mask.

An hour later he felt well enough to drive me home.

We said goodnight, knowing we would never attempt a date with each other again. Once you almost kill a man, you don't get asked for a second date.

I looked at the clock; the dance would be starting now. I put on some music and danced around the living room by myself.

I won't give up... I want to love and to be loved. I don't want to spend the rest of my life alone. Just because five thousand men rejected me and just because I nearly killed the only man who did agree to take me out (but only after someone else died), that doesn't mean I should give up hope.

I believe every kettle has a lid.

I believe in love.

— Holly English —

Speed Dating

When you're open to receiving them,
the possibilities just keep on coming.
~Oprah Winfrey

dging toward my sixtieth birthday, I realized that I had been divorced longer than I'd been married. And even though I had been engaged twice in that span, I finally came to realize that I was going to be just fine as a single woman "of a certain age."

It was actually rather liberating to let go of the desperate need to find a man to "complete" me.

I had a great career with a private practice in a prestigious clinic. My dream condo had a spare bedroom and bath for my children and their families to sleep over on holidays. My free time was filled with live jazz and art events with good friends, as well as some volunteer activity for my church.

Then, on a rainy weeknight, a business acquaintance called asking for a favor. She and her husband had consulted me for marketing advice for their dating business. Now they needed another woman to even out the numbers for a speed-dating event at a local restaurant. Right away. They even offered to waive the entry fee and buy me a drink!

Hmm, let's see, I thought. *Leftovers and watch some mindless sitcom or a night out for free on a Thursday?*

It didn't take me long to refresh my make-up, spritz on some perfume and say goodbye to the cat.

Now, the way speed dating works is this: Each person gets a name badge with only their first name and a code number. There were fourteen guests: seven men and seven women. All had been pre-screened and were single, available to date, and between the ages of forty-five and sixty.

The ladies sat at high-top tables for two. Every seven minutes, a timer would ding, and the men would move to the next table. Each person had a pad for taking notes. We were allowed to ask about hobbies, favorite date ideas, pets, occupation and general niceties. But we were not permitted to ask for last names, addresses, phone numbers or exact age.

If the woman wanted to know more about the man, she could write his name and number on her pad and submit that request at the end of the event. And if the same man had also submitted an interest in getting to know her, that was considered a "go." The planner would supply the gentleman with the lady's telephone number and suggest he call her to invite her to lunch or coffee.

Well, out of seven men, I asked to meet four guys. And there were five men who wanted to know more about me, including the four I was interested in. So, I had four potential dates.

The first man talked almost two hours on the phone the very next night. After what felt like a friendly job interview, he decided that I was too busy with my family to devote enough time to him. Fine! So long.

The second gentleman was an art professor. We had a lovely lunch, and he invited me to the open-air theater. Since the show changes every two weeks, this was a safe bet for an easy first date. Shirley, a family friend, worked at the concession stand, and I trusted her character judgment. She scowled as soon as he approached her cash register with a thumbs-down. I still cannot recall the play, but I know it seemed like the night would never end. He was so nervous that he talked through the entire show!

The third man was rather quiet and shy, so I offered the summer theater idea again. I was eager to walk this handsome fellow with the easy laugh right up to the snack counter. I ordered popcorn and a diet soda. Shirley took one look at his rosy cheeks and neatly trimmed beard and flashed him a big smile with a thumbs-up! I felt my shoulders relax as we laughed and enjoyed the show. Kenny was so easy to be with that I didn't want the evening to end.

But when this handsome farmer from Topeka asked me out for another date, I had to be honest and say, "Maybe."

I explained that there was one more guy on my list for a coffee date from the speed-dating night.

Kenny just looked down at his shoes and said softly, "Okay."

I asked how many ladies were left on his list. His face turned bright red as he looked into my eyes and said, "Well, you're the only one I wanted to see again."

Yikes, I thought, *no pressure here!*

Kenny looked so sad. I agreed that I would call him right after the last man's date and promised to tell him the truth about a second date for us. He seemed slightly encouraged, but we parted with just a handshake.

The fourth guy took me to see the last play of the season, but he was more interested in the snack bar than me or the show! My friend was laughing as he kept adding items to his order. He acted like we were about to go on a cross-country journey, not watch a two-hour, open-air play. After enduring his lip-smacking and greasy fingers on the arm of my chair, I politely declined his offer for dinner the next night, telling him that I really wasn't looking for daily dinner dates. I guess he was just as happy to move down his list of women.

After my date dropped me off, knowing that Kenny worked the night shift anyway, I couldn't wait to call my "Lucky #3 Guy" and tell him that he was the one for me.

He asked me if I'd like to see a new movie, a controversial docu-drama, and when I instantly agreed, I think we were both surprised.

I just kept thinking that this farmer dude was not a braggart, not a foodie and certainly not like the rude, middle-aged guys I'd met who truly were "just after one thing."

After our movie date, Kenny suggested we grab a bite to eat. I was so relieved because I really didn't want to have to wait another week or so for a next date! As we walked to The Cheesecake Factory, we talked about the film and realized we think alike in politics.

"Wait," I said. "Are you a Democrat in Kansas?"

And with that smile that I've come to adore, he quietly replied, "I sure am."

"And I was the only woman you asked to see again at the speed dating?" I added.

He replied softly, "I saw your eyes light up when you looked up at me, and I thought, 'Wow! I finally got a pretty one.' Why would I look for anyone else?"

I was at a loss for words.

But I was pretty sure that warm glow around my heart was new-found love.

And I was right.

—Valorie Fenton—

Experiment

*All life is an experiment. The more
experiments you make the better.*
~Ralph Waldo Emerson

y freshman year of college, I experimented. But not in the
sense that would make most parents squeamish. In high
school, I found my niche. I had a set group of friends, I was
a member of clubs, I was a part of sports teams, I wrote for
publications, and I felt comfortable knowing I had a place I belonged.

In college, I entered as a guppy in a sea of students who meant
nothing to me. In this new world, I was undefined, and I immediately
searched for a place where I fit in. I tried out for the cheerleading squad,
to no avail. I tried out for the dance team and left tryouts intimidated.
So I moved on to Plan C. Second semester of freshman year I decided to
take a swing dancing class. I wanted to meet new people and I figured
what better way to do so than in a completely forced social setting. This
was the best decision I made throughout my college years — next to
refraining from going out and drinking that Tuesday night before my big
test, and deciding not to spend the night with the fraternity boy who
asked me to his formal.

Swing dance class met every Tuesday and Thursday in the basement
of the university gymnasium. I could not have been more nervous — a
little freshman, unsure of what to wear for swing class, what shoes to
bring, or who my classmates would be. I didn't know the first thing about
swing dancing. The class consisted of about seven girls and four boys,

one of whom caught my eye. Standing at 6'2" in his jeans, tight T-shirt, and sneakers, I knew I had seen him before but I couldn't place him. Then I realized that he was in my communications class the previous semester. He was the outspoken one who sat in the middle of my row and was always on his laptop. I remembered being impressed by him and his quick, witty responses when the teacher called on the student least likely to be paying attention. That was how I remembered Eamon Brennan. The story of how we fell in love is much more remarkable.

Swing class began with the choice of a partner. Rather than being forward and running over to the cute boy to ask him to dance, I waited on the side of the room to be selected. Unfortunately, one of the socially awkward boys in the corner decided to make his way over to me and asked if I'd be his partner. As I glanced at Eamon, who had made eye contact with me, I felt the urge to say "I'd rather dance with the sexy boy over there..." but instead I said, "Sure."

Luckily, I soon found out you switch partners, moving clockwise after every count of eight. Three partners later, I was in Eamon's arms... literally. We officially introduced ourselves and danced as if we had been friends, maybe even more, for years and years. Our eyes locked and even when we weren't partners we made eye contact across the room. Our secret glances were betrayed by the mirrored walls, and the chemistry could be felt across the room. Two or three weeks went by with us exchanging flirtatious glances, and one night after class Eamon asked if he could walk me home. I ecstatically accepted and so began our series of dates.

Eamon and I have been dating for nearly two years now and my college experience has been greatly shaped by my decision to take that swing dance class.

I wasn't looking to find love when I enrolled in a swing dance class and I wasn't looking to find a lifelong hobby. I was exploring my options. The best advice I can give a college student is to experiment. Don't experiment with sex, drugs, and rock and roll—but experiment with the things that will matter in ten years. Experiment with the things that help you find your own current in a sea of swimming fish.

—Jamie Miles—

Damaged Goods

The only sure thing about luck is that it will change.
~Wilson Mizner

When you are over sixty, it is hard to find someone to date. In fact, it is nearly impossible.

I asked my friends to introduce me to their brothers, cousins, neighbors, anyone, but according to them, they didn't know any unmarried men. I didn't believe them and suspected they were hoarding all the single men for themselves.

I had joined clubs, gone to lectures, volunteered for practically everything, tried sports I hated, visited different church senior singles events and checked out the Internet. Nothing had worked. I think the last time I had a date Reagan was President. Okay, I could be wrong about that, but it had been a while.

My friend, Marsha, started dating a very nice man and was annoyingly happy. She said she'd met him at the grocery store between the carrots and green peppers. By the time they reached the checkout, he'd asked her for a date.

Well, that might be fine for Marsha, but I was hoping for something a little more romantic, like meeting him in a field of daisies or seeing each other across a crowded room and experiencing love at first sight.

Sometimes, you can wake up on a perfectly ordinary morning and feel like something wonderful is going to happen to you.

Thursday morning I woke up, went into the kitchen to make my coffee and promptly turned around and hit the left side of my face on a cupboard door that had swung back open. It only took a few minutes before my eye was black, puffy and nearly swollen shut. It also kept tearing up so that I had to keep dabbing at it to keep it from leaking down my face.

I also had a root canal scheduled that morning and the tooth happened to be on the left side of my face. The dentist was so repulsed by the way my eye looked that he laid a paper towel across my eye so he wouldn't have to look at it. He said he did it to protect my eye, but I think it was because he was repulsed.

After the root canal I decided I'd better stop at the store on my way home and get some soft food to eat that night. I was bending over the frozen dinners trying to find something that would require very little chewing when a man stopped beside me on my right side. I glanced up at him with my right eye. He was tall, in my age range, and wasn't wearing a ring.

"It's hard to find a frozen dinner that tastes better than the box it came in," he said. "When you live alone, it really isn't worth trying to cook a meal."

"Yes, you're right," I said. I'm a brilliant conversationalist.

"I get tired of frozen dinners but it's no fun to go out and eat alone. Sometimes it would be nice just to have someone to have dinner with once a week," he smiled.

My mind was racing. He's nice, he's tall, he's mentioned twice he is single. Marsha was right! You could meet a man in the grocery store. This was my lucky day!

"Yes, it would be wonderful to have someone to have dinner with, someone to talk to." I stood upright and turned to face him.

He stared at me.

"Oh, I'm so sorry, were you in an accident?" he asked.

I reached into my purse and took out my compact. My eye was black, swollen shut, and leaking tears. My jaw was the size of a baseball from the root canal and I was drooling just a little from the corner of my mouth because my lips were numb and swollen.

I looked like I should be ringing a bell in a tower. The only thing missing was a hunch on my back and the day wasn't over yet.

"I've had a bad day." I started to explain that I didn't always look like this but he was already backing away.

"Try the roast beef dinner; it's pretty good," he said and pushed his cart down the aisle as quickly as he could.

I decided to accidentally bump into him at the checkout to explain why I looked hideous but he was too clever. When I reached the tea and coffee aisle I saw his abandoned cart. He'd left without his bananas, onions and bread.

Well, his loss. He'd left behind his groceries and possibly the great love of his life. If all he cared about was superficial looks, then he wasn't the right man for me anyway. In another week my eye wouldn't be black and leaking and my cheek wouldn't be swollen and I wouldn't be drooling and even if I ran into him in the store again, I wouldn't speak to him. After all, I have my pride!

I think I'll call Marsha and ask her where she buys her groceries.

— April Knight —

Shortcut to Disaster

When we can begin to take our failures non-seriously,
it means we are ceasing to be afraid of them. It is of
immense importance to learn to laugh at ourselves.
~Katherine Mansfield

n 1974, my college campus was filled with uniformly "noncon-forming" males and females clad in T-shirts and worn jeans. Against that backdrop, Luis's entrance into my film class was nothing short of revolutionary.

With all the confidence of John Travolta's swagger in *Saturday Night Fever*, Luis invaded my world. His thick, dark hair had an impressive sheen that hinted at professional care, and his bright hazel eyes offered intensity rarely glimpsed in the frat boys who surrounded me. He offered his 500-watt, whiter-than-white smile like a movie star.

His starched white shirt seemed tailor-made and his slim black pants and leather shoes completed the outfit that set him 180 degrees apart from his classmates. I found myself staring helplessly. He looked like the hero from the cover of a romance novel. Instantly, I decided that I would become his real-life love interest.

After class, I managed to "accidentally" bump into him in the quad. He seemed as eager as I was to begin a conversation. Over an orange freeze, I learned that he was a foreign-exchange student from Guadalajara, Mexico.

His family owned a plantation there. This explained his style of dress and added one more thing to my list of adorable Luis traits: his softly accented voice.

All went well between us, and soon we were dating steadily. Language was no barrier as he was determined to perfect his English.

We might have lived happily ever after if his three sisters, who spoke little English, hadn't decided to visit. By that time, I was madly in love with Luis and determined to make a good impression on his family. The only problem was that I was too busy with my classes and part-time job to take a Spanish class. Instead, I decided to take the Spanish-English cognate shortcut.

I discovered that I could add a vowel to the end of many American words and voilà! Instantly, it became Spanish. Thus active was *activo*, ranch was *rancho*, habit was *habito*, and abrupt was *abrupto*. I should also have known that stupid was *estupido*, and I was about to become an *estupendo estupido* very *rapido!*

When his sisters arrived, I was invited to dinner at Luis's apartment. I thought the dinner went well since the three girls continually returned my friendly smiles. Little was said, and no one seemed to find the silence awkward.

Then Luis excused himself from the table to go to the restroom. Though his absence couldn't have exceeded two minutes, the companionable silence we'd enjoyed throughout the meal took an ominous turn. With three sets of eyes focused on me, I felt compelled to speak.

I chose to play it safe by simply complimenting the fine meal they'd made. "*Me gusta dinero*," I said, beaming at each girl in turn.

The gentle traces of their former smiles completely evaporated with my final syllable. The oldest folded her arms across her chest in the international symbol for contempt.

Confused, I decided to try again. This time, with feeling and enthusiasm, I repeated in a slightly stronger voice, "*Me GUSTA dinero!*"

Three pairs of angry eyes stared me down as Luis re-entered the room. Loyal to his family, he looked at me suspiciously.

"What did you do?" he asked evenly.

"I just complimented your sisters on this delicious dinner," I uttered weakly, suddenly questioning my limited Spanish vocabulary.

"*¿Cuál es el problema?*" Luis addressed his sisters.

All pretenses of quiet, serene, demure little ladies were gone now. The three spoke at once, each managing to point an accusing finger at me to punctuate some aspect of their diatribe.

Near tears, I pleaded with Luis to tell me what I'd done to offend his sisters.

"You told them that you like money. They say you're a gold miner."

"That's gold digger," I corrected lamely as if this minor distinction would win anyone over to my side.

I can't say that this ended my relationship with Luis, but things were never quite the same between us after that fateful night. My social faux pas may have robbed me of my fairy-tale ending, but it also served as a valuable lesson. It was always the shortcuts that got me in trouble.

— Marsha Porter —

Marry Her Off!

*Family is a treasure chest worth more
than a mountain of gold.*
~Author Unknown

For years, I avoided dating like the plague. I was the type of person to give 110% in love and life and I decided not to date around casually. I reasoned that my heart was too fragile, and I was busy traveling the world. I also never found anyone interesting enough to bring home.

This just wouldn't do for my big Italian family. After one of my younger sisters married early, the family started looking to me. Why wasn't I even in a relationship? Better yet, what could they do to change that?

Dad was the first in the family to break the silence. On one of our father/daughter coffee dates, Dad got straight to the point. "Have you been seeing anyone?" This had become routine questioning in an effort to help me find a man. I had crafted a reply that seemed to satisfy my family's curiosity, but this time was different.

With furrowed brow, he followed it up with, "Well, if you are waiting for my permission to date, you know you have it. How are you going to meet anyone if you don't date around?"

"Thanks, Dad, but that's not what's going on here," I said. As I tried to explain that I was happily single right now, something dawned on me.

Perhaps more than marrying me off, my dad was looking for

reinforcements in a son-in-law. Our estrogen-dominated family was getting the best of him. While he had two sons, he also had three vocal daughters who were much like their mother in various ways. I'm sure the thought of another couple of sons-in-law was his only hope.

Next it was Mom who had a hard time understanding why I hadn't met the right one. So she reasoned her way through my singleness.

"You know, some people like the same gender," she said casually to me one day. "Not everyone likes the opposite sex. Don't worry, we will love whomever you bring home, no matter what."

At first, I didn't get it. Then I realized she thought I was a closet lesbian. After I reassured her that I do in fact like men, she was relentless in trying to set me up.

Mom just couldn't resist the cute cashier at Costco. "My daughter is single," she would say to him in front of me. "She loves to travel, and she…." Her voice would fade as I walked away inconspicuously with my sisters. Then she would find us and say, "He's a babe alert. Don't you think? What about him?"

In her defense, Mom loved my dad very much. She had shared that love with five children, and she just wanted me to find the same kind of happiness that she found in life. Her desire for more grandbabies was also a motivation, I'm sure.

The most epic moment was when my brother called me with urgent news.

"Sis, I just want you to know that Mom and your sister are setting up an eHarmony account for you," John said. "It's not cool that you have no idea what they're doing."

I laughed out loud.

"Wait, what?" I said. I could hardly believe it. "Are you kidding me right now?"

"No, I just left her house, and they're checking out your matches," he said. Later, I found out both my sisters were there with Mom.

"I really don't think she's going to like what we're doing," my other sister said. Somehow, her voice was drowned out in the excitement.

To this day, I have no idea what they put on my profile page. Matches were chosen by eHarmony based on my profile. What information did they include? Which pictures did they use?

I could hardly believe my potential love life was now unfolding in their hands.

At my brother's suggestion, I called them back and played a prank. I pretended that I had a dream they were at my sister's house, and they had set up an eHarmony profile. For a quick minute, they were fooled. But it didn't last long.

Once they figured out that my brother had let me in on their little secret, they pleaded shamelessly with me.

"Come on, Jenny, what's the harm?" said my mom. "This guy's profile says he lives in Huntington Beach, and his passion is Jesus!"

Who were these people? Oh, yes, my crazy but very well meaning family.

Mom knew I loved the beach, and at the time I wasn't living too far from there. She knew that my faith was important to me. I think she was hoping her words would seal the deal. Sorry, Mom. I just wasn't ready.

A few years prior to this incident, I was engaged to a good man but for various reasons I had reservations about my decision. Although I hadn't told anyone at that point, my brother made it very clear that he wasn't at all impressed and didn't think I would go through with the engagement. He told me flat-out, "You won't marry him." And, for various reasons, I actually didn't.

Looking back now, I'm thankful for all of my family's love and support, even if it was shown in different ways. They tried to figure out why I was still single. Deep down, they worried about me. They wanted to see me happy and in love.

Today, I'm happily married to a man I met on a dating site, and my brother approves. He let our wedding guests know at the reception, too. In front of hundreds gathered for the day, my brother's toast to the new couple went something like this. "This guy is way better than the one you almost married. I approve of him."

Well, thanks, Brother. Your opinion matters to me.

Behind these uncomfortably funny and sometimes crazy family incidents is a lot of love. In the end, our families keep us grounded.

Sometimes, they go about doing things for us in a way that we don't understand, but it helps us see there's more than one way of doing things. We can't choose our blood relations, but we can choose to see their better intentions.

—Jen P. Simmons—

Catching Snowflakes

Love is like a virus. It can happen
to anybody at any time.
~Maya Angelou

I was twenty-seven years old. I don't know why I did it, but I turned down a dream job in Vancouver, and flew home to Toronto two weeks before Christmas.

As I unpacked at my parents' country estate, Dad endured -15 Celsius whipping winds while barbecuing steaks for us outside. We chatted over dinner at the pine table, and it was over butter tarts that my mom sprang the news. My dad had fixed the rusty red sedan I'd left behind in his shed. My insides jumped — I had wheels! I immediately called my friend Steph and made dinner plans at her house for the next day.

Waking early, I baked a loaf of bread and popped it into a gift bag to take with me. I styled my long blond hair and dressed in a black velvet skirt and black high heels.

"Aren't you dressed a bit fancy?" Mom queried. "There's a snowstorm coming. Those are not exactly sensible winter shoes."

I scowled. "I'll be inside."

"Still," said Mom, retreating to the laundry room.

"I'll be home late," I called, as I headed out.

Snowstorm, eh? Despite my bravado, as I began the forty-minute drive I decided I'd better stick to the main roads. Halfway there it started to snow like mad. Cars slowed. I strained to see even with the wipers on high.

The sound of a siren announced the approach of an ambulance and I pulled aside to let it pass. As I inched back into my lane, the traffic light ahead turned red. I stopped. My stomach grumbled. The bread made the car smell like a bakery. I realized I was starving.

The light turned green. I pressed on the gas, and then that old car sputtered and died.

I tried to start it. One click, then nothing. Before I could do anything else, two scruffy guys raced over from the nearby sidewalk. I rolled down my window a crack.

"Give us a sec," one of them said. "We'll get ya outta here." Before I could reply, they had started to push. While they pushed and guided me, I steered into a parking spot in a strip mall beside a fast food chicken joint.

"You'll be fine now," they said, and before I could even thank them, they took off into a dark lot behind the plaza.

The snow fell faster. I rolled up my window and called Steph on my cell phone to cancel. Next, I called my parents to come get me. I was parked in front of a brew-your-own-wine shop. Luckily it was open, so I went inside and explained to the well-dressed, older couple behind the counter that my car had died, and I hoped to stay in their parking spot and eat chicken while I waited for my folks.

"Certainly!" they said.

I was very hungry. But there I was in my high heels, with soaked feet. I walked to the fast food restaurant and back. My mother was right. I sighed, wondering why I'd gotten dressed up in the first place.

I feasted on chicken thighs from a cardboard box inside my frigid car. The steam rose and fogged up the windows. I wiped off a spot and looked out. There was a man coming toward my car, approaching from the dark lot where the scruffy men had gone. He was alone. As he drew near, I saw he wasn't scruffy.

Nervous and confused, I locked my car doors and sized him up. He was about my age, clean-shaven with wavy, blond hair to his shoulders, dressed in jeans and hiking boots. He looked kind of rugged.

I cracked the window.

"Hello," he said.

"Hi," I said, wiping my greasy mouth with a napkin.

"This is my dad and his wife's store," he explained. "I just took the garbage out. They said to invite you in to warm up."

"Thanks," I said, "but my parents are coming, plus I'm eating chicken."

"You can bring your food inside," he said with a smile that was very nice.

"That's nice, but I'm good," I said.

I wasn't about to pig out in front of a handsome stranger.

"But it's snowing — really, really hard," he said, tipping his head toward the black sky.

The flakes were now huge, more like goose feathers than snow. Opening his mouth, he tried to catch them on his tongue. He stepped back and dodged a little to the left, then a little to the right, and back. In that split second, I changed my mind.

"Actually, I will," I said.

"Great," he said, "'cause it's really snowing."

I smiled. "I'll just finish my chicken first."

"Sure," he said, and went inside.

Shortly after, I entered the store to a warm welcome. We all sat on high stools in the shop's rear, and chatted about the storm and holiday plans. The young man, whose name was Ian, was quiet, shy even, but he asked questions, grinned a lot, and brought me a glass of fruity red wine. My parents arrived not long after and jumpstarted my battery. After saying my thanks and goodbyes, I left the store.

"Let's go before the roads get worse," my dad said, heading for his truck. "We'll follow you in case you have trouble."

As my mom went to join my dad in the truck, I suddenly yelled, "Wait! I need to go back in."

"What for?" she asked. "You heard Dad. He wants to get home."

"Yes, I know, but… the wine store guy, Ian, I have to see him again."

"Oh for Pete's sake, don't be boy-crazy."

"No, this is different," I said.

"Sure," she said, shaking her head.

"No, it is," I insisted. "I have to go back in."

"Be fast!" instructed Mom.

I grabbed the bag of bread from my car and ran inside. Ian was not in sight, so I gave the bag to his parents, took a business card and left.

The next day, I mailed a thank-you card to the wine storeowners. In a P.S., I invited their son to join me snowboarding sometime, "as friends," and included my phone number.

The months passed and I didn't hear from him. I figured that was it. Then, in March, the night before St. Patrick's Day, my phone rang — and it was him. The next day, over green drinks, I learned his parents had sent my bread home with him the night we met, and he enjoyed it. But they had wisely kept my thank-you card — the one with my phone number, until he split from his then-girlfriend.

It turned out I was right — this was different. Eight months later Ian asked me to marry him — and I said yes! Not long after we took a trip to Vancouver, and I taught him to snowboard on Cypress Mountain. We married October 3, 1998.

This past March, we stood as giant snowflakes fell and watched our seven-year-old daughter Gracie, and our ten-year-old son Reece enjoy their first snowboard lesson in Calabogie, Ontario, proof positive that sometimes during a snowstorm in Canada you can catch more than snowflakes on your tongue — you can catch true love!

— Patricia Miller —

Doors Wide Open

Falling in love consists merely in uncorking the
imagination and bottling the common sense.
~Helen Rowland

could see the white sedan pulling into the driveway through the half-open blinds of my home office. My first instinct was to scream. I felt like a giddy sixteen-year-old schoolgirl instead of a forty-two-year-old mother of three going on a blind date.

I had agreed a few nights before at a moms' night out, glass of chardonnay in hand, to go out with Rob, the best friend of my friend Florence's husband. She passed along my number, and he called the next night. It was a surprisingly easy conversation. My children, ages ten, eight, and six, had just vacated for the weekend with their dad, and Rob was dead-on when he asked, "What did you do first? Clean up or catch your breath and relax?" From there we shared lighthearted stories about our kids (he had two, ages seven and five) and dangled tidbits about our failed marriages — enough that I was curious about how a man could be as relieved and positive about his divorce as I was.

It had taken me almost a year to get to this optimistic place. At first, when my husband moved out on the notion that he needed "a break," I felt defeated. I'd already gone through the pain of caring for and losing both of my parents within eighteen months, and now my husband was leaving me alone with three young kids.

I couldn't help feeling punished — like everyone except me deserved loving husbands and nearby extended families. At Back-to-School Night and on the soccer fields, I felt my singleness the most. And then right before the holidays, we got hit with lice (yes, all four of us had live bugs). As I picked nits out of hair for hours every night and waded through piles of laundry, I wondered if for the rest of my life I would have to tackle every obstacle alone. That included the thirty-six inches of snow that was dumped a few days later, the day after Christmas. I had to climb out my kitchen window to attempt to shovel, only to realize my kids had played with the shovels the night before and they were all buried. It was all too much, and I found myself paralyzed on the couch. (Later, I would say: "My mom died, my dad died, and my husband left, and I survived. It was the lice and snow that nearly killed me.")

So what changed? In February, as I approached my forty-second birthday, I went to one of those women's "change your life for the better" workshops, led by a woman I knew who had also gone through a divorce. I learned some important lessons that night from women who had come through way worse than I had, including breast cancer and abusive marriages.

I, Jennifer Chauhan, was the only person responsible for my happiness. Not my ex-husband. Not my children. Not my mom's six surviving siblings or my brothers who lived on the other side of the country. Not my friends.

Nobody owed me anything.

If I believed in my heart that my life could change for the better, it would.

Shedding my victim skin, I began reciting very Zen-like (slightly scaring all those around me), "I choose not to suffer. I choose to be happy."

I wrote down in my journal everything I wanted in my life: to sell my house for the asking price; for my divorce to go amicably and for me to get what I needed; to be successful professionally and do well financially.

I paused a moment before writing, "to find a true partner who loves me for me." Could this really happen?

The night Rob and I met was my thirteen-year wedding anniversary.

Exactly one year prior I had slid off my wedding rings and asked for a divorce (just one week after my husband had moved out).

So much had changed in a year.

Coincidentally (or not, as I'm more and more inclined to believe) Rob had moved out the same weekend Chris had. He'd been married just about the same length — twelve years.

We were traveling on paths winding toward one another.

We spent that first night together at an outside bar overlooking the ocean, talking and laughing as we shared stories about our kids and opened up about our marriages. We laughed until we cried as I realized my six-year-old son was obsessed with all-boy bands, namely Big Time Rush, and how I told my friends the best way for them to be my friend was to stop giving advice and "hold my hand and shut up."

Rob's given me a fairytale romance — strolling through Washington Square Park and kissing for hours on a park bench (serenaded by an NYU violin student), taking me to the ballet, sending me late-night love texts — that is still as passionate and romantic and real nearly three years later.

At times, I've been guarded. Having lost so much in such a short time, I have a fear of abandonment — I'm wired to expect people to leave me. But Rob shows over and over again that I can trust him. He wants me to open up and be real, share my fears, my concerns. He wants me to cry when I miss my mom and tell him when I think he's not doing enough.

There are no games. No lies.

Our kids have met, get along wonderfully, and even though we live an hour apart and are not sure how logistically we can get married anytime soon (there's alimony, I don't want to uproot my kids, etc.) we know we will always be together.

And because he believes in me and in us, I have gone on to do braver things than open my front door to a blind date in a white sedan. I've sold my marital home and discarded the belongings of my former life, including my favorite white everyday Williams-Sonoma dishes, the brand-new king-sized bed that was never shared, even my still-sealed-in-plastic framed wedding photo.

I've opened my own business, a writing studio, and offer creative writing workshops for teenagers and adults. And now I'm starting a nonprofit to help disadvantaged kids achieve academic success and personal growth through writing.

Most of the time, I have no idea what I'm doing and just plunge ahead, figuring it out as I go. Having been thrown too many curve balls, I know this is the better approach.

Life is messy; it's unpredictable. The only known is that we get to choose how we want to experience it. And I want to live mine with doors wide open and believing that anything is possible.

— Jennifer Chauhan —

My Ray of Sunshine

Being deeply loved by someone gives you strength.
Loving someone deeply gives you courage.
~Lao Tzu

Life is as good as you make it. I made the most of my time and I loved my life, fitting work, school, homework, and fun with my family and friends into my busy schedule. I was an outgoing, energetic, fun-loving twenty-something, with an optimistic attitude and strong faith. I valued my relationships and worked hard at achieving my goals.

I was living with a close friend while working at a few jobs to put myself through university and become an elementary school teacher. In my last semester, life turned upside down. It was a clear morning on September 25th in 2009. I was working as a traffic controller, wearing my high-visibility gear. As I was holding up my stop sign, I was hit by an SUV at approximately eighty kilometers per hour. I am 5'0" tall and weighed 120 pounds. I flew across the street, out of my steel-toe boots, and landed in front of my coworker.

I was in critical condition. I am told that I technically died but was revived while being airlifted to the hospital. I was admitted to the intensive care unit where I was in an induced coma for six days. After several surgeries, the medical reports indicated that I had bilateral carotid artery dissection and severe brain damage to my frontal lobe, occipital lobe and hypothalamus. In addition, my pelvis was shattered, all of my ribs were cracked, and my sternum, sacrum, cheek, nose, and arm were broken. My spleen was ruptured. The doctor informed me that I would never walk again and that I had retrograde amnesia.

I thought that I was in a strange dream. I couldn't understand what was happening or who people were. I could barely move and only knew basic facts. But I felt that God was with me and would help me to recover. I told the doctor that I would walk down the aisle at my wedding someday.

During my recovery at the hospital, I had many visitors. I was informed that one was my boyfriend, so I assumed that it was the guy who I was most attracted to. I was told the name of my boyfriend, so I called the best-looking one by that name... but I was mistaken. Ray was not my boyfriend, but I thought he was perfection! I zealously declared my love for Ray to all of my visitors. My friends told me that I was just confused, but I was certain that he was the one I wanted. This ended the relationship with my unknown boyfriend. Fortunately, Ray drove an hour to visit me every day.

I had only met Ray ten days before the accident, yet it seemed like he was the only person that I could remember. I tried telling him some events that I thought I remembered, but he corrected me. Somehow that caused my brain to switch back into reality. The realization that I hadn't been dreaming had left me extremely confused, but even more surprised that Ray was real! He showed love, patience, kindness, thoughtfulness, and every other virtue that I admired. I recognized how selfless it was for him to support and encourage me, while constantly trying to make me happy.

My memory didn't last longer than the present moments that I was experiencing, so Ray constantly tried to make sure that I felt special. He'd bring me a rose and a slushy drink daily, he'd give me compliments, and he'd take me to get my hair done professionally. Whenever he could, he'd also lie by my side to comfort me. He made me feel unconditionally loved!

Aside from Ray, my life was very difficult. I had lost all of my independence. For a long time, I required help to be fed, bathed, moved, dressed, and even taken to the toilet. I couldn't sleep. I could only lie down or sit in my wheelchair. I had also lost my sense of smell and taste, so I always ate until I was full. This resulted in weight gain. I was very depressed about that. Ray just said there was just more of me to love.

I was slow to process information and my vocabulary was very simple, I couldn't follow people's conversations and I lost my creativity. I also couldn't grasp the concept of time and frequently repeated myself without knowing it. I always felt stupid and confused. Without visual memory, I couldn't distinguish fruits, vegetables, meats, animals, or even people that I should have known. I also often made people feel uncomfortable in conversations by blurting out comments that I didn't know were inappropriate; I didn't have a filter. I'd even interrupt speakers because I couldn't hold onto a thought. Ray noticed my struggles and was aware that I could only retain information with focus and repetition, so he encouraged me to ask questions, he repeated answers, and he summarized previous conversations for me. I had so much to relearn.

Although everything was wonderful with Ray, I yearned for the strong friendships that I had before the accident. I needed to expand my social horizons. I had a hard time paying attention, but I tried my best to focus, listen, and not speak until my turn. When I'd talk, I'd ask basic questions. Each night, I tried to review the day, repeating as much "new" information as I could. I found that the amount of information I was able to remember was increasing daily. I spent all of my time learning. I frequently studied a thesaurus to increase my vocabulary, and Ray regularly played games with me to improve my mental faculty. My brain injury no longer seemed obvious to others.

On the other hand, my physical disabilities continued to limit my independence, so I worked very hard with a kinesiologist to strengthen my muscles and improve my range of motion. I had to push through the pain to stand and take my first step while using a walker. I eventually progressed to a cane. Now, I am proud to say that I don't need any assistance with my walking! I knew what I wanted to do, and I have exceeded all expectations. In May of 2011, Ray and I blissfully walked down the aisle and now we are expecting our first child!

Through my constant pain and distress, I am still the same girl that I was. Being disabled is tough, and people can't see my cognitive struggles. But with prayer, appreciation, and effort, I will keep moving forward. It is unnecessary to focus on the pain; I focus on positive distractions. I am determined to enjoy my life with my best friend. It's been a challenge in so many ways, but I am grateful that my Ray of sunshine carried me through the storm!

—Jennifer Wiche—

12

Lucky for Love

A cat assures its owner of good luck.
~Chinese Proverb

On a rainy December morning on Long Island, I drove thirty miles to Save-A-Pet animal shelter to look at kittens. Among the chaos of kids, barking dogs, and parents, I picked up a black kitten. She appeared to be six months old. She clung to me and purred as I petted her silky coat. How could anyone find a black cat unlucky? I had to take her home.

But I was just there to look. I didn't have a pet bed, food, or bowls for her. Furthermore, that night I was going out with Ed. We had been friends for quite a while, but this was our first "official" date.

I had to leave the kitten. "Goodbye, Muffin," I said and handed her to Kyle, the shelter volunteer.

As I drove home, sheets of rain beat against the car. And I cried tears for my kitten. *Why did I have to name her?* I thought. *Now, she is a part of me like a heart or a lung. I can't abandon her now. I should be excited about my date, so why am I sad?*

At home, I looked at the clock: 3:00 p.m. *If I hurry back to the shelter, there will still be time to adopt Muffin before it closes.*

I tore off my wet clothes, pulled on dry ones, and ran to the car. The rain had turned to hail. Golf-sized lumps of ice pummeled the vehicle. I struggled to see through the blurry windshield as I rushed back to the shelter to save my Muffin.

I must have looked like a madwoman when I got back, but Kyle brought Muffin to me. "She's been waitin' on you." I opened my wet coat and held her against my chest. She stretched her neck, stuck out her pink tongue, and licked me. Looking into her huge green eyes, my heart filled with warmth, love, and happiness.

"How did you know I'd come back?" I said to Kyle.

"Oh, you were hooked big-time. And the little girl, too." He scratched her head. "I'll get the adoption papers started."

"But I don't have any food, a bed, or a cat carrier." Through my shirt, I felt her heart beating. The winter chill was gone as she warmed me.

"No worries. We have some food and a box to take her home in," he said.

At the checkout counter, I signed Muffin's paperwork and paid a small fee.

The volunteer gave me a bag of dry food and put Muffin in a carton. He carried her out to the car for me and put the box on the passenger seat. Outside, the rain had stopped. A glimmer of sun fought through the clouds. Muffin let out some meows.

Kyle said to Muffin, "It's okay, girl. This nice lady's goin' to make you a good home."

Shivering in my soaked jacket, I thanked Kyle and opened the trunk. I put the food inside, closed it, and got into the car. Then I peeked inside the box. Muffin was gone!

I looked on the floor, under the seats, and in every corner I could find. No kitten. I ran into the shelter. I came back out with Kyle, and we went to my car. He pulled a lever on the bottom of the front passenger seat and pushed it forward. Muffin was huddled inside the small space.

"What are you doing in there?" I said. I patted her head. She peered up at me. Kyle picked up Muffin and put her in the carton.

"How did you know where she was?"

"'Happens all the time."

"Thanks again for rescuing us."

"Any time." He went back to the shelter.

I grabbed a blanket from the back seat, tucked it around Muffin, and made sure she had plenty of air. On the ride home, she cried. That was heart wrenching. Maybe I had made a mistake.

Inside my apartment, I gathered blankets and pillows. I made a place for her next to my bed and filled bowls with food and water. But she was not ready to take a nap. Muffin wanted to explore. Sniffing the air, she dashed under the bed, around the furniture, and into the kitchen. I got ready for my date even though I really wanted to stay home with my new kitten. It was too late to call Ed and cancel, but I thought that perhaps I should make a spaghetti dinner and invite him to eat in.

An hour later, I was dressed and ready. When Ed arrived I introduced him to Muffin.

She meowed, "Hello."

He kissed me on the cheek and I said, "Her name is Muffin. I adopted her about an hour ago. Would you mind if I cooked dinner? I can't leave her alone on her first night."

"Hey, Muffin. Sure, we can stay here."

We ate, laughed, talked, and played with her. I hoped there would be more dates with Ed.

Ed and I celebrated our thirtieth wedding anniversary this year. And Muffin, an indoor cat, lived for sixteen glorious years.

Often, we reminisce about the joy she brought us. Black cats are good luck after all — especially for love.

— Marilyn June Janson —

13

How to Find a Husband

I once decided not to date a guy because he wasn't
excited to meet my dog. I mean, this was like not
wanting to meet my mother.
~Bonnie Schacter

always heard that German Shepherds were obedient and protective. What I didn't know was that they could actually pick out a husband.

Soon after I chose my German Shepherd puppy, I thought I'd made a mistake. My puppy ate through the carpet, right down to the foundation, and then continued to eat the concrete and break off his canine teeth. Thus, I named him Trouble.

Trouble grew into a handsome Shepherd indeed! His black and silver coat gleamed after his baths and his ears stood at attention if he heard a noise. He seemed to understand that it was his job to protect me since I lived alone.

After a troubling divorce, I became accustomed to cuddling up with Trouble. Of course, he took up a good deal of the bed. But he never thought he was too big to plop down on the couch with me to watch a movie. We took long walks together and often shared the same food in the evenings. Steak was his favorite.

A few months after the final papers for my divorce were signed, I started dating again. I met a few gentlemen through work, and my girlfriends were always ready to fix me up with a blind date. Since Trouble had been my only companion, I felt almost giddy when it was time to open the front door to a date.

Little did I know that Trouble had his own agenda. I opened the door to greet Paul, and Trouble trotted close to my heels, almost shoving me to one side. This was a blind date, so I didn't know what to expect. As I put my hand out to shake his, Trouble leapt between us and stood stiff, growling, his eyes shooting nasty glares at Paul. "I'm so sorry," I apologized. He took a step further into the house while saying, "Oh that's okay. I love dogs." This is when Trouble grabbed hold of his pant leg and almost made Paul do a face plant on my tile floor.

This pattern repeated itself many times over the next year. I even went back to obedience basics with Trouble. I tried everything short of putting a muzzle on him. I locked him in bedrooms only to have to replace doors or at the very least repaint them.

As long as I didn't have a date, Trouble was a perfect, calm, obedient dog. I started to meet dates outside my home. I became rather attached to one gentleman in particular. Ray was a funny, charming man who dazzled me when he cocked his cowboy hat to one side. He loved to sing and had a great voice. What girl wouldn't want to have someone serenade her?

The weather turned chilly. I started a fire in the fireplace and planned a quiet romantic evening for Ray's first visit to the house. I worked on new obedience skills with Trouble — hand signals and commands — in hopes he would behave. The doorbell rang.

"Hi Ray, come on in." I put my hand out flat toward Trouble and cautioned him to sit and stay. He amazed me by sitting tall and didn't move a muscle. The evening started smoothly with the tasty meal I had prepared and cordial conversation. Trouble was perfect. He lay quietly by my side at the dinner table and walked alongside as we headed to the living room to enjoy the fireplace. Ray and I sat fairly close together on the couch.

Then Ray put his arm lightly around my shoulders. That's when we both heard the snarling growl from behind the couch. The next thing we knew, Trouble's nose was between our heads. His bright white teeth sparkled within his open mouth. He stared at Ray as his nose came under Ray's arm. Still growling, he pushed Ray's arm slowly to the side, away from my shoulder. Ray smiled. "I guess he doesn't want me to do this?" I laughed and apologized for Trouble. We resumed the evening without touching as Trouble's keen, unblinking eyes watched.

Ray visited often. Trouble continued to growl, sneer or nudge him with warnings not to touch me. Slowly, Ray's gentle ways convinced Trouble that he meant me no harm. During this courtship I continued to date other men, but every date turned into disaster when I brought him home to meet Trouble. He didn't just growl, but was always ready to clamp his pearly whites on a leg or arm. Ray seemed to be the only man he tolerated.

Trouble spent more time with Ray than with me during visits. He relished the fact that Ray threw balls for him and played rough games with him. When Ray left, Trouble sat by the door and whined. I didn't whine when Ray left but I realized I'd like to have him around more often. It occurred to me that Trouble might have found the perfect mate for me. I never imagined my dog would be the one to pick out a new husband.

Ray and I married. Trouble became Ray's best friend. They were inseparable, which made me believe all the more that Trouble had a keen sense for picking out husbands. We've been married twenty-seven years and often look back on our courtship and tell friends about how Trouble brought us together. My advice: if you are looking for a new husband, first get a German Shepherd.

— Alice Klies —

14

When Richard Met Cindy

When you realize you want to spend the rest of your life
with somebody, you want the rest of your life to
start as soon as possible.
~From the movie When Harry Met Sally

t was a Saturday like no other. "Dad, I don't know how to tell you this." He took my hand in his, put his other hand on my knee, lifted his little-boy face, looked me square in the eyes and said, "Dad, you need a girlfriend."

Being a single parent had prepared me for just about anything—except this.

"Oh, no, I don't," I replied with a smile. He said nothing and sat rather poised for a child. I continued, "For the sake of discussion, if I did—which I don't—how would you know?"

"Dad, when your nine-year-old son tells you that you need a girlfriend, you need a girlfriend."

"And just what would I do with this so-called girlfriend?" This was risky territory.

"Dad, do I have to tell you everything? You could go to the beach, the movies, dinner… And if you really liked her, you could kiss her!"

"Okay, we've covered this plenty. I'm happy being your dad. That's enough for me."

As we hugged, he said, "If you say so, Dad, but you still need a girlfriend."

Then he added rather speedily, "You're the best dad, and if you find the right person and want to make me a brother or sister, that's okay, too. But I'd rather have a brother first."

This wasn't the first time I was told I needed a girlfriend. Baseball Mom from Little League also told me. I told her, "Not interested." She assured me I was, but I just didn't know it yet.

I love old movies and romance stories. One rainy Sunday, I had the afternoon to myself. I had plenty of time to finally watch *When Harry Met Sally* uninterrupted. I settled in with my favorite blanket, coffee, and bonbons. Halfway into the movie, Baseball Mom called.

"Are you going to bother me about dating?" I asked.

"Only for a minute. I figured you're sitting on the couch with your favorite blanket and coffee, eating bonbons, and watching *When Harry Met Sally*. Why is that one of your favorites?" she asked.

"It's a good movie."

"If you say so, Mr. Blanket and Bonbons. Got to go. Oh, the reason I called: Go online to a Jewish dating website and at least consider it."

"Not my style," I replied.

"Take it from a Catholic Baseball Mom. It'll be good for you."

"I don't think so."

"Okay, Mr. Sensitive. Got to go."

After the movie, I thought about it. Being a parent meant everything to me, but I was also terribly lonely. It took my little boy, *When Harry Met Sally* and Baseball Mom for me to realize I was available.

I wanted a woman of good moral character, as well as someone who was smart, sassy, sensitive and had a sense of humor. A woman like that doesn't just show up at the door and say, "Hi, I'm perfect for you. Let's fall in love, go through hard and great times, grow old together and share a million laughs along the way. Also, without being too forward, Mr. Sensitive, would you like to join me for dinner sometime?" It just doesn't happen that way!

Reluctantly, I signed up for the dating website and proceeded with caution. A month later, I dedicated an entire day to finding the right woman. I read hundreds of profiles, disregarded easy check-off items as well as anything fluffy or overly boastful. Profiles without pictures were more likely to be reviewed. I wanted a relationship where we loved each other heart and soul. Anything less just wouldn't do.

Somewhere around #200, I found her. She lived in a house south of Boston, got her education in a library, liked being home with her children, said that sometimes a party is just the thing to lift her spirits, liked a good cup of coffee, and announced that her annual salary was none of anyone's business. Now that's my type of woman!

We met at the bookstore where a local artist was debuting children's music. At the very least, it would be good coffee. Cindy apparently had a surveillance team. An unusual number of fortyish women were strategically browsing aisles while whispering in their cell phones. After the music, we took the kids to eat. She didn't seem to like me, and I didn't know what to make of her.

We had a number of second tries and decided we were better as friends, but we would each try finding someone else for the other.

We met for lunch a few days later, and as we were leaving, I leaned in to kiss her unexpectedly.

"What are you doing? I thought we were going to be friends," she said.

"I think I want to kiss you instead," I replied. I realized I had no intention of finding her a man.

Come to find out, she had no intention of finding me a woman either. It was a rocky beginning, but neither one of us was letting go.

I'd contacted two people on the dating website based solely on their profiles. When profile #2 responded, I replied that I was already talking to another woman, and talking to two women at the same time wasn't appropriate.

A few months later, Cindy was on the phone with her friend Lauri. "He's here right now. Get over here and meet my cyber-date, dream-date."

Lauri was over in a flash. She wasn't in the door ten seconds when she said, "Oh, my god, you're that guy who wouldn't talk to me because you were already talking to another woman."

Cindy piped in, "You two know each other?"

"Cindy, that's the guy I told you about who wouldn't talk to me because he was already talking to another woman. You're the other woman!"

Turns out, Cindy had helped Lauri write her profile and only submitted her own profile because Lauri insisted. Cindy had no intention of responding to anyone. That's why her profile had been down around 200. But she responded to mine, and that's all that mattered.

Cindy and I have had our share of challenges. Through it all, we've managed to build a strong, deeply loving relationship.

Many years ago, my therapist asked how I could be so happy with so many problems. I told her, "It's easy. So many people go through life never getting the right person to share it with, but I got the girl."

I always knew what she'd be like, and with some help, I found her. It took my nine-year-old son, *When Harry Met Sally*, a Baseball Mom, a dating website, and Cindy's friend Lauri to get us together. We've been together more than fourteen years. I definitely got the girl.

— Richard Berg —

15

Canine Cupid

Love makes your soul crawl out from its hiding place.
~Zora Neale Hurston

I was aimlessly punching buttons on the remote, trying to find something on TV that would occupy my mind for a while. The sky outside was as dark as my mood. A thunderstorm rolled in just before dusk. The heavy rain and blowing wind intensified my gloomy disposition, and soon I was engulfed in self-pity.

After three years, you'd think I would have adjusted to being a widower. Though I coped fairly well during the day I had a tough time getting through the nights. My friends and family urged me to get out more, but I didn't seem to know how to socialize without Marie at my side. I was lonely. I was ready. I just didn't know how.

Boredom had taken me to the edge of sleep when the soft rap came at my door. For a moment I thought it was the TV, but when I glanced at the screen there were cowboys riding across the desert. Blinking the sleep from my eyes, I turned and looked at the door. Had I been dreaming? Who would come visiting in this weather? Then the rapping came again, soft, hesitant.

I jumped up and hastened to the door to let whoever was on the other side come in out of the rain. I had no porch so they must be getting soaked. When I pulled the door open I was surprised to see a small, attractive woman peering back at me, her face full of question marks. In the few seconds she had stood at my door, she had gotten a good soaking. In her arms she carried an equally wet small black puppy.

She opened her mouth to speak, but before she could utter a word, I pulled the door open wider. "Come in out of the rain, miss. No need to get any wetter than you already are." I figured she needed directions or was looking for a neighbor and had ended up at the wrong house.

Giving me a grateful nod, she stepped inside, apologizing at the same time for dripping water on my carpet. Even with wet strands of hair in her face, I noticed how pretty she was.

I was about to comment on her puppy, when she thrust him toward me. "I almost hit your puppy. It was raining so hard and he is so small that I almost didn't see him in time to stop. When I slammed on the brakes he ran into your yard, so I thought he must be yours."

She must have noticed an odd expression on my face, because she blushed and blurted out, "He is yours, isn't he?"

I took the puppy from her. "Thank you. This is very kind of you. Not many people would stop in this kind of weather to bring a dog home."

She grinned. "Well, he sort of brought himself home. I just wanted to make sure he was safe." She reached over and scratched behind his ears. "I love dogs. I would have been devastated if I had hit him."

"Look," I said, surprising myself at my boldness. "You must be miserable. Why don't you take your coat off and let me make us some coffee. The least I can do is let you dry out a little before you go."

She hesitated, biting her lower lip and sizing me up. "A cup of coffee would be nice," she said, apparently deciding that I didn't look like a serial killer or a crackpot.

She took the puppy from my arms. "If you'll get me a towel, I'll dry him for you while you make the coffee."

When I carried the coffee into the living room, the pup was curled up in her lap fast asleep. "He sure likes you," I said, grinning at the warm sight. She had pulled her legs beneath her, and in the soft light she looked almost like a little girl.

"Animals know when someone likes them," she said. "He knows he is safe with me."

She was easy to talk to, and her warm laugh seemed to awaken my heavy heart. Her presence made me realize why my house had seemed so empty for so long. It needed the hundreds of little things that a woman does to breathe life into a house and make it a home.

When she stood to leave, my heart leaped inside my chest in a surge of panic. I had to keep her longer. Her voice, her laughter, her mannerisms were a soothing balm to my loneliness and pain. "Let me take you to dinner," I said.

She shook her head. "You don't have to do that."

I stood up and faced her squarely. "I want to," I said.

"Okay," she said, gently sitting the yawning puppy down on the floor. "If you're sure you're not just being kind."

When we walked to the door, the puppy trotted after her, whining. I laughed. "He wants to go home with you."

"I'm sorry," she said, bending over to pet the pup. "I didn't mean to get him so attached to me."

"I don't blame him," I said. I fought down the urge to tell her that I wanted to run after her too.

Ronda and I became a couple soon after that. Whenever she came over to my house, the puppy would run to her eagerly, clearly preferring her to me. On one such occasion, when he rushed over to give her kisses, whimpering with joy at seeing her, I blurted out, "You may as well marry me, Ronda. Cupid is miserable when you aren't around." I took her in my arms. "So am I."

With tears in her eyes, she nodded happily. "You never did tell me why you named him Cupid," she said.

"There's a story behind it," I said. "Someday I'll tell you."

Some day, when the time is right, perhaps on our first anniversary, I'll tell her why my dog is named Cupid. I'll tell her that I had never seen the dog before in my life until she showed up on my doorstep with him in her arms. I called him Cupid because he brought us together.

I figured the three of us were destined to be together because I had tried in vain to find his real owners when she first left him with me. But from the very beginning, Cupid obviously wanted her. I'm glad that they both tolerate me.

—Joe Atwater as told to Elizabeth Atwater—

Man of My Dreams

16

Surprise! You're Getting Married

Love isn't something you find.
Love is something that finds you.
~Loretta Young

My mother kept asking me why I didn't find some nice young man and settle down. At age twenty-two I hardly felt that was a priority. But, because she married at age seventeen, I guess that a twenty-two-year-old daughter who didn't date seemed rather odd to her.

I was happy in my career as an administrative assistant and was considering ways to get a promotion. I wasn't even sure that I wanted to get married. Finally, my mother asked one too many times. I replied rather forcefully, "I don't have to go out and beat the bushes for a husband. When the time is right, he's going to come right up and knock on my door." Mom must have finally gotten my message, because she quit bugging me about it.

Three months later, I had the strangest experience. I woke up one day and found myself saying, "Prepare, for within six months you'll be married." I was mulling this over when I started having thoughts about a specific man, a man I had never met who I seemed to have conjured up, complete with random facts about him. I was so taken aback by this that for several days I could hardly concentrate on my job.

A month after that I called a high school friend, Theresa, whom

I kept in touch with, and asked if I could come over and tell her about my premonition or whatever it was. She and I always loved talking about weird things that happened to us, but this time I was sure she would think I was delusional.

I told Theresa everything, starting with the mysterious six-month timetable. "I kept having all these facts bombarding my mind. He has deep blue eyes and a smile that could melt your heart. He loves the outdoors, hunting, fishing, hiking, camping, anything outdoors. He has something to do with Colorado." This didn't sound at all like a man I would marry, because I was definitely not the outdoors type. "He's athletic and loves all kinds of sports." Again, that's not me! I don't have an athletic muscle in my body. "He loves reading and has lots of books. He wants a wife who can cook, sew, keep house, loves kids, and is a strong Christian." That was more like me. I continued, "He's quite a bit older than me, but doesn't look it. And, he drives a little blue sports car." Then, I sat and waited for her to burst out laughing.

I wasn't prepared at all for what Theresa said. "I know that man! He's exactly like that and he goes to my church! He's hunting in Colorado right now. And he just bought a little blue sports car!" She had a shocked look on her face.

"You're kidding!" I exclaimed.

"No, and he desperately wants a Christian wife who wants to raise a family, loves cooking and sewing, and would enjoy his library with him. And," she said, "I think that he said he's in his thirties. He sure doesn't look it."

At this point, I was staring at her, not knowing what to say. "Okay, you're serious, aren't you?"

"You've got to come to church and meet him as soon as he comes back." So, we planned our assault on poor, unsuspecting Lyle.

A few weeks later, I went to church with her and her family. Even though she had not described how he looked, I spotted him in a church of about one hundred people. I just felt like I should be sitting next to that man. When I met him face to face, his smile melted my heart. Of course, Theresa agreed to keep my secret.

A few weeks later, Lyle called and asked me for a date. When he came to our front door and knocked, I told my mother, "That will be my husband." Since I had not told her about my premonition, she just laughed at me.

Although I didn't tell Lyle about my experience until months later, he said that he felt like he had known me all his life. I felt the same. He asked me to marry him. Five months after my strange experience, and five weeks after our first date, we were married. I always wanted wedding bells to ring on my wedding day, but the church didn't have bells. So, I asked God to fill the trees with birds and have them all singing. Lyle thought that was funny and not likely to happen because it was February. But we had a beautiful spring-like day for our wedding and the trees were filled with birds singing joyously, which had everybody talking. God gave us his wedding bells.

On our honeymoon, Lyle told me how his friends had tried to fix him up over the years, but it never worked out. As he told me about a co-worker who tried to get her cousin to go on a date with him six years earlier, I realized that co-worker was my cousin and I was the girl who wouldn't go out with Lyle on a blind date!

Then he told me that he once knew a waitress who had taken in a single woman as a roommate. He invited her to bring her roommate and attend a concert with him. She tried, but her roommate didn't want to go, so she brought another friend. We were dumbfounded when we realized that I was that roommate.

Lyle told me about another set-up that hadn't worked out. He was expected for dinner at a friend's house, when a single woman dropped in on them unexpectedly, just an hour before he was scheduled. They invited her to stay for dinner, but she decided not to, because she didn't want to be considered a blind date. I was that woman!

Three times over the course of six years I nearly met Lyle. I guess I needed a more direct push to finally meet him. We enjoyed thirty-three years of marriage, and had two children and eight grandchildren. My soul mate and best friend died of cancer on Easter Sunday at home, with our daughter and me by his side. I greatly look forward to meeting him again and being by his side forever.

— Rebecca Gurnsey —

17

Happily Ever After

The way to a woman's heart is through her children.
~Author Unknown

Early one morning, I awoke from a dream and found myself grinning from ear to ear. It had been eons since I felt this content.

In this vision, I saw the figure of a large, muscular man. His face was blurry, but I could distinguish that he had dark features. His warmth and affection were very comforting, and his presence was homey.

I wished this dream had lasted longer and tried to savor this blissful state.

During the following week, I was haunted by the image of this enigmatic man. I believed that this dream was more than a fantasy, perhaps a message, but trying to keep the memory alive by being overly analytical did not bring me any closer to understanding what it all meant. I even replayed this dream in my head while trying to fall asleep, hoping to encounter this mystery man again in my slumber, but I couldn't make it happen. As time passed, key moments of this dream remained strong, but the rest faded. Other matters took priority in my life, and I was no longer obsessed with figuring out what my subconscious was trying to tell me.

A year later, I was invited to view a friend's new house, which was under construction. I showed up one hot summer afternoon with my two-year-old son, Lee.

"I really like the design and layout of the home," I said as we walked around the various rooms. "It's going to be beautiful!"

The carpenters on site noticed Lee's animated face as he observed their labor, and they seemed pretty amused.

"All little boys love tools," the head of the crew said with a grin.

For some strange reason, this carpenter looked familiar. I ran through various possibilities in my mind, but I just couldn't place him. I gave him a friendly smile, reached for my son's hand, and continued to explore the house with my girlfriend.

"You're welcome to pop in anytime," my friend said to me. "I can see how much Lee loves watching the guys work."

"Yes, he does," I agreed. "I will. Thanks."

In subsequent weeks, I found myself, with Lee in tow, heading over to my friend's house, even without her presence, in order to give my little guy more access to carpenters swinging hammers and sawing boards. I sensed that as long as my son was not getting in the way, they didn't mind our presence.

Many trips later, I confessed to myself that I had an ulterior motive. Dave, the large, muscular head carpenter, was the main reason I made excuses to visit the house so often. This man was fun loving, easy to talk to, and had a great sense of humor. I was also charmed by the way he interacted with my son.

"How's my little buddy?" Dave would say to Lee as we entered the building.

He remained on his break noticeably longer, chatting with me and demonstrating "guy stuff" with various tools to my toddler. In time, a strong connection was forming between us, which I couldn't ignore. I considered inviting Dave over for dinner, but I was conflicted. *Was it the right decision to be allowing another man into our home and my young boys' lives? Would it be damaging to them if our friendship didn't work out?* I weighed the pros and cons, and then listened to my heart.

The next time I saw Dave, I struck up my nerve and asked, "Would you like to come for supper?"

"I'd love to," he answered without hesitation.

The initial time Dave spent with my family was truly unforgettable. During that evening, the phone rang just as Lee vied for my attention.

To avoid a typical two-year-old outburst, I scooped up my son and answered the call while Lee sat on my lap trying to grab the phone. After a few seconds, to my astonishment, I watched as two strong arms reached out and relieved me of my pesky little boy.

"Let's go over here," Dave said to Lee while carrying him away.

I sat there in awe, almost moved to tears by the sensitivity of this large man.

From the onset, Dave established a caring relationship with both Lee and his older brother, Nathaniel, and made an effort to spend time with my "little men." I learned early on in our friendship that Dave had two girls whom he saw every other weekend and missed terribly. His younger daughter, Cheryl, was five, the same age as Nathaniel, and Jana, his older, was eight. It was obvious that being around my children and soaking up their kid energy definitely helped him fill that void.

"Why don't you bring your girls over sometime?" I suggested to him.

"I would really like that," Dave said enthusiastically.

The next weekend, two sweet girls arrived, accompanied by their dad.

"It's great to see how well all four kids are getting along," Dave said as his face lit up.

"It sure is," I agreed with a smile.

We exchanged warm glances while watching my boys share their toys with the girls. Over the next few months, Dave visited regularly. He had many entertaining stories to tell, and conversation between us was effortless. In time, our friendship grew and developed into something more intimate. Witnessing my sons bonding with Dave added to his attractiveness and was a strong extension of our friendship.

One day, as I pondered my relationship with my new boyfriend, it struck me that Dave was the mystery man in my dream. I was thrilled by this awareness and realized that the dream was a premonition, which was why it impacted me so strongly. I instantly felt more settled and was anxious to relay my dream to this wonderful man. After the children were asleep one evening, I told Dave in great detail about this vision that had puzzled me so many months earlier. He sat quietly and listened. After a few seconds of watching him deliberate, Dave looked at me and said, "I've been in love with you for quite a while now."

"I feel the same about you," I said.

It was enough to reassure us that we were meant to be together. Twenty-one years have gone by since we revealed our love to each other. The highlight of our relationship has always been sharing the upbringing of our four children. In the past few years, both Jana and Cheryl have provided us with beautiful grandchildren, and we recently celebrated Nathaniel's wedding. Life doesn't get much better than that! I will always remember and am eternally grateful for the dream that connected me with my soul mate. Sometimes, by listening to your heartstrings, you can make your dream come true.

— Dalia Gesser —

18

My Big, Burly Guy

Hope… is the companion of power, and the mother
of success; for who so hopes has within him
the gift of miracles.
~Samuel Smiles

Saving every dime to support my ten-year-old daughter, Milan, was my goal even as I was receiving eviction notices stapled to the door of our small, one-bedroom apartment. I worked at Milan's private Catholic girls' school so I could get a hefty discount on her tuition, but it meant taking a huge pay cut from the public-school teaching job I had given up in order to send her there.

I could never foresee that, within the first two years of her attending this prestigious school, her father and I would divorce. I had instantly become a single mom, and I had been doing everything in my power to keep her at the school she loved so dearly. Dealing with the emotional strain of divorce was now coupled with the financial burden of rarely receiving child support. I decided I would have to leave Miami, the city I was born in, to move five hours north to Jacksonville to live near my sister. It was much cheaper there, plus I could be near family.

One night, I had the most vivid dream of sitting at Scotty's Landing, the waterfront restaurant my daughter and I frequently visited. It was our usual spot every Sunday evening after spending a long day at the beach. She and I were sitting at a table, listening to the live reggae band, and at a nearby table sat a man who gently smiled at us. He had broad shoulders, light hair and eyes, and a big physique.

The next morning, I called my sister and told her about this "big, burly guy" dream I experienced, and she suggested this could be a premonition of meeting a man in her city. We laughed it off, and I told her to keep her eyes open for him. A week later, I had the exact same dream and called my sister once more.

"It has to be a sign," she told me, so I started thinking seriously about this possible premonition. And as I prayed each night for God to answer my prayers, I secretly wished this dream was his sign that I would find happiness again.

Two weeks later, I was invited to a wedding as the date of the best man, Gerry. We had gone out a few times in the past, but decided we would make better friends than a couple. Since we ended on good terms, I didn't hesitate to accept his invitation. Not knowing anyone at the wedding, I sat alone watching my date at the altar. I couldn't help but feel bittersweet when I watched the loving couple say their vows to each other. But I smiled politely throughout the ceremony and finally made my way to the reception.

Gerry led us to our assigned table and introduced me to everyone. There were three couples and a man named Mike, who had come without a date. Since Gerry was away from the table doing best man duties, I sat alone once again. The three couples at our table seemed friendly and engaging, but I couldn't stop staring at Mike. He had a great smile and was very handsome. We talked all night, and I was intrigued by him, finding myself feeling a little jealous as he danced with other women as I danced with Gerry.

I decided I would pursue him, something I'd never done before, because there was this pull toward him that I couldn't explain. I got up enough courage to ask him more personal questions like his last name and where he worked. He was a firefighter and obviously Irish, with his red hair and green eyes. As I admired his broad shoulders and husky physique, I guessed he was around 6'2". I left the reception giddy as a schoolgirl even though I didn't know if I was going to see him again. That night, I called my sister and told her I had met my "big, burly guy." At first, she squealed with delight, but then hesitated and asked, "Does this mean you're not moving up here?"

The next couple of days, I thought about how I was going to meet him again. I didn't want to look like a stalker showing up at his fire station, so I decided to look him up in the phone book. I couldn't believe that in a city with over four million people, Mike lived within two miles of me. Mustering up the courage I had left, I called him… but his voicemail came on. Nervously, I stuttered, "Hi, Mike? This is Angie from the wedding a few days ago. I was calling because I thought that maybe you and I could go get some coffee some time and talk. So call me if you're interested… bye!" My fingers were crossed that he'd be interested enough to call me back.

The next morning, my phone rang, and it was him! "Angie," he said softly, "it's Mike. I have something to ask you. Aren't you with Gerry?" When I explained our history, he asked if I liked sushi.

"That's my favorite food," I practically yelled back.

"Then it looks like we have a date," he concluded.

Our first date was magical. We talked for hours while we ate sushi and drank sake. I couldn't stop staring at his handsome face and I felt a strong connection with him. His calm demeanor and gentle smile were mesmerizing. Then I nearly fell out of my chair when I learned he used to work at Scotty's Landing as a bartender — the restaurant in my dream! A wave of peace came over me afterward, as if I knew he was God's answer to me. "Give love a chance again," God must have been saying. "Here he is."

I listened to my gut and continued to date him. Eventually, he met Milan, and they hit it off. We've been together for twelve years now. I can literally say that Mike is the man of my dreams. My big, burly firefighter rescued me, although he swears that I rescued him.

— Angelene Gorman —

19

The Date

Love recognizes no barriers. It jumps hurdles,
leaps fences, penetrates walls to arrive at its
destination full of hope.
~Maya Angelou

ur mother was the one who taught us the technique. Cut a hard-boiled egg in two, salt it, eat only the white part, and then somersault into bed and sleep with your head at the foot of the bed. "Do that," she told us, "and you'll dream about the man you're going to marry."

The first time I tried the technique, I was twelve years old, and a stranger did show up in my dreams that night.

A long, dark car pulled up in front of the house, and a man stepped out of the driver's side and approached me. He didn't say anything — he just stood there gazing at me, which enabled me to get a good, long look at him. He had black hair cut neatly above the ears, and a handsome face with sharp, angular features. I could tell he was an intelligent man; I could see it in his eyes.

I don't remember how the dream ended, but I know that the stranger and I never spoke to each other. He probably just got back into the car and drove off. But even though I'd forgotten the ending, my mind never let go of the central part of the dream. I'd replay it in my thoughts every now and then. The car. The black-haired stranger. That face. Those intelligent eyes.

One winter day, some five years later, my good friend Jean called me to ask a favor. "Jane, I need you to go on a double date with Ralph and me."

I'd never been on a double date before. And this would be a blind double date. I asked Jean for more details.

"Ralph's buddy from the Navy is in town," she informed me. "He's nice. His name is Joe. I think you'll like him."

"And what if I don't?" I asked.

"If you don't like him, we'll all say goodbye at the end of the night and go our separate ways. Come on, Jane. It's just one date."

I agreed to do my friend a favor and go on the double date. That evening, after getting myself ready, I sat in the living room and waited for the three of them to come and pick me up.

Seven o'clock came and went, and my friends didn't show up. At 7:30, I called Jean's house. When I learned she wasn't home, I figured she'd be arriving with the guys any moment.

Eight o'clock came and went, and still there was no sign of my friend.

By 9 p.m., I was beginning to get agitated. Of course, I worried that maybe something had happened to them, but only for a few fleeting minutes. Somehow, I knew that they hadn't gotten into an accident, and nothing bad had happened to them. They were simply being irresponsible and had lost track of time.

By 9:30, I'd decided that I definitely was not going on a date that evening. It was too late for me to leave the house. I was only seventeen, and my mother would worry about me if I went out after 9:30, accompanied by a stranger no less! I sat there in the living room and fumed. How could my friend be so rude?

It was just before ten when a knock came at the front door.

I marched to the door, prepared to tell Jean and the guys that they'd have to do their double date minus one. I wasn't leaving the house this late, and if they had any sense, they'd have known better than to show up now!

But when I opened the door, my attitude immediately softened. Jean and Ralph were there on the front porch, but I didn't pay any attention to them. Standing right in front of me was a stranger... a stranger I had encountered five years earlier. Same black hair. Same handsome, angular face. Same intelligent eyes. How could I ever forget those eyes?

"I'm Joe," he said, smiling as he shuffled forward. "Nice to meet you."

He put his hand out and waited for me to shake it. But instead of shaking his hand, I pointed at him and said in a voice brimming with certainty, "You're the man I'm going to marry."

"I am?" Joe replied, visibly taken aback by my bold remark.

I held his gaze as I allowed the moment to settle in. Then I glanced over at Jean. "Let me get my coat."

Joe and I had a wonderful time that evening. In the weeks that followed, we shared many other wonderful days and evenings together. That double date was in December. By March, less than four months later, Joe and I were married.

My sweetheart passed away a number of years ago, but prior to his passing, Joe and I enjoyed forty-four years of wedded bliss. We built a life together—and a legacy. Five children. Ten grandchildren. And now so many greats and great-greats, I practically need a spreadsheet to keep track of them.

Sometimes, at family gatherings, I look around the room at my children, my grandchildren, my greats and great-greats, and I think about that December night in 1950. One thing I know for sure: I wouldn't have accompanied Joe on that date if he hadn't appeared in my dream some years earlier. I would have gone to bed and missed out on sharing a life with the black-haired Navy man.

If I hadn't experienced that dream, it's often occurred to me, none of these beautiful people around me would exist. None of them would have been born. There would perhaps be other people in my life, other children and grandchildren, but not these specific people—the wonderful, talented individuals I've come to think of as the jewels in my crown.

It's amazing what a dream can lead to if you listen to it and act on it. You can build a life on one dream, as I did. If you're fortunate—as I was—you might even create a legacy that lasts for generations to come.

—Jane Clark—

20

The Right Man

In all the world, there is no heart for me like yours.
In all the world, there is no love for you like mine.
~Maya Angelou

"**W**ait. This is wrong. Why is it you? You're not supposed to be here!" I woke up just after he smiled and shrugged. Then I realized I was smiling, too. What a silly dream!

I was newly married and forging a life with my husband Andy in New York City. I was slowly getting used to the fast pace, strong language, and absence of personal space. I landed a job in a gift shop to help pay bills between theater auditions, and I was starting to feel like I fit in. But all the hustle and bustle, even at my young age, took its toll. I was exhausted when I returned to our apartment on Staten Island every evening, and I slept like a baby every night.

My slumbers were so sound, in fact, that I rarely dreamt, which is why that particular night was so peculiar. Not only did I have a dream, but it was vivid, the kind where I had to look around when I awoke, making sure it wasn't real.

I was walking down the aisle at my wedding on the arm of my father, except this didn't look anything like the actual church wedding I'd celebrated just a few months earlier. This wedding was outside in a beautiful garden in front of a white gazebo. Still, there Dad and I walked, nodding to family members seated around us, smiling and happy.

Then I reached the clergyman standing in front and turned to my handsome groom. It wasn't Andy. It was my high-school boyfriend, Alan, whom I hadn't seen since graduation over five years earlier. We had parted friends, wished each other luck, and went our separate ways. But now here he was, about to marry me in my dream. I gasped and exclaimed, "Wait. This is wrong. Why is it you? You're not supposed to be here!" He smiled and shrugged. He never spoke. My goodness, he looked handsome!

I woke up, laughed, and told Andy about the bizarreness of it all. He laughed too, and we agreed my brain was probably overtired. We never gave it another thought.

Nearly four years later, Andy came home one day and asked if we could talk. He announced that he no longer loved me and he didn't want to be married anymore. He packed a bag and left, leaving me sitting frozen in a chair, too shocked to speak. The months that followed were bleak as I struggled to get on with my life. There were good days and bad, and I was fortunate to have amazing family and friends to support me. But I was broken.

Then one day there was a message on my answering machine. I listened to it once and then hit "Repeat" because it was too surreal to believe. "Hi. My name is Alan. I'm looking for a girl I used to date in high school named Joan. Is this you? If so, I'd love to catch up. Call me back." I rewound it again. It had been eight years. How had he found me? *Why* had he found me?

I called him back, and we talked for hours. Then he called again the next day. And the next. He listened while I told him about my failed marriage, and he told me about his own. He understood all the pain and shame, and we helped each other heal. We also reminisced about high school, all the marching-band trips and homecoming dances, and the years melted away. By the time we finally reunited in person, I already knew I had fallen in love with him. It took a few years because we were both so gun-shy after our previous failures, but one evening he asked me to marry him, and I replied "Yes!" without hesitation.

We started looking for venues and found a lovely resort that specialized in weddings. As they walked us around to the back of the hotel to show us the grounds, I stopped dead in my tracks. I hadn't thought of that dream in years, but here it was in front of me. There was the garden. There was the white gazebo, exactly as it had appeared in my dream. "This is the one," I simply told Alan.

The day of our wedding was glorious. Surrounded by the family who had so lovingly supported me through all the dark days, I walked down the aisle holding onto my father's arm. I reached the clergyman and turned to my smiling, handsome groom. He was definitely supposed to be there.

Today, a lovely framed photo of my groom and me standing in front of that gazebo, overlooking that garden, hangs on our wall. I study it every day. I'm still not sure what that dream meant. Was God trying to warn me that things were going to get a little rough, but there was a greater plan down the road? Who knows? I just tell people that it took me a while, but I finally married the man of my dreams and I wouldn't change a thing.

—Joan Donnelly-Emery—

21

Take Me Out to the Ballgame

*When two people are meant to be together,
they will be together. It's fate.*
~Sara Gruen

The divorce had been rough, and the ongoing legal struggles were exhausting. I slumped in the pew one gloomy Sunday morning. The gray day seemed to penetrate the inside of the church and my mood as I sat there and prayed, "God, if you just get me out of this mess, I promise I will *never, ever* get married again!"

I think God must have smiled at my offer. Immediately, I was given a vision or a premonition — and it scared me to death!

I saw myself getting ready to walk down the left aisle of our church with my adult children, Darren and Michele, my son-in-law, Tim, and my grandson, Kristopher. Although Kristopher was their only child, Michele was carrying a little, dark-haired girl about two years old. Coming down the right aisle was a tall man holding the hand of a little girl. The altar was filled with beautiful, pink flowers!

The vision only lasted a few seconds, but it was so real that I was shaking and confused. I thought about it for a few days and then forgot about it as I struggled to survive. Working two jobs, I had no social life at all.

I did enjoy watching our local baseball team, the California Angels, on TV. Finally, at my friends' urging, I joined the Angels Booster Club. It was fun to attend the baseball games as a group and hand out give-away items at the gates. While working the gates, I met John, one of the club members. He was so friendly, and we talked and laughed a lot.

Whenever the team was out of town, a group of us would gather to watch the Angels on TV. John was always present and hopeful of a relationship, but I told him, "I enjoy being with you, but I'm not interested in anything more." He would just nod his head and smile.

One day, John's parents invited me to their house for a party. John had an adorable daughter, Jamie, and it was her sixth birthday. I knew he had a little girl, but he was pretty protective of her and hadn't introduced us until he was sure about his feelings for me. She and I bonded immediately, but I told John, "I still don't want to get married again — ever." John just smiled and nodded his head in that infuriating way of his. I responded with an adamant, "I mean it!"

"I know you do — now," he replied, grinning.

I took the problem to God. "Why won't he believe me? I don't want to hurt him, God, but I just don't want to get married again."

One day, John and I were sitting at the park watching Jamie play on the monkey bars. "You know," John said quietly, "we might as well get married. We're together all the time, and we get along so well. I can't imagine my life without you."

I had a lump in my throat as I sat there staring at him and then at his sweet girl. Neither of us spoke for a long time, and then I said, "I can't imagine my life without both of you, either."

We decided on a February church wedding and a reception at Angel Stadium where we had met. Michele and Tim came from Minnesota to visit us in October and arrived with Kristopher, now four years old, and two-year-old, Kelly, my little, dark-haired granddaughter.

On Wednesday of their weeklong visit, Michele said to me, "Mom, we're going to start building our new house, and we won't be able to come back in February for your wedding."

"What shall we do?" I asked John.

With his usual calm, he asked me, "What's more important to you — to have all the kids there or to have the wedding we planned in February?"

When he said that, I remembered that vision from three years before. "It's definitely more important to have all the kids there," I replied, "but how can we pull this together so quickly?"

"We'll just split up all the tasks, and everyone can help," he replied confidently.

I called my friend, Betty, who worked at a nursery. "John and I are getting married on Saturday. Can you help with the flowers?"

"Of course, I wouldn't miss it," she replied calmly. "What color is your dress?"

"I don't have one yet!" In fact, I hadn't even thought about it.

"Okay," Betty said, "your flowers will be pink. Pink will go with any color you choose."

I called our Booster Club friends to see if they could serve refreshments. They jumped right in and even planned to wear their Booster Club shirts.

Another friend, Isobel, offered to make our wedding cake. "No one else can make your cake and put all the love into it that I can," she said.

Everyone pitched in. Some made calls since we had no time to send invitations. Others offered to decorate and make punch. "I'll get napkins, plates and cups," my future father-in-law volunteered. I wondered if it would all match when the pieces were put together.

At the rehearsal, I told our pastor about my vision. "I think it was a picture from God," I explained, "so I want to walk down the left aisle with my children and grandchildren while John walks down the right aisle with his daughter. Then we can all come out the center aisle together as one family."

"I think that's a fine idea," he agreed, smiling.

On Saturday, I walked into the church reception hall, and everything looked beautiful! Everything that our friends and family had prepared fit together beautifully. Isobel's cake looked like three layers of love and deliciousness. There were the plates and napkins with our names printed on them as promised. And — everything was pink!

Just before we were to walk down the aisle, Kelly slipped and started to cry, so Michele picked her up and held her, and we walked down the aisle together just as I had seen in my vision.

The pastor even included all the kids in the ceremony. After we said our vows, he had us all clasp hands on top of my Bible and asked my children, "Do you promise to respect and honor John and this marriage?"

"Yes, we do," they promised.

Turning to Jamie, the pastor asked her, "Do you promise to respect and honor Judee as your stepmother?"

"I do," she answered in a solemn, small voice.

"Then I pronounce this family is one in the sight of God and these witnesses!" announced the pastor.

As we started our journey together down the center aisle, we laughed out loud as the organist played a dignified rendition of "Take Me Out to the Ballgame" on the church organ. We had heard that song hundreds of times, but now we would hear *our* song at every baseball game!

— Judee Stapp —

22

Love and Purpose

*In the process of letting go you will lose many things
from the past, but you will find yourself.*
~Deepak Chopra

"I s everything okay?" Trina asked as we walked toward the park. I wasn't sure how to answer, but I couldn't say that everything was fine. Trina knew me better than that.

"I had a weird dream last night," I told her.

Trina looked concerned. "What was it about?"

I stopped for a minute, trying to figure out how to respond. There weren't any scenes or events in the dream. That's why it had felt so strange, almost not a dream. "It felt like a bunch of voices speaking a language I couldn't understand, but somehow I knew what language it was."

She cocked her head and raised an eyebrow, waiting for me to finish.

"They were people from India," I told her.

"Do you think the dream meant something?" she prompted.

I felt tears spring to my eyes unexpectedly. Blinking them back, I started walking again. I was afraid of the meaning, but I couldn't deny it. "I got the feeling I'm meant to go to India," I told her. I had had dreams of moving to Ireland or Scotland, maybe becoming a midwife like my mom. But India? I had no plans to even visit.

My friend didn't laugh. We were both daughters of former missionaries, both entering our adult years, trying to figure out our direction in life. My parents had lived in India when I was very young, but I hardly remembered it. I had mainly grown up in central California and moved to Southern California the previous year after graduating from high school.

There was another impression the dream had left me with, but I didn't have the courage to share that part with Trina. It felt too personal and specific. I decided to keep that part to myself.

"Why don't you give it some time?" Trina suggested. "Maybe talk to a few others about it. What about Angie?" Angie was a mutual friend who had spent a year in southern India and had recently returned.

"I'll do that," I told her. I had mixed feelings, but as the days went by, I couldn't forget the dream or the strong impression it made on me. I started making plans to visit India. To my delight, Trina decided to come along. A few other friends joined us, and it felt like an adventure as we landed in Bombay (now called Mumbai) and adjusted to the changes in weather, culture and lifestyle.

Then, almost before the adventure started, it was nearing its end. Trina had only gotten a three-month visa, and our friends decided to stay only as long as she did. When they returned to California, I stayed in India, somehow knowing this was what I was meant to do. Although I began volunteering my time in tutoring and other social work projects, I felt aimless and homesick.

One rainy day in early monsoon, I got a phone call from a friend of Trina's. Her voice broke as she told me the news. Trina had been bicycling on a mountain road and had been hit by a truck. After twelve hours in a coma, she passed away. My vision clouded, and it felt as though someone had sucked the oxygen from the room where I sat, unable to respond to the voice on the other end of the line. I managed to get out a word or two and ended the call.

The next few days passed in a haze. I couldn't get through a conversation without crying. I had no appetite. I just wanted to go home, but I knew nothing would be the same again, no matter where I went.

Why did she have to die? The question burned inside me. There was so much she wanted to do. She had talked about adopting a dozen boys or starting a school in some remote place where children didn't have the chance for education.

One night, tossing and turning in the oppressive humidity, I fell into a restless sleep.

I woke with a start, knowing I had had a dream, an important one, but I couldn't remember the details. It was beautiful, but not a single scene remained in my mind. All that stayed with me was a single phrase spoken by a voice I knew well.

Trina's voice.

She said, "If you only knew…" She didn't finish the thought, but the feeling behind her words was full of joy and awe. I knew that she was in a place of perfection and beauty.

I sat up in bed and looked outside my window at the early dawn in a land that I didn't call home. One day, I would be home, but I knew I couldn't leave India. If nothing else, I had to make a difference for Trina's sake. I had to live as she would have lived — with a sense of purpose. I needed to do it for both of us, even though I was comforted by the thought that she was happy and content.

I traveled to southern India to attend a conference for young people, many of them foreign volunteers looking for a place to settle in and a ministry to devote themselves to. I attended a workshop by a man named Ajay from New Delhi who worked with deaf people. He mentioned that there were over ten million deaf people in India, and that many of them did not have opportunities for education and training. He had started more than a dozen deaf friendship clubs in and around New Delhi, where deaf people could join a community with others who had shared common experiences. They also received training, education, and various kinds of assistance from Ajay and his co-workers.

After the workshop, I approached Ajay and introduced myself. I told him I had taken several classes and knew some American Sign Language.

"Why don't you come visit us?" he asked. "There are plenty of ways you could get involved in the work. You really could make a difference."

He sent his friend Daniel to pick me up by train so I wouldn't have to travel to New Delhi alone. I went for a visit, but I ended up staying. India became my home for the next decade.

Remember the part of the dream I didn't want to share with Trina? I had been embarrassed because it seemed like nothing more than a young woman's foolish hope: that India was the place where I would meet my future husband, and that he was waiting for me there.

Two years after Daniel picked me up at a crowded train station not far from Bombay, he took my hand, and we exchanged vows. He had been waiting for me.

— Bonita Jewel —

23

Bad Patch

Angels have no philosophy but love.
~Terri Guillemets

The spaghetti had extra Parmesan just the way I liked it. My mother's smiling face leaned in as she handed me the steaming plate. Her cooking had been an attempt to mend my broken heart.

"I have extra Parmesan if you need it." Her voice trailed off as she headed back to the kitchen. She added the next words casually. "He wasn't right for you, you know. Your man is out there somewhere."

The hot tears welled in my eyes. The wounds were still fresh and the sting of my disappointment still burned.

The sound of running water almost drowned out yet another overused expression that I was tired of hearing. "You just gotta get right back in that saddle. You're in a bit of a bad patch. That's all."

Bad patch? My entire twenties had been a bad patch in terms of love. It was overrun with the weeds of awkward blind dates and soured relationships. Either I was running from love, or more recently, it seemed it was running from me.

My life was complete in every other area. I had a fulfilling career. My strong friendships and family ties had bolstered me as I sailed the rough seas of my relationships. But now I was one week shy of my thirty-first birthday. My inability to find love and create my own family hurt. I felt like a failure: a lonely failure.

The physical pain that accompanies heartache is sharp. It cuts into your heart and constricts your throat. Tears bring temporary relief. But, the pain needs to be ridden out. Sleep helps, too. So, I decided to spend the night in my mother's guest bedroom that evening. I turned in early, eager for sleep.

I was in a very deep sleep when I felt the blankets pulled up over me. A warm pair of hands lovingly soothed the bedding over me, untangling it and shifting it up over my shoulders. I could feel the deep concern as this person leaned over me, peering into my face.

My eyes were heavy but I managed to open them slightly. It was just enough to see a woman standing over me. I closed my eyes quickly due to the brilliant light that filled the room. My eyelids fluttered as I squinted in an attempt to get a better glimpse. The woman was wearing a white dress and the moonlight shimmered upon her in such a way that she seemed to cast her own light. Her light hair flowed around her face, but I couldn't feel the breeze rippling against her. My eyes closed again just as she leaned in closer to my face. At this point my dream state must have taken over because her warm hands seemed to melt into my body as she smoothed the blankets over me.

"Oh, Michele... you are loved." Her words were full of deep compassion as she whispered them into my ear.

I padded into my mother's kitchen the next morning. My mother had her head in the refrigerator, obviously eager to cook up yet another remedy for my broken heart.

"I must have really worried you last night," I said as I grabbed a coffee mug. "You haven't tucked me in like that since I was a kid."

"Tucked you in?" She emerged from behind the open door of the refrigerator, hands full of eggs and butter.

"Yeah, didn't you come in the guest room last night? And, where did you get that pretty white nightie...." My eyes affixed to her red flannel nightgown. "And, your hair was..." I looked at her graying hair that was up in curlers, a bit confused.

"I didn't come into your room. I turned in early and slept like a ton of bricks." She patted my head as she headed for the stove. "I always sleep better when you're home, hon."

"Well, someone came in. Maybe you don't remember. Maybe you

just came in to check the light?"

She cracked an egg. "Weird dreams again?"

My heart was lighter that day. That woman's hands had simply shooed away the darkness that had been eating away at my heart. I knew I had seen the lovely woman. I had felt the blankets move around me and I certainly felt the hands as they moved over me. More importantly, I had sensed her soothing comfort. Whoever she was, this woman had cared enough to show her love and compassion for me. She had also ignited hope.

After that day I approached dating differently. I was a woman who had an angel around her, an angel that loved me fiercely.

Within a year, I had met the love of my life. I had gotten back in that saddle, as my mother had suggested, and bravely went on yet another first date. I knew he was the one immediately, as did he. It was a whirlwind relationship and we were married a year later. Today, we have been married ten years and we have two wonderful young daughters. I realize now that all of those dead ends to love were just God's way of putting me on ice. I was being saved for a rare love that only a few are lucky enough to find. And, I will never forget the woman who had paid me a midnight visit. I believe she serves as a reminder that everyone has that kind of love watching over them every single day.

— Michele Boom —

Meant to Be

Mango Love

When I am with you, the only place
I want to be is closer.
~Author Unknown

t was our first date. He'd asked me to a movie, and I had suggested we each bring some food and have a picnic first. I was pretty excited; it had been a while since I'd been out with anyone, and I could tell this guy was special. Besides that, he was gorgeous.

It was a warm summer evening so I chose to wear my new sundress and sandals. I gathered some food, nothing special: half a loaf of bread, a block of Vermont cheddar cheese and I was just about to throw in some apples when I glanced at the fruit bowl. Oh yeah! A few days ago I had bought a mango. When we buy mangos in Vermont they're hard as a rock, and you have to wait forever for them to ripen. Even then you never know if they'll be any good, and they are expensive to begin with, so it's rare I would even buy one. This mango had gone from green to a beautiful yellow/orange with reddish streaks. A gentle squeeze showed me that it was ripe so I added it to the paper bag and headed out the door.

We met by the movie theater and walked to the river. I had that little heart-poundy thing that happens if I'm excited, nervous, and extremely hopeful. We found a grassy spot to sit by the water and started to unpack our picnic. While he pulled a green pepper from his backpack I noticed how far away I had sat down from him. I tried to be nonchalant as I inched closer, pretending I needed to brush some pine needles off my dress.

"This is from my garden," he said. His hair had this way of parting on his forehead in just the right way to make him look, well, dreamy. "I thought we could slice the pepper and dip it in this." He took out a container of hummus. His hands were so big. He pulled out his pocketknife and sliced up the pepper. He carries a pocketknife, I thought, and inwardly swooned.

"There's more," he said, "but let's see what you have first."

What I have? I had gone into a teenage daze even though I was in my thirties. The guy was so darn handsome! "Oh, yeah. What I have." I pulled out the bread and cheese.

"Is that the Cabot extra sharp?" he asked. He reached out to take it and his hand touched mine. It sent a spark through my whole body. I'm sure I turned bright red. Pretending to look for something, I stuck my head into my picnic bag, trying to hide my pink face. I realized I never answered his question about the cheese.

"Yeah," I said from inside the bag. "It's the extra sharp." I was feeling lightheaded from the way his eyes sparkled and I thought maybe it was a good thing I was inside the bag. Isn't that what you're supposed to do if you are about to faint? Stick your head in a paper bag? Breathe, silly, I told myself. He's just a guy. "Oh, here it is!" I said pulling my head out and retrieving the mango. Could he possibly believe I had to search that hard for a mango inside the now empty paper bag?

"A mango?" he said. Uh oh. What if he doesn't like mangos? What if they make his tongue go fuzzy or his throat seize up? "Yum," he said and he smiled.

Oh no! That warm thing was happening again and I was afraid I would have to dive back into the bag. Deep breath, I told myself.

"Maybe we should eat," I somehow managed to say, trying to swallow tiny little gasps.

He sliced the green pepper, cheese and bread with his pocketknife. We drank from his water bottle and ate our picnic while a duck family swam up and asked to be included in the feast. The river quietly flowed by, the wind whispered through the leaves above us, and my heart flip-flopped inside me as I began the journey of falling in love with this gorgeous man. Quietly we sat next to each other, letting the grassy smell of July fill the space between us. Andy picked up the mango, and said, "Shall I?" All I could do was nod.

He peeled and sliced the perfectly ripe mango and placed the whole thing in his massive hand, offering me a piece. The combination of his hand and the juicy mango made me unbalanced. I reached out and grabbed a slice, but then ended up jostling his hand, which made him drop the rest of the mango onto the sand and ant-covered grass. Our eyes met and I was amazed that in deep crisis he could still take my breath away. We turned our gazes to the mango slices. They were a loss. There was no way to get the sand off them. The duck family looked at us as if to say, "We'll eat it! We love sand and ants!"

I didn't know if I should laugh, cry or stick my head back into the paper bag. Andy nodded toward the slice in my hand. "Go ahead," he said, a twinkle in his eye.

"No, no, it should be for you! I'm the one who knocked it all to the ground. Here." I handed the mango piece to him. He took it from me and bit it in half. Then he reached out and brought the other half to my mouth. Oh lord, help me stay alive for this, I silently prayed. He placed the mango slice in my mouth and I tried really, really hard to leave his finger alone. The mango was perfect. Sweet, juicy, tender.

Maybe we should get going, I thought, and I started packing up our little picnic.

"Not so fast," Andy said. He reached into his bag and pulled out... a mango! He had brought one too! It was yellow, orange and red. He peeled it, he sliced it and in an incredibly trusting move, he offered me a slice from his giant hand.

Slice by slice we ate that mango, the sweet juice dripping through Andy's fingers. The duck family sat close by and watched us eat and fall in love.

Today, whenever we eat a mango, the kids ask us to tell the story about the time Mom flung the mango out of Dad's hand onto the sandy, ant-covered ground.

— Lava Mueller —

25

Miracle Meeting

Therefore, what God has joined together,
let man not separate.
~Matthew 19:6

rowing up with a last name like Miracle made for a lot of puns. When I was born, my parents could honestly say without boasting that I was a Miracle child. On the playground in elementary school I heard, "Hey Miracle Whip!" In junior high school, "It's a Miracle!" echoed through the halls as I carried a toppling stack of books. It wasn't until I reached high school and college that I really found consolation in my name.

I didn't believe I would ever marry, even though that is what I wanted. I would laugh and tell my best friend, "At least I have a good last name because it is never going to change."

Years after my pessimistic marriage prediction, I started my career as a fifth-grade teacher. One day I was walking innocently down the hall, minding my own business after taking my students to the bus. Beth, one of my fellow teachers, emerged from her classroom into the empty hallway.

"There is someone you should meet," she said. Her eyes danced and her lips curled into a smile.

"Oh no," I thought to myself. "Not another blind date." A thousand alarm systems shrilled in my head, and I imagined myself making a U-turn and sprinting, Olympian style, to the nearest exit. I was a single newcomer in town and everyone seemed interested in plotting out my love life. As afraid as I was of never getting married, I was becoming more and more afraid of blind dates.

I politely said, "No thanks, I'm already seeing someone," which was true.

Despite my refusal, Beth, without pausing for breath, continued to tell me about Jesse, the nice man she had met at church. Jesse's mother, Sharon, had taught at our school, but died tragically in an automobile accident long before I could ever meet her. Other teachers and past students fondly remembered her kindness, and each year a senior at the high school was awarded a scholarship in her memory. I was sure this devoted woman had raised a nice son; I just didn't like blind dates. Dating in general could be troublesome, and I certainly didn't want to intentionally invite trouble into my life.

Persistence became Beth's mantra. Each time during the school year when she asked if I would like to meet Jesse, I adamantly refused. I explained that I was dating someone and I was comfortable with that.

Then that relationship went south, literally.

That summer the man I had been dating left the country on a mission trip, mailing a letter from the airport revealing his decision to end our courtship. Tearing into his letter with great expectation only brought stinging hot humiliation to my cheeks.

It felt like my love life had died a death so dark it was far beyond resuscitation. My faith told me God was with me, but my doubt made me wonder where He was in my love life. I decided my youthful declarations might be true; it looked like it really would be a miracle if this Miracle ever married.

School started again and I moved to a new apartment. It wasn't my first choice. Plans for another apartment fell through, and by word of mouth, a friend found this one for me near the school.

Those days were filled with definite highs. I loved learning and laughing with my wide-eyed students. When they said, "Miss Miracle, you're the best teacher ever," it softened the hard edges of life. But I was still lonely and wanted to meet someone special — someone with whom I could have a future.

Day after day I graded papers and looked out my new back patio window into the carefully maintained square. A variety of vibrant pots filled with looping vines and late summer flowers clung to neighborly-looking balcony rails. The common area was shared by twelve apartment buildings. I could have lived in any of them. Initially I hadn't considered how choosing this particular building, overlooking this peaceful plot, would be such a good plan for my life.

Months went by. The summer pots disappeared from the square, replaced by snow and ice that clung to the balcony rails instead.

One wintry February morning, I was scraping my car windshield and talking to one of my new neighbors who lived downstairs in my building. He was tall, friendly, my age, and it hadn't taken long for me to notice his movie star smile. When our paths had crossed in the stairwell, we would say hello and engage in brief conversations. If the truth be known, I was developing a crush, and we had never even been formally introduced.

That particular February morning, this handsome neighbor was concerned for the other tenants' safety, as the sidewalks were slick with a thick sheet of ice. He warned each person who walked by of hazardous spots, and I saw how kind he was. We talked as we de-iced our cars and he asked me where I taught.

"Second Street School," I answered, as my scraper flicked shavings of ice that melted on the warming car hood.

His whole face lit up with interest, igniting his perfect smile. "My mother taught there," he told me with pride.

"Really?" I said enthusiastically. "Would I know her?"

"No." In a quiet voice that sounded far away and tinged with sadness he said, "She died in a car accident."

This tall friendly man began describing his mother's beautiful qualities and telling me about the scholarship that family, students, and friends had started. But his words were muffled, as if making their way down a long tunnel to my brain. My breath caught in the frigid air. My neighbor, who introduced himself as Jesse, was the man I had refused to meet for more than a year. And yet there he was, standing before me.

Much has happened in the nine years since that memorable

discovery. My students and I raised money for the Sharon Lewis Scholarship Fund by recycling aluminum cans. My gloomy guess at how life would turn out was wrong. My last name changed after all, and I taught at the school until two days before our handsome baby boy was born.

Now on wintry icy mornings I snuggle close to my husband Jesse in our warm little home and I feel like I'm still a Miracle.

— Janeen Lewis —

26

We Dreamed a Little Dream

*If two people are meant for each other, it doesn't mean
they have to be together right now or as soon
as possible, but they will… eventually.*
~Nina Ardianti

From the time I was a very little child, my dreams were vivid and real. Most of them were filled with images of playing in sunny meadows or flying over surreal places, so dreams of the more ordinary sort simply passed through my consciousness like the blur outside a train window. But there was one particular dream that felt very special, and I knew it, even though I was only about five years old.

My great-grandparents emigrated from Japan to the Hawaiian Islands at the turn of the 19th century. Four generations later, my family still held onto some Japanese cultural practices. One of them was the *furo* bath where, after washing with soap and water outside the tub, we would enter the hot water to soak. The temperature of the water is notoriously hot. In the old country, it would be heated over burning coals. The entire village would take turns soaking in a large public bath.

Although our modern day *furo* was not heated with coals, but just very hot water from the faucet, I recall being worried that the water would cook me. Boil me alive. I learned to enter very slowly, one toe at a time, as my body acclimated to the searing heat. By the time I emerged, my skin was lobster red. Cooked lobster red. But I loved it. We all loved soaking in the *furo*. It made us feel clean inside and out.

One night, I dreamed that I was sitting in an old-fashioned Japanese furo. *My great-grandmother, with her white hair pulled into a tight bun, sat nearby crocheting and looking up occasionally to be sure I was safe. Next to me was a little blond boy. He was a little older than I was, and we didn't speak to each other at all. But we were friends. That much I could tell because of the overwhelming feeling of wellbeing and happiness I felt while with this playmate.*

And when I woke up, that was all I could remember: A sweet joy. All I knew was that I wanted to spend time with my friend. But waking life compelled me to focus on growing up, and so I did.

Little did I know that thousands of miles away and across the vast Pacific blue, a little blond boy was growing up, too.

And he, too, had had a dream.

Nearly twenty years later, I was living in California and struggling to end a five-year relationship. One night, I went to bed, sad and uncertain, and prayed to God: "Please, God, help me to know what to do. If it is your will that I marry this man, I will stay with him. If not… if there is someone else for me, please let me know."

That night, I had a dream that I saw a filmy veil that hung like a curtain across the window. I saw the shadow of a figure of a man. And my heart skipped a beat. There was someone else for me.

The next day, I made a clean break. And then, like an ensign that signaled my new beginning, I got a new job, in Newport Beach in advertising. And one week into my new job a blond man walked through the door.

When our eyes locked, something tangible occurred. We both felt it. There was something so familiar about us together. So much so that the company secretary who had been sitting at the front desk came to me later to ask, "What was *that*? Something *happened*. What's going on?"

I didn't know, frankly. All I did know was that there was something remarkable and alluring about this man, and all I wanted to do was be with him. We had our first date of many that night. As time passed, we talked about everything from our families to our career goals, and then finally, our childhoods.

As I explained a bit about Japanese culture, I talked about the practice of *furo-ba*, or hot-tub baths, and how I loved them. He fell silent, and his eyes grew teary. Quietly, he recounted a dream he had had when he was just a little boy living in Texas, in an all white area where no one had ever encountered an Asian family.

He was in a large hot tub with an old Asian woman sitting in the background. Next to him sat a little girl with short black hair. She looked Japanese. And although they did not speak, he felt very happy to be with his playmate.

He said that the sweet dream replayed for three nights, and he was anxious to go to sleep each night. When the dreams stopped, he felt a terrible loss that took him a while to get over. And he was only about eight years old.

What are the odds that two little children separated by thousands of miles had the same dream about each other and then met twenty years later? But we knew it was true because, for some inexplicable reason, we couldn't bear to be apart. And so we weren't — for the next thirty-two years and counting!

Now we have grown children of our own. And sometimes we sit in a large Japanese *furo* together like we once did in a very happy dream, one that continues now even while we are awake!

— Lori Chidori Phillips —

27

The Man of My Dreams

*So, I love you because the entire universe
conspired to help me find you.*
~Paulo Coelho, The Alchemist

One morning in July 2012, I woke up remembering fragments of a very vivid dream in which I was having dinner at a restaurant with a handsome, dark-haired man named Marco. As I lay in bed recalling the dream, I thought about how real it had seemed. But I didn't know anyone named Marco, and anyway, it was just a dream. It didn't mean anything.

Besides, it was some years since I had been in a serious relationship and, at the ripe old age of thirty-one, I had given up thinking I would ever be in one again. "It was a nice dream, but it'll never happen," I thought to myself, as I got out of bed and carried on with the rest of the day.

The days went by and I forgot all about the dream.

At the time, I was living in Melbourne, Australia and I began to think of moving to another city. I couldn't explain it, but it was as though something was compelling me to move to Fremantle, a coastal city in Western Australia I had always loved visiting. So I booked myself into a backpackers' hostel until I could find more permanent accommodation and on the 19th September, I checked in to the Sundancer.

While I didn't know it at the time, on that exact same day, a twenty-eight-year-old Italian man had boarded a flight from Venice to Melbourne. He stayed in Melbourne for a few days, did some sightseeing and decided he would prefer the west coast of Australia. So he took a plane to Perth, just sixteen miles from Fremantle.

The flight ended up being delayed by some hours, and by the time the young man arrived at Perth airport, it was well past midnight — too late to go searching for a hotel room. He began to settle in for an uncomfortable night's sleep on the chairs at the airport when, as luck would have it, a flight attendant who had just finished her shift approached him.

He explained the situation to her and she offered to drive him to the hostel that was on the way to her house. He thanked her for her generosity and followed her to her car.

The flight attendant dropped him off outside the backpackers' hostel closest to her house — the Sundancer in Fremantle.

And the name of the handsome, dark-haired Italian man? Marco.

We have since moved back to Melbourne to start our life together, and we have been together for two and a half years. I am not sure if it was fate, premonition or just a strange series of coincidences that brought us together, but I cherish every day with this wonderful man who has restored my faith in love.

And wherever she is, I'd like to thank the flight attendant who, through an act of kindness to a stranger, delivered the man of my dreams straight into my arms.

— Rachel Lee —

28

Complementary Attraction

A critic can only review the book he has read,
not the one which the writer wrote.
~Mignon McLaughlin, The Neurotic's Notebook

"That was so bad, I had to turn my hearing aid off," the older woman said after I finished reading aloud a scene from my novel. She tapped her red pen on the printed handout as an exclamation point.

I suppressed the urge to correct her split infinitive and, instead, giggled, believing the hearing aid comment a group initiation prank. But I spied others nodding.

Another woman said, "You know, this will never be published." And yet another suggested I seek mental-health counseling since the plot was too depressing for a writer with a healthy psyche.

I thought back to the eye-catching flyer posted at the recreation center, claiming the critique group provided positive feedback in a supportive environment. As my chest and neck flushed, I controlled the desire to stand and rip my manuscript in half, to yell "never mind" and flee the building. Instead, I waited for someone to give me a reason not to quit this writing gig while I still retained a sliver of pride.

Having recently moved to town, I envisioned the evening as an opportunity to make new friends who shared the same passion and to bond with those who understood the difficulties of writing a novel.

Unfortunately, the stern-faced writers meeting my gaze didn't care about my need for camaraderie or support.

After the group expressed their overall displeasure with my prose, the founder of the group announced it was time to critique my work page by page. "Time to nitpick," he warned.

Flipping through my handout, I cursed myself for bringing an entire chapter rather than an excerpt. The group exuberantly discovered missing commas, unnecessary adjectives, and missing end quotes, as if unearthing golden treasures.

Soon, a "can you top this?" attitude surfaced, and they began critiquing each other's critiques, pointing out one another's inadequacies in perfecting the craft. While they battled for the Best Editor of an Edit Award, I sat quietly, summoning enough strength to endure the rest of the evening. The reprieve didn't last long, and the group refocused its assault on my self-esteem. What made me think I could effectively write my name, let alone a book? Whatever possessed me to call that number on the flyer? Why did I move to this stinking town? I offered an occasional "uh-huh" and "I see" as not to appear ungrateful to them for revealing my grave oversights.

Once the meeting adjourned, the leader invited everyone out for drinks. I politely declined, believing the drinks would have been more effective before the meeting. Besides, I couldn't imagine what they'd say to me with a few drinks in them. As the members shuffled out, patting each other on the back for such an insightful critique, I stumbled to my car.

"Hey, Cathi," the leader called before I reached safety. I turned, bracing for one last discouraging word. "I hope they didn't scare you."

I waved off his concern, and a member named Michael made his way over. "They can be a little rough, especially with new members."

Did he actually think I'd become a member? "Rough? I hadn't noticed," I said.

We all laughed.

"You held up well tonight," Michael said. "We've had others leave in tears right in the middle of a critique. I was sure they'd break you."

And there it glimmered — the gauntlet — lying at my feet. Never one to turn down a challenge, I announced, "I'll see you both next Wednesday then."

The following week, as I listened to Michael get a tongue-lashing from the group, I realized why he wanted me to return. Why he needed me to return. Self-preservation. My writing served as a temporary distraction to the group's larger plan to thwart his chances at publication.

After the meeting, Michael and I stood in the parking lot. I said, "Wow, you took a beating tonight. I was certain they'd break you." I smiled. "They can be a bit rough, especially with the old members."

"Yeah. They've never liked my writing."

"Then why do you still come?"

"The same reason you came back, I suppose. Searching for that elusive praise from someone... anyone. Writers are good at beating themselves up, you know. Besides, it's become a game of sorts."

"A game?"

"I'll score a compliment from them before the end of the book." He smiled. "In fact, before you get one."

"Oh, really?" Yet another challenge I couldn't pass up. "Game on."

For my next critique, I set out to dazzle the group with my deft prose. I offered a killer simile. Not exactly a cliché but too close, they thought. A line of alliteration. Too sing-songy, like a nursery rhyme. I added symbolism. Too transparent, some believed. Too unclear for others.

"I thought you had it," Michael said after the meeting.

"Well, technically the word 'okay' can be viewed as a compliment," I said.

"Come on. Everyone knows that's code talk for 'not so good.' Merely adequate."

We watched the others pull from the lot. "Hey, how about dinner?" he asked.

Ah, an opening. I smirked and said, "Okay."

He paused. "Good one."

We found a new reason to stay in the group — each other. Over the course of numerous rewrites and months of laughter and compassion, Michael proved himself not only a keen editor, but also a soul mate.

While the group continued to whittle away at each other's self-esteem, they hadn't noticed Michael and I helping one another along the path to publication.

Then one day, Michael asked, "Have you considered dropping the first fifteen pages of your novel? The story actually starts with the second chapter."

What? Had he been a spy for the enemy all along? Stunned, I went home that night, betrayed by my confidant, my only fan. Then I reread the first chapter, and he was right. I cut it, trusting Michael acted in my best interest. What were a mere fifteen pages of writing besides days of work and a chunk of my ego? I learned to listen to Michael and improved my novel.

Our relationship inside and outside the group flourished as we shared our love of literature and writing. Besides, any man who could convince me to drop the first chapter of my beloved novel could certainly convince me to say "yes" to marriage. And with this simple word, we not only gained a loving partner for life, but we also acquired an in-house editor: a major bonus for any writer.

These days, I say, "Hey, honey, what's a synonym for lethargy?"

"Somnolence," Michael tosses over his shoulder.

We no longer search for that elusive compliment. We complement each other just fine.

— Cathi LaMarche —

29

Adopt a Soldier

Sometimes the most beautiful thing is precisely
the one that comes unexpectedly and unearned,
hence something given truly as a present.
~Anna Freud

Another school year was beginning. I had thirteen excited first graders eager to learn and ready to fill my classroom with giggles, tears, and everything in between. I realized that I had a uniquely small class size and got excited about the special projects we could do. One project that I had been particularly interested in was adopting military members as pen pals for my students.

I began by sending out an e-mail to our school district employees asking for names and contact information of any military members they knew of. I was able to gather four different contacts and sent an e-mail to each one asking if we could "adopt" them.

I only had one reply: Captain Denisar, who was deployed to Afghanistan. Since six-year-olds' attention spans are rather short, and many of the students were just learning how to read and write, I thought it would be best to correspond through e-mail. Captain Denisar quickly became a reward system. If students practiced and could read a book fluently, I recorded it and e-mailed it. If they finished a writing assignment, I would scan it and e-mail it. If students were misbehaving, I caught myself saying, "What would Captain Denisar think about that?" We also used the information Captain Denisar included in his e-mails as learning opportunities. As we communicated with him, we learned more about him. He was twenty-nine, a year older than me, wasn't married, and didn't have any children. I quickly found that we had a lot in common.

At one point, I learned that one of his soldiers had been killed in action and noticed it was taking a toll on him. We started to lighten things up by recording songs and jokes, and sending art projects and care packages. He was so appreciative of the communication and looked forward to being included in the everyday drama of first grade. The communication between my classroom and Captain Denisar continued when he returned stateside. We even sent a banner down to welcome him home! Even though he was home, we continued to communicate with him, as my students had gotten quite attached. Communication dwindled some as he re-deployed, but he promised that he would make a trip to our small town in Illinois to meet my class when he could.

The school year was beginning to wrap up when he contacted me in April about coming up to visit in May. For the first time, we began talking on the phone to coordinate his visit, and somehow our conversations on the phone started getting longer and turning more personal. Before long, our phone conversations turned into a daily event, and Captain Denisar became just Brad.

As the day of his visit approached, I began getting nervous that this man who had stolen the hearts of my students — and was sneaking into mine — wouldn't live up to the hype and the chemistry that was so present through e-mail and phone calls. Did I mention that Brad's father was my school superintendent (my *boss*)? So I was a tad worried that if things didn't go well, it could affect my reputation within the school system. His dad and I drove to the airport together to pick him up, which was somehow not awkward. And before too long, Brad was there, walking toward us in the flesh. We hugged, and as we headed to baggage claim, he turned to me and wiggled his ears. As crazy as that sounds, I wasn't anxious from that moment on. I knew he was exactly the man I thought and hoped he was.

The next morning, he came to the school and stayed all day. I had planned a huge day with my students. Because he was deployed for an entire calendar year, we wanted to catch him up on the holidays he missed. We went all out with an Easter egg hunt, exchanged valentines, had a Thanksgiving dinner for lunch, and sang "Happy Birthday" with a cake for dessert. We wore costumes and had a haunted house for Halloween, and exchanged Christmas gifts. Brad brought an Army T-shirt for each student with his or her name on the back, and we gave him a school T-shirt. We ended the day with a school assembly at which Brad told all the kids about being in the Army and serving in Afghanistan. He showed pictures and answered *a lot* of questions.

We spent the entire weekend together and had dinner with my parents, his best friend, and his father. Things were great. But one week after Brad's visit, I got a frantic call from him telling me that his father had just had a massive heart attack. He didn't know anyone else to call who was in close proximity to his dad. I was the first person to the hospital and met Brad there. He stayed with me for two weeks until his father was able to leave the hospital and recover at home.

The day after the heart attack, we were driving back to the hospital after being up most of the night, and he looked at me and said, "This is it. You're the one." I was speechless for the first time in my life. Things moved quickly. I was able to meet his whole family, who lived all over the country, as they came and took turns helping his dad through the recovery process. By the end of June, we had booked a church, and I purchased a wedding dress. Then we picked out rings. He asked my father's permission for my hand in marriage, and then he proposed. It was not quite in the traditional order.

We were married on January 1, 2011, just seven months after his visit to my classroom, in the church that I grew up in. It was the same church in which his parents had taught Sunday school before he was born, just miles from his grandparents' farm where he visited as a child. It was a beautiful winter wedding with a large military presence and the beginning of my life as an Army wife. Never in my wildest dreams did I imagine that adopting a soldier would lead to a lifelong commitment and the love of my life.

— Katie Denisar —

30

Collared by Love

*He stirred my soul in the most subtle way
and the story between us wrote itself.*
~Nikki Rowe

My husband of fifteen years and I had separated, but we shared joint custody of two finches. I was standing in the local pet store in our Northern California town looking at bamboo nesting houses for them when a vibrant dog collar caught my eye.

Our two Shetland Sheepdogs had died two years before, and I longed for another canine companion. The finches were nice for noise and funny when they cheeped along to Lady Gaga, but the birds were not much to pet and didn't contribute anything to my exercise routine.

The collar that caught my eye was intricately patterned in a rainbow of hues and tightly loomed like an Oaxaca rug. Symbols representing mountains, sun, stars, and rain had been incorporated into the detail. It was handmade in Guatemala, the card clipped to the collar read. With its sturdy brass D-ring it was the ideal size for the German Shepherd, Husky, or Malamute I wished I had. What I did have was a job that put me on more than 100 airplanes over the past eleven months, a lifestyle that was neither dog-friendly nor sustainable.

I purchased the collar anyway, in anticipation of a different future.

Fast forward two years. I was thankful the high-stress job and I had parted ways. I now worked for myself and loved every minute of it. It was why I could pop up to Seattle to spend time with friends before flying to Japan to deliver sixteen paintings to my new distributor. On a surprisingly clear October day, I sat in a diner where a dozen people had pushed together four tables to celebrate a birthday. My best friend and former co-worker, thirty years my senior, sat at the far table. She grinned a little too knowingly as she placed me next to her only single son, across from two of his teenaged children.

Rick and I had met at a picnic when we were both married, and he was chasing his three kids around. (He didn't remember.) And then our paths crossed again in 2008: at his stepfather's memorial service, and during his mother's breast-cancer surgery and recovery. In October 2013, we bonded for three hours over greasy breakfast food and beamed so much at each other that his kids texted each other: "Never seen Dad smile so much." Hours later, Rick asked me out after realizing I'd only be in town for one more night.

The next month, I returned to Seattle and met Nacho, his Red Heeler Cattle Dog. Rick had warned me that Nacho could be wary of strangers. They had rescued him from a high-stress situation where Nacho had lived with six other dogs and a few cats cramped in a small house with a smaller yard.

During our introduction, Nacho greeted me at the back door of the house by baring his teeth and growling. If Rick hadn't been holding his choke collar, he might have lunged at me. I steadied my nerves and held my fist out to let him know it was okay to sniff; I came in peace. His nostrils flared a bit as he took in my scent and relaxed, but Rick still held onto him until he was sure the dog would do no harm.

Over the week of that first visit, which was during Thanksgiving, I played with Nacho outside several times a day. I chucked the orange-and-blue ball, and the dog ran to retrieve and return it, charging toward me so fast that I was sure he would knock me over. I respected the power of his build: barrel chest, short legs, and a head and body that could withstand cattle kicks. I chucked the ball for him over and over until he lay exhausted and panting, his extra-long tongue hanging out of his mouth. We still didn't completely trust each other but we were working on it.

Finally, on the day I was to return to California, Nacho bade me goodbye by slurping my left cheek. Rick, a witness to this kiss, said, "I hope he remembers you next time."

When I returned for Christmas, Nacho was tentative at first. He growled, then sniffed me, and then, instead of baring his teeth he gave me an exuberant kiss.

For Christmas that year, I spent the holidays with Rick and his kids. I brought gifts for everyone, including Nacho. I gave him organic grain-free treats, tennis balls, and a stuffed alligator. Nacho seemed thrilled with these offerings and wanted to use them right away, so we went outside to play.

Throughout the new year into spring, I worked alternately from my house in California and from Rick's house outside of Seattle. Rick, Mr. Tough Guy, admitted to tearing up every time we parted. I said it would make sense when my lease ended in the summer for me to move, since he couldn't easily relocate.

In May 2014, Rick gave me a birthday gift wrapped in paper covered in cartoon dogs to which he added even more dog stickers. He declared the rubber garden shoes were from him and Nacho. Later that night, during an elegant supper at an award-winning restaurant, he proposed. In the spirit of our relationship, he included in the proposal the effect I'd had on his life, his kids' lives, and the dog's life.

Later that summer, I moved to Seattle, bringing that colorful dog collar. Though Nacho's legs are much shorter than a Shepherd, Husky, or Malamute's, his neck circumference is about the same. Suddenly, I understood that I had bought the collar for him, this loyal, now very loving dog who came with an equally loving man. The first time I clicked the collar closed around Nacho's neck, he sat up a little taller. This collar is now the only one he will wear.

— Jill L. Ferguson —

31

The Funeral that Made a Family

It is never too late to give up our prejudices.
~Henry David Thoreau

He was the love of her life, but most of his family never knew she existed. They loved one another for more than fifty years, but they never married, never shared a home, never had a child together.

When they met, my grandmother was a pretty, lonely young widow with a toddler daughter (my mom) and he was a handsome, young bachelor who dated widely but had never found "the right one." From the beginning, they knew they had found something special. They knew they had discovered a lifetime love.

But there was a problem. A big one. She was from a strict Baptist home, and he was from a family of Jewish immigrants from the Old World. Their parents told them that if they married, they would not be their children anymore.

It was agonizing — they loved their families and they loved each other. They were told they had to choose. But how do you rip your heart in half? How do you tell your heart whom to love?

And so they lived more than five decades in a delicate balancing act — loving one another intensely yet never marrying and never living together. We, her family, knew him well. But most of his family never knew of her existence. They thought he was a lonely bachelor all his life. Those who did know never spoke of her.

They had great happiness. He was a gourmet cook who came over every Tuesday and Thursday to create an amazing meal. They were avid about fishing and spent one day every weekend in their boat on the lake. They took amazing trips every summer — they visited all the latest restaurants — they celebrated birthdays and "anniversaries" and holidays. For more than fifty years, they shared their lives and were happy.

But they also had the sadness of never being affirmed as a couple, of never sharing a home, of never sharing events with his family, of never having a child together. It hurt even after decades.

After fifty years of the same happiness and the same sadness, my grandmother passed away. Not long afterwards, her companion of a lifetime died as well.

Somehow, in the midst of his final days, his family learned about the great love of his life. Our two families came together at his funeral. They asked us to sit with them at the service and the burial. (The rabbi was confused but supportive.) Afterwards, we shared a meal. Around those tables, stories abounded. Having never known my grandmother, they had not really known him.

You didn't know that he loved to fish? Well, they went fishing together every week. Let me tell you about the time she caught the biggest fish. You didn't know he was a great cook? Well, let me tell you about his terrific spaghetti.

You never heard about their trips? Well, we have these great pictures of them down in Florida.

It was at the lunch that my young daughter Kate met his equally young grand-niece Abigail. They looked at each other curiously — two little girls in the midst of a room full of grown-ups.

They were shy at first. They were not sure how to get started being family with someone they'd never met before.

Then Abigail had an idea. "Would you like to see the doll I got for Hanukkah?" she asked. Kate nodded. The doll came out.

They began to play, quietly at first. Before long they were chasing one another through the room — shouting and laughing. Then they joined hands and started singing "Ring Around the Rosie." Round and round they twirled — smiling, giggling, and holding hands.

All of a sudden everything got quiet as every adult in the room noticed them. All the aunts and uncles and cousins and grandparents — those who had always known and those who had just found out. They all stopped and watched. Then they smiled. Then they laughed. After all those long years of being apart, two families had finally come together, all because of two little girls and a doll.

A decades-long love was finally complete.

Kate and Abigail are friends.

Kate and Abigail are family.

And now we all know.

— LeDayne McLeese Polaski —

Not Your Typical Senior Year

He who has a why to live can bear almost any how.
~Friedrich Nietzsche

S enior year of high school is supposed to be about three things: friends, picking a college, and graduation. My senior year wasn't like that... not at all.

Brian and I met when I was a freshman and he was a sophomore and dated throughout high school. He enlisted in the United States Army the summer before my senior year, the year he graduated. When he first enlisted, we didn't think that he would be shipped off right away, but we were wrong. He enlisted in May and was sent to Fort Benning, Georgia two months later, three days after my senior year began.

On top of the usual voices saying, "This is your last year of high school, make the best of it," and, "You need to pick your top choice school," I also had to worry about Brian. The mailman and I became very good friends during the time Brian was in basic training. I remember when I got that very first little green envelope. My school's theater department was putting on one of our biggest musical productions yet: *Peter Pan.* My mom and I had been texting sporadically throughout rehearsal, with me mainly asking if anything had shown up in the mail yet. When she brought me my fast food dinner, she also handed me that little green envelope. I tore it open as quickly as I could, trying to save as much of the envelope as possible.

Reading that short letter, I knew that he made it to Georgia and they were getting him processed. I lived off that feeling until the next letter showed up. The letters kept coming until December, and then my soldier himself made an appearance at the airport. We were just supposed to pick him up, but I had to run out of the truck and attack hug him. It had been four months since I'd seen him, the longest we'd ever been apart. Christmas was fantastic, despite coming down with the stomach flu. No present in the world could compete with the man in the digital camouflage ACUs sitting beside me.

Sending Brian back to Georgia to complete basic training was nearly impossible. But, much like I did before Christmas, I lived week to week off letters.

Until that one night. Who knew a person's whole world could change with one simple phone call? I was at a basketball game playing in the pep band when Brian called. Naturally, I lied to my band director and told him my mom was calling and I had to take it. In the period of a fifteen-minute phone call, Brian told me that he would have three days off after basic training graduation, and then he would have to get on a plane and go to his base station... in Germany. After he told me he was going to be stationed in Germany, he gave me the worst news I had ever received.

"There are rumors going around that the company I'm going to is getting deployed in about two months." And in that moment, I felt my whole world crashing down. I wasn't strong enough to do this. There was no way on earth I was going to make it through deployment, no way, no how! With the news of his shortened vacation time and his possible deployment, I gathered up the resources I could and found a way to Georgia. Which, I came to find out, was a good thing.

Seeing Brian graduate basic training was one of the happiest days in both of our lives. But what happened the next day was even better. Brian's mom and two little sisters joined us in Georgia after the friends who brought me to see him had to return to Indiana. Little did I know that Brian's mom was carrying a very important package. On the way to dinner with his mom and his sisters, Brian seemed really nervous.

He kept telling me that it was the traffic, but I knew him too well. Something else was going on.

After we got to the restaurant and ordered our food, Brian's mom asked if she could borrow my camera. Confused, I handed it to her and she started taking mindless pictures of Brian and me. Well, that is... until he turned to me and asked me something that went like this:

"Hey baby."

"Yeah?"

"Will you marr —"

"OH, MY GOD!"

That was the gist of my proposal on March 6th, in Columbus, Georgia. Now, on top of finishing my senior year, Brian being stationed in Germany, and the possibility of a deployment on the horizon, I had a wedding to plan. I left Brian in Georgia that weekend, and my heart sank. It sank even lower when I found out that the rumors of the deployment were true. My fiancé was being deployed to Afghanistan.

My story isn't very common among teenagers, but I know that there are more than a few of us out there who are dealing with something like this on a daily basis. Brian just returned home from his deployment in June of this year, and we were married eight days later. After my first semester of my sophomore year at a local college, I plan on packing my bags and making my way to spend a year or two in Germany with my now husband. You see stories of girls becoming teen moms out there all of the time, but it's very rare you find a story of a teen military wife.

I am not a very strong person, or at least I wasn't before Brian joined the Army. Now, I am an army wife, so I have to be Army Strong. For any girl, or boy for that matter, dating a man or a woman in the United States Military, this one is for you. I know that you are strong, and I have faith in you. Hold on to those letters and those ten-second phone calls. They may be all you have right now, but at least they're something.

I made it... you can, too.

— Paula Perkins Hoffman —

Man of My Dreams

In dreams and in love, there are no impossibilities.
~Janos Arany

When I first got to college, I tried to be someone I wasn't. I'd never dated in high school, and the only guys who had expressed interest in me were hoping for an easy hook-up (which I angrily declined). The conclusion I drew was that there must have been something wrong with me personally. I was, you see, a pretty huge nerd. (I still am, in fact.) Any free time I had that didn't involve reading fantasy novels was absorbed by playing videogames. But boys don't like nerdy girls, right?

So I ignored my personality, my actual wants and desires, and became what I thought a college girl should be like. And it did get me dates. With losers. I finally turned to my last resort: online dating.

On my profile, I started to be a little more honest with myself. I listed some of the books I liked, said I was hoping to find someone who could make me laugh, and even admitted to being a "nerd" (though I said this with the hopes of sounding like a flirty and fun nerd as opposed to the type of nerd who literally spent the last sixteen hours playing *World of Warcraft*).

A few weeks passed, and I had gotten a date or two (with losers), when I got a message from "SilverMan." It said simply: "If you're looking for a nerd who can make you laugh, I'd appreciate it if you gave me a shot," followed by his phone number.

I looked at his picture and recognized him from my psychology class. I'd noticed him the first day of lectures, in fact. He'd come in a little after me and was kind of hard to miss.

He was tall and lean, wearing blue jeans and a nice, button-down shirt. His eyes were so piercing he could probably see through brick walls, and they were accented nicely by his high cheekbones, regal nose, and just exactly the right amount of facial hair. If you had asked me about him at any other stage of my life, I probably would have swooned. But there was just something about him, and I never could pinpoint what, that just seemed a little nerdy. Maybe it was his attentiveness in class and willingness to ask questions. Maybe it was because he frequently printed extra copies of his notes to share with others in the class. There was just something about him that made me categorize him as a nerd.

And college girls don't like nerds, right?

I read his message over twice, ignoring the strange tingling excitement running through my chest. "Oh, great," I said aloud to my empty apartment, "it's that nerd from my psychology class." I promptly deleted my account.

That night, I had a dream about him:

I was in our usual psychology classroom. Class had either just gotten out or had not yet started. Faceless students milled around making conversation I didn't try to hear. "SilverMan" stood beside me, smiling. He said something that made me laugh. I felt warm and comfortable. Accepted. It felt like being a toddler after playing in a bath with a soft towel wrapped around me in a hug. We chatted about nothings and flirted shamelessly. Toward the end of the dream, I remember taking his hand.

I woke blearily to the sound of my alarm, the dream still vivid in my mind. My heart felt like it had tripped down a flight of stairs.

"Huh," I said, blinking at the sunlight that had forced its way through my thin blinds.

Try as I might to ignore it, the dream clung to my conscious mind. Its implications were obvious, but I spent almost half the day trying to talk myself out of it.

"This doesn't happen in real life," I insisted quietly as I finished my make-up.

Tromping down the stairs, I muttered, "I'm not going to have a dream about him, then fall madly in love with him and get married and live happily ever after."

"That sounds like the premise of a bad romance novel," I told myself after breakfast.

"Besides," I thought while walking to class, "my account's been deleted. I probably won't have access to his number anymore anyway."

I studiously avoided him in psychology and rushed home after my classes were finished.

By dinnertime, I'd exhausted all my excuses and still couldn't get the dream out of my head.

"Fine!" I said at last, prying open my laptop. "If his number is still there, I'll send him a text. I could use the dating experience anyway. But it probably won't even be there anymore."

I got online and reactivated my account. Most of my messages had been erased. Only three were still in my inbox. One of which was from SilverMan. So I sent him a text.

We'll be celebrating our seven-year wedding anniversary this December.

— Mary T. Whipple —

34

Healing Heartache

*Fun fact: According to the Delta Society, the presence of
an animal produces positive results in safety, self-esteem
and in dealing with loneliness and depression.*

The guy I was interested in fell for a nun instead of me. When I first heard the news, I called an old boyfriend who I could depend on. I cried, "Now I'm losing guys to nuns! These women aren't even trying!" He responded with all the compliments I needed to assuage my humiliation, but his true opinion on the matter manifested in a package he sent to me three days later containing a calendar called "Nuns Having Fun" and a note that read simply, "Hahahaha! Nuns really DO have all the fun!" The vintage photos on the calendar showed nuns on roller coasters, nuns doing tricks on bikes, and nuns having more fun than I'd had while dating in my thirties. These were single women the world didn't pressure into finding love or living a fairy tale, and they were happy.

I decided to move out of my apartment and into an actual house, one where I could set down roots and redefine my version of "happily ever after." I found a sweet, historical home previously occupied by an elderly couple. The wife had died, and the old man wanted to live near his children, but he would have to leave one thing behind. "Will you please take good care of my cat?" he asked. "She's spayed and doesn't need anything but food and some attention now and again. It would mean so much to me if you could take care of her." His eyes were so earnest, I couldn't say no. I had never owned a cat, but I understood his broken heart. I told him I would pamper her. He smiled, then said, "Well, if you're a woman living alone, you'll need a good cat. Her name is Ms. Thang, you know, like slang for 'thing.'"

My first act as the owner of this gray fluffy creature was to change her name to Edie. She responded with approval to the new name with my first pop of a cat-food can. Edie ate her food like a lady, and then spread out like an odalisque on the patio table. Then the others appeared.

The neighborhood cats apparently received a newsletter stating that a single woman had moved in and was serving posh food to all the other singles. They descended on my house and hung around as long as Edie let them. Regardless of the number of cats that came and went, it remained her territory. Even the neighborhood dogs respected the invisible boundaries. Edie regally sat on my porch railing, presiding over the yard. She never left the property — after all, she wasn't seeking a mate and had no need to do anything other than hang out and be free. I understood this and found myself adopting a similar lifestyle. I shopped for books, went to movies, and had no obligations to anyone. It was glorious.

Together, we formed a daily routine with minimal effort, even as my house became a revolving door to friends visiting for summer beach weekends, including Andrew, a friend who came into town for a few job interviews. We had agreed that he could stay and share the rent if any of them worked out. Before he arrived, several people asked if I had romantic prospects with Andrew, which I always denied. I had known him for years, but the timing was never right for us, and we remained comfortable friends. Lots of my girlfriends had crushes on him. He was handsome, freakishly smart and had the sort of wit that made you wonder why Jon Stewart hadn't yet discovered him. He was everything I should have wanted, but I can be guilty of missing the obvious at times.

Two days after Andrew arrived, a hurricane developed in the Gulf that seemed to be on a direct path to my town. Rather than leave, he climbed on my roof to check the durability of my shingles. He also checked the sewage lines, the storm shutters and our cars in case we needed to leave town. He went to the store to buy supplies. When he got back, his mother called to try and convince him to leave.

Andrew was in the kitchen, but I could hear him say, "Mom, I know you're worried, but I'm not going to leave her. If it becomes clear that we need to leave, then I'll help her with that, too, but I have to make sure she's okay through this." He loved me and had patiently waited for the right time for us. More importantly, he knew I was beyond the fantasies of dating life and spared me the discomfort of wooing me with sappy songs or deep thoughts on Dostoyevsky. Instead, he demonstrated an ability to share my life as couples really lived, completely committed to each other despite potential storms.

I walked over to help with the supplies and found that he had purchased enough provisions for Edie to survive Armageddon. I reached for a can of cat food and smiled. It was the posh kind.

"Andrew, we're getting married, aren't we?" I said.

He looked at me and smiled. "I hope so."

Fortune was on our side, and the storm never came. We married the next year, and Edie remained a fixture at our house long after the birth of our son. She was sitting on the porch with us when we got word that Andrew had a new opportunity that would move us out of town. Edie had become frail that year and she quietly disappeared before we started packing. She had seen me through the aftermath of heartache and helped me learn to embrace myself before I embraced anyone else, and I am a better wife and mother for it.

— Tanya Estes —

35

A Snowstorm to Remember

*Why don't we embrace them (snow days) for exactly
what they are; a rite of passage, a part of being
Canadian. The snow day — it should
be put on a stamp.*
~Rick Mercer

t began as a typical January day. The grey skies were heavy with
snow and a brisk northerly wind played havoc with the drifts in
front of Valleyview School. I was in my first year of teaching and
had no idea that this approaching snowstorm would change my
life forever.

When gentle snow began falling the principal kept a careful eye
on the brewing storm. It soon took on qualities of something more
vicious. By mid-day he called the school buses back so the three
hundred kids could get home safely before it was too late.

My students gathered their belongings. They were excited to be
going home early. "Snow days" are not uncommon in the snowbelt
region of southwestern Ontario. It's "the lake effect" from Lake Huron,
we're told, which delivers more than our fair share of winter storms.

The buses arrived but the storm suddenly escalated before the
waiting kids could board and it was quickly clear no one was going
anywhere any time soon.

Snow fell relentlessly, whirling and whipping itself into treacherous whiteout conditions. Gusts of wind blasted the school windows with such a fury we feared they would shatter. Menacing snowdrifts wafted in silently under the doors.

By now the bus drivers and a couple of snowplow operators who'd been forced off the road were discussing the situation. There were over three hundred children, staff, bus and snowplow drivers barricaded inside the school.

As night approached and the storm showed no signs of abating, we realized we were prisoners until Mother Nature decided to release us from her grasp. None of us guessed it would be three days before the storm relented enough for us to finally go home.

We faced some basic questions. What would we feed several hundred children for dinner? Where would they sleep?

Earl, our school janitor, began working non-stop to keep the old groaning furnace running, but what if it quit? Concerned about the old pipes freezing, he wrapped them with whatever material he could find. With our hydro lines swaying under the increasing weight of ice and snow in heavy winds, what would we do if we lost power? A plan was definitely needed.

After every parent was called to reassure them their children were safe, a few silent prayers were said, and then people who lived close enough to brave the elements were called and asked if they could help. Soon, a handful of people had managed to wade through the heavy drifts and blinding snow bringing bags of sandwiches, tinned juices, blankets and a couple of board games.

One woman, who lived right on the edge of the school property, bundled herself up and trudged through the blinding snow with a huge kettle and enough ingredients to make tomato soup for at least half of the school. Those who didn't get soup feasted on peanut butter and jam sandwiches delivered by someone else. There wasn't a lot of food, but everything was shared, no one went hungry, and no one complained.

When night fell we worked out sleeping arrangements for the kids. Exhausted by the tensions of the day, most of them slept relatively well on the carpeted floors, drifting off to sleep under coats and donated blankets. I watched with a warm heart as three little first grade girls snuggled up under my own large, furry coat.

Some of the older girls acted like it was a huge pajama party, snuggling, giggling and telling stories as if nothing unusual was happening. Finally, they too gave in to sleep. It became an adventure; no one seemed homesick or even upset about having to stay at school overnight.

The next morning the treks down the long, cold hallway to the washrooms began early. On hall duty, I watched as two little boys in grade one walked down the corridor hand in hand. Jason turned to Jamie and said, "I wonder what we're having for breakfast?" Jamie, in wide-eyed innocence replied, "Eggs and bacon, of course. That's what I always have!"

Well, it wasn't eggs and bacon, but instead a piece of soft toast broiled in the school oven with half a cup of lukewarm cocoa. The bread had been retrieved from a stranded bread truck and delivered to the school by several young men on snowmobiles who were eager to help out however they could. With their parkas and helmets and all those hungry children to attend to, I didn't notice, but one of them noticed me as he trudged back and forth loaded with donations. My life was about to change.

Meanwhile, although the storm continued to bluster, it gradually began to diminish. As it did, some fathers began arriving on snowmobiles to collect their children. One man, well bundled against the elements, arrived on an open tractor pulling a small covered trailer to carry home his kids as well as every other kid that lived along his concession.

As the day progressed our numbers slowly dwindled. We kept those who remained busy playing basketball and volleyball in the gym, watching films or reading in the library.

On the morning of the third day we awoke to the sun shining in a clear blue sky. With the roads now plowed, the last of our students were soon safely on their way home, and all the staff breathed a sigh of relief. We had survived three days of the worst storm on record for our region in the past century. But what might have been a disaster had instead resulted in a strengthening of bonds — first between the community and our school, but especially between the teachers and students.

When the principal finally gave the teachers the "go ahead" to return home, I headed out to my car and went to start it. That's when I was approached by one of the snowmobilers who had delivered bread from the stranded bread truck.

He opened my passenger door, introduced himself as Bob, and asked me if I was planning to go somewhere.

"Home of course," I responded with a laugh.

"Well," he said, "after three days of sitting in a raging blizzard, your car is not likely going to start." Then he continued, saying that as he had been going in and out of our school bringing supplies, he had noticed me. He also admitted that by speaking with some of my co-workers he had learned I was "unattached."

I had to admit that because I had been so busy with my young charges I hadn't paid much attention. "Besides," I laughed, "most of the time your faces were totally covered with toques and helmets."

Undeterred by my initial indifference he asked me if I would go on a date with him sometime. Whether I was too exhausted to say no to his boldness, or whether there was a certain twinkle in his deep blue eyes, I really don't know. I accepted his offer, but it was June before we managed to go on that first date. When we finally did, we got along so well and shared so many common interests it seemed as if we'd known each other forever. Romance blossomed quickly. Soon we were engaged, and in November, less than five months later, we were married.

Throughout the years we have weathered many storms together, but that first storm was the one we both remember. Who could have guessed that the storm of a lifetime would have brought me the love of my life!

— Ardy Barclay —

36

Hometown Girl

He is happiest, be he king or peasant,
who finds peace in his home.
~Johann Wolfgang von Goethe

rms crossed over my chest, I lean against the doorframe of my lovely, two-bedroom apartment where I have lived happily for the last three years. I will miss the two luxurious bathrooms, the great-room's hardwood floors, my balcony facing the lush green pines, and even the family sized dining area where I often ate alone. At my feet, my Shih Tzu, Chelsea, gives a half-hearted "woof" that echoes throughout the empty apartment.

It is time to leave, and yet a part of me wants to unload the waiting U-Haul, return all the furniture I worked so hard to buy and all of the hand-selected decorations to their carefully chosen places, and to continue with my single, independent life. Part of me wants to stay here because I love this haven that I created all by myself, and another part of me wants to stay because I fear the changes that remain in my future.

I was a small-town girl when I left the Midwest and moved to Houston, Texas, to make a life for myself. I knew I could never really be independent living anywhere near my old hometown, my family, or my childhood friends. To be truly free, I would have to rely on myself for survival. Houston offered grand experiences, the doorway to travel to many different places, and mostly, a chance to set myself apart from those "simple" kids I grew up with. I wanted not just more — I wanted something bigger and better — and Texas seemed like just the place to discover it.

Liberated life was exactly what I expected — most of the time. I did my student teaching in Rio de Janeiro, Brazil, and learned a great deal about Brazilian culture. I ate *feijoada* every chance I got; I sunbathed on Copacabana Beach; and I took overcrowded buses to remote villages for the weekend.

I went to graduate school and won a grant that allowed me to explore Ireland while I was studying to be a librarian; I thumbed through yellowed books in the Long Room, admired Ireland's literary history and cultural heritage. In the evenings, I tossed back a few Guinnesses with the locals in neighborhood pubs. I married another teacher, and we honeymooned in Mexico where we visited the ruins at Chichen Itza and snorkeled above the world's second-largest barrier reef. On a whim, I hopped a plane with co-workers to Beijing where I walked on the Great Wall of China, then took a night train across the country to see the ten thousand Terracotta Warriors of the first Emperor of China. Life outside of my tiny hometown was an adventure, and I had the whole world to myself.

Yet liberated life was often challenging and sometimes even heartbreaking. My husband loved my strong self-assuredness, my sense of responsibility, my obsession with adventure, and my naiveté. Unfortunately, that naiveté blinded me to my husband's serious problems, in business and with prescription drug addiction. I made ends meet for as long as I could, and made sure his doctors' bills were paid and that he had proper treatment. Eventually, when it was impossible for me to stay, I did the strong, responsible thing and moved on with my life alone.

I was always at my strongest alone.

I gaze at the living room wall where the couch used to sit and where I had my first post-marriage kiss. The dining room wall has a barely visible outline of a painting I had commissioned with my first solo income tax refund. Turning my head slightly, I imagine myself standing at the kitchen bar preparing hors d'oeuvres for my first-ever hostess gig — a book-club meeting. Then I look over at the guest bedroom where the carpeting reveals the indentations of a bed and dresser — the bed where my mother and a few other guests slept when they visited me.

My eyes sweep past the master bedroom door where I curled up so many nights to read myself to sleep and on to the balcony off the living room. My wind chimes are packed away now, and I will never again sit at my patio table here in Texas and watch the birds feed while the breeze plays with the ends of my hair. A sudden nostalgia and longing begin to weaken my resolve.

"You ready, baby?" says a husky voice behind me.

I take one last look at the apartment, turn, and close the door behind me. Looking up, I see the bright blue eyes of my fiancé, Terry, shining down at me. Those crisp blue eyes have been glinting with mischief at me since second grade when Terry would pull my braid and run, since middle school when he would tell off-color jokes and those piercing blue eyes would light up with amusement at my reaction, and in high school when he would invite me to go for a drive with him and then wink one baby blue before walking away. I smile up at the boy from my hometown who is now a man.

"I'm ready," I say. I scoop up Chelsea and scratch behind her ears.

It's hard to believe that I'm blissfully married and have been living in my hometown for nearly two years now. My old hometown is no different than it was twenty years ago when I left. Yet this little town is a different world compared to Texas. I stand at the window in the front room of the house where I live with Terry and my two stepchildren. Fat white flakes fall from the sky and coat the gentle rise and fall of the fields around our home. Birds peck at the feeder hanging in the flowerbed, and Chelsea lies curled up in an upholstered armchair. The wood floor creaks as I lean over and reach for a sweatshirt, then pull it on to fight against the winter chill. I haven't lost myself here as I had feared, haven't lost the independence I valued, or the feeling of being special that I fought so hard to discover during my travels.

Florence + the Machine blares from my stepdaughter Teresa's room, and I hear Thomas, my stepson, laughing at something funny on television. I smile when I picture those "simple" kids — small-town kids like me. Terry walks through the front room, talking on the phone, and stops to playfully swat my behind. I laugh. Later, I will go shopping with my mother and call my brothers to arrange a weekend movie with the nieces and nephews.

I have discovered something bigger and better, and it was here in my hometown all along—something more exciting than my solo life in Texas. I am a part of that something now. I am strong, I am independent, and I am complete.

—Erin E. Forson—

37

Police Report

'Tis sweet to know there is an eye that will mark our
coming, and look brighter when we come.
~Lord Byron

"Gee, what a hunk!" I thought, as the blue-eyed RCMP officer strode towards me from behind the police counter.

"How can I help you, Miss?" he asked, very formally.

"My father's missing," I said without preamble. "He's overdue from driving back from a job in Edmonton, and we haven't heard from him. My mother's frantic. She thinks he's gone off the road somewhere."

"I'm acting, here, for my mom," I made sure to stress, even as I felt myself shrinking to the size of a six-year-old. "She's the one who wants to file the report."

The dashing Mountie asked me a few questions, and then filled out a missing persons report.

"I'll pass the report on to the CNR Police in Edmonton," he said. "I'm not on duty tomorrow so someone else will call you as soon as we hear something."

I repeated my phone number for him — twice, seared his nametag into my memory, thanked him, and left.

It was an exceptionally cold winter. The snow, both in town and on the highways, was above average, making for dangerously icy conditions. It certainly was out of character for my dad to not call my mom along the route from Edmonton to our hometown in northwestern British Columbia — a driving distance of over 800 miles.

When I walked into the house I shared with my twin sister, I blurted out, "I've just met the most wonderful guy on the face of the earth. And… I got his name!"

"You'd better phone Mom," she said, rolling her eyes.

The next day someone, not Blue Eyes, called from the RCMP detachment to announce that my father had been located, safe and sound.

"Your dad was a little embarrassed at being pulled over by a police cruiser," the officer added. I relayed the good news to Mom and the family breathed a collective sigh of relief.

Days later, after Dad had arrived safely home, he confronted me. "Do you know how embarrassing that was? I've never been pulled over by a cop in my life."

"But Dad," I retorted in self defence. "Mom made me do it!"

Crisis passed, I searched for Blue Eyes in the phone book but he wasn't listed. Darn it, I thought, I'll never see him again.

From then on, every police car I saw took on new meaning. No longer trying to avoid them, I was now aiming for them, hoping to catch a glimpse of Blue Eyes' face. But no face was his, and a few Mountie faces even scowled at me as I nearly drove into them! After a few weeks of near misses with every police car in town, Blue Eyes was still nowhere to be seen.

Several months passed before I saw him again. As fate would have it, we crossed in the doorway of a local pharmacy. He was dressed in civilian clothes, wearing a suede leather jacket that was quite becoming. After saying an initial "Hi," I thanked him for his assistance three months earlier, we engaged in light conversation, and then slowly retreated from the doorway to get out of people's way.

Then, under the stares of other shoppers, he said the magic words: "Do you want to go somewhere for coffee?" Inside I was jumping up and down. We went to a restaurant a block away where we drank hot chocolates and talked about ourselves and our families, including my no-longer elusive dad. Before parting, we exchanged phone numbers.

"You know that wonderful policeman I told you about?" I enthused to my sister, "Well, I just had hot chocolate with him at a restaurant!"

As of this writing, we've been married thirty-eight years, and two of our four children have followed in their father's law-enforcement footsteps. I've always had an aversion to ice and snow, but when those exact winter conditions forge warm hearts, as they did with us, there's no complaint from me.

— Chantal Meijer —

Chapter
4

Keeping Love Alive

38

Love Letters

Relish love in our old age! Aged love is like aged wine;
it becomes more satisfying, more refreshing, more
valuable, more appreciated and more intoxicating.
~Leo Buscaglia

Normally, my husband had a lot to say when he got home from work, but so far he hadn't uttered more than a few words. I waited while he slathered his tacos with a mountain of salsa and sour cream before I finally broke the silence.

"So, how was work?"

"Okay," he shrugged, picking at his food, "except the women I work with called me a lousy husband again."

"What for this time?" I asked.

"Our anniversary," he said. "They couldn't believe I didn't take you out for dinner last night or buy you an expensive gift."

Valentine's Day, Christmas, my birthday—these women loved teasing my husband for not coming through in the "romance department," even though he'd explained several times that I'm the kind of wife who would rather get a bag of Brussels sprouts, a package of gumdrops, or a scenic ride in the car as opposed to a diamond necklace or an expensive dinner. Besides, we loved celebrating at home.

"I hope you reminded those women that I'm not high-maintenance," I answered, shaking my head at their nonsense.

Suddenly, his face lit up like a Christmas tree. "I did remind them.

I also told them that obviously I'm not *that* lousy of a husband since I get daily love letters from my wife — and *their* husbands don't."

I couldn't help but smile. My husband adored his "love letters" and had often mentioned them to the people he worked with, although what he calls "letters" are more like little notes.

Early in our marriage, I'd confessed to my husband that I never wanted to become one of those loving but crotchety wives who barked at their husband over trivial issues. Yet, after wading through several stressful months, that's exactly what I'd done, and I hadn't even realized it. Horrified with my actions, I wanted to ensure that I never turned into that kind of wife again.

Throughout the many years, I've left sticky notes in my husband's cooler for him to read during his lunch hour. He never knows when he'll get one but enjoys my notes and even writes back to me. That gave me a brilliant idea.

Each day, I decided to set aside time to think about my husband and why I was grateful for him on that particular day. On a piece of scrap paper, I scribbled him a note and left it on his nightstand where he'd find it after he got home from work each evening.

My notes are simple but sincere.

"I am grateful for your understanding."

"I'm grateful to you for taking me to my doctor's appointment yesterday."

"I'm grateful for your sense of humor and your laughter on a day when I needed it most."

Once in a while, I get carried away, and his note overflows with mush. I always end the note with "xoxoxoxox."

Of course, my husband thinks that I started the tradition to show him how much I love and appreciate him, but I actually wrote the notes for me.

When life is hectic and disasters abound, when the bills pile up and money is tight, even when all is peaceful and right in our world, I never want to forget the many chapters it took to get us together and on the same page. I feel so blessed to have my husband by my side and never want to take him for granted or forget how I feel about him.

Initially, I planned on leaving him notes for one month, but those little expressions of gratitude meant so much to my husband and made such a difference in my life that they've become a part of our world now. Even though he knows I love him, and I know I love him, it's like feeding the fire one more log — those daily "love letters" keep our love burning a bit warmer and brighter each day.

I think it's pretty neat that my husband tells everyone that he gets daily love letters from his wife, especially since we're old farts who have celebrated thirty-one years of marriage so far. As an added plus, when it comes to his co-workers, his "love letters" are a great defense and prove to those women that no matter what they think, I'm crazy about my husband!

— Jill Burns —

39

Best Breakfast Ever

One good mother is worth a hundred schoolmasters.
~George Herbert

My dad worked in construction. His day started early and ended late. All he wanted to do was crash on the couch and relax when he got home. For the most part that was what he did. No one complained; we were just happy when he was home.

But one hot and muggy summer, when my parents' nineteenth anniversary was coming up, they made plans to go out, just the two of them. The big day finally arrived and Dad got home at seven. Mom had fed all five of us early. She was dressed in her finest and wearing his favorite pair of high heels when he came in. They kissed, as they always did, when he came through the kitchen and headed for the family room. It was obvious he was hot and tired.

"Honey, I just need a thirty-minute nap and then I'll get ready and we will go out to eat," he said as he sat down on the couch.

Mom was already on her way over to the couch to give him a fresh cup of hot coffee. She bent over and kissed him on the head and said, "I'll be ready whenever you are."

I knew how important this evening was to my mother, but before long Dad was fast asleep. Then I watched my mother do the strangest thing. She reached into the refrigerator and took out eggs and bacon. Soon she had a batch of biscuits baking in the oven. I never said a word. I just watched her.

Breakfast was my dad's favorite meal. Before my eyes she piled a plate full of his favorite foods. As she set another fresh cup of coffee on the end table she bent down and kissed him while whispering in his ear, "It's time to wake up, honey."

He ran his fingers through his head of natural curly snow-white hair and sat up on the edge of the couch. As he looked up he found my mom standing in front of him with his dinner. I will never forget the look of love that passed between them as they made eye contact.

"Honey, I promised you I would take you out to dinner and I meant it," he said sincerely.

Mom sat down beside him on the couch as he took the plate of food. She kissed him on the cheek. "I know you would, but I also know you've had a hard day and you're tired. What's important is that we are together. We can go out any time for dinner."

I was seventeen then, and that lesson in love is still with me today, five decades later. Dad died nineteen years ago and Mom lived into her nineties. One day, I found her holding a picture of Dad in her hands. I watched her kiss him and then, as she emerged from the cloud of dementia, I heard her say, "Baby, it won't be much longer until I can come home to heaven to be with you forever."

Three years ago, Mom entered heaven's gate to be greeted by the love of her life. When I miss them I just imagine how happy they are to be together again. Then a sweet peace and comfort falls over me, the same way I felt when I saw their tremendous love for each other on that night when my mother made my father a special anniversary breakfast for dinner.

— Sylvia J. King —

40

Starting Over

A successful marriage requires falling in love many
times, always with the same person.
~Mignon McLaughlin

"This is it," said my husband as we pulled up in front of a funky, little house with a couch on the front porch. My heart sank, but I didn't voice my disappointment. We'd just sold a beautiful two-story home in a city an hour away. Now we were going to live in the college town where my husband had a new job teaching military history at the university. This funky, little house was a rental with four college boys moving out so we could move in.

"It's nice of them to leave that couch for us," I said, thinking how our three small children would look jumping on that broken down thing for all the neighbors to see. With my husband in the Army, we'd lived in a lot of different places in the past twelve years, but never had living room furniture decorated the front porch of any of our homes.

"The couch will be gone by the time our stuff gets here." My husband pointed to a nearby park. "We can walk the kids down there every night to play. I'll be home for dinner now. Won't that be great?"

I swallowed hard. I wasn't sure I wanted my husband home every night. I wasn't sure I wanted him home at all. For years, he'd been a helicopter pilot away on missions. This new ROTC job was my husband's attempt to restore our marriage. I'd been trying to leave him for a year. I just couldn't take being married to a military pilot.

And when he was home, we fought because I didn't trust him. Our children were the only thing holding us together. That, and the hope perhaps we could start over again in this rental within walking distance of my husband's new job.

When we moved in, I didn't care much about the rental, although I did clean it like a mad woman, realizing we'd now be living with bugs, mice, and perhaps a raccoon once we settled into this rattrap place (literally, I placed traps everywhere). My husband put a foosball table in the living room. Each night he and the kids banged up a storm on that table, laughing and loving being together while I plugged my ears and prayed that God would restore our marriage and help me like this dirty old house and that foosball table in our living room.

When my mother-in-law came to visit she was horrified by our move. "How could you sell your beautiful house for this place?" She looked around at the battered rental, the jungle in the back yard, and threw up her hands. "You must really love my son to move here for him."

I kept my mouth shut since I wasn't feeling love. This was something new I was learning. To give thanks for a roof over my head, and three little kids safe in their beds, children so happy to have their dad home every night to play with them before bedtime.

"This house isn't so bad," my husband said a few weeks into our new life. "If we cleaned up the back yard we could sit out there around a fire pit. The kids could make s'mores and we could talk and share a glass of wine." My husband's blue eyes sparkled with longing.

"We could have kept that couch and put it out there too. The kids and the critters would have liked that in this crazy yard."

My husband laughed and I thought how handsome he looked at that moment. After several weeks, my heart was softening towards him and this place. "How about we put the foosball table out in the back yard? You guys make a ton of noise playing that game at night in the house."

"I like it in the living room," my husband said. "It's a lot better than zoning out in front of the TV. Besides, we can't play in the dark. It would be dark out there at night."

"Tarzan might join you out there," I said, looking at all the lush green vines covering the backyard trees and the forest of weeds that had once been a lawn.

"We'll work on the yard this weekend," said my husband.

Within a month, we were sitting in the yard circled around a fire pit as a family. We nearly had a lawn now and I'd picked out a spot to plant a small garden. I'd left my job working for a newspaper in our old town. Now, with only our three-year-old son at home with me and our two older girls in school, I was ready to put my hand to the plow. Any plow. But I decided not to work outside our home because my heart was coming home, and that's where I wanted to be even though this home didn't belong to us. Thank goodness this house didn't belong to us! I couldn't imagine the money it would take to fix it up and get all the bugs and rodents out, but our family was healing here.

Cleaning up that yard, and then growing a garden in a corner of it, my first garden ever, made me love that funky, little rental all the more. I also loved watching my husband become the dad I never realized he could be. The husband I never realized he could be. I also made going to church a priority, and God seemed to be answering all those prayers, because I was falling in love with my husband all over again.

And then September 11th happened and I thought I'd lose him to war. Yet, the Army allowed him to stay at the university teaching cadets instead of sticking him back in the cockpit of a Black Hawk helicopter. I cried when my husband's cadets graduated from the university and were sent into battle, and I cried when my husband arrived home safely every night. I cried because I was crazy in love with him again, and I really liked our rental house now. I was so grateful my husband wasn't in a Black Hawk on the battlefield. I loved walking to the park with my family, and I loved sitting around our fire pit in the back yard. I loved listening to my husband and our children laughing in the living room as they beat the foosball table to death.

That rental wasn't much to look at, and I never succeeded in trapping all the critters scurrying through it night and day (once a mouse ran over my slipper as I ate breakfast at the kitchen table), but that funky, little house became our home. The place where our family started over and the war in Afghanistan passed us by. A baby was born to us there, too, before we moved on to buy another beautiful home. That baby was the first of four more sons we would have!

—Paula Bicknell—

Distant Promise

To watch us dance is to hear our hearts speak.
~Hopi Indian Saying

After more than thirty years of marriage, I thought our days of romantic secrets were over. That is, until Loren announced, "Don't plan anything for your birthday. I have a special surprise."

On the evening of my birthday, we dressed up and drove into town. We pulled into the parking lot of a strip mall and I scanned the storefronts. Hmm… a costume store, Harbor Freight Tools, the driver's license place, and then I saw it. The sign on the corner building read "Arthur Murray Dance Studio."

Loren wasn't kidding when he said he had a surprise. We had never danced, not even in high school, and I had always wanted to learn. Though he didn't think dancing was manly, early in our marriage he promised, "Someday I'll take you dancing."

Instead, life's well-worn routines took over our days and we never found the time. What followed were years of raising kids and long hours of hard work building a career. Middle age found us changing jobs, helping our aging parents, and busy with seven grandchildren.

Now here we were, more than a few pounds heavier and our hair a little grayer. My girlish fantasy of whirling across a dance floor had faded, long since tucked away in the place of surrendered dreams.

Heather, our instructor, a tall slender blonde wearing a short tight skirt and stilettos, welcomed us at the door of the studio. She showed us to a desk where we had a short interview. Her eyes glistened with tears when she learned Loren was making good on a thirty-two-year-old promise.

"Why now?" she asked him. "What took you so long?"

"I guess I had to grow up," he said, giving my hand a squeeze. "And it's important to me to make her dreams come true," he added, as he looked at me with a love far deeper than the young man who had made the promise decades earlier. I giggled when our eyes met and he blushed with a grin he couldn't contain. No doubt, we seemed like a pair of infatuated teenagers to our twenty-something instructor.

Heather described the various dances taught at the studio. We decided to focus on the waltz for our two introductory lessons. Between Loren's hearing loss, two knee surgeries and a back surgery, and my arthritis, we felt like stiff old broomsticks.

We stumbled through our first awkward steps with enthusiasm while he tried to lead and I attempted to follow. Loren looked forward to our lessons as much as I did. When the trial period ended, we agreed to continue.

We signed up for eight more lessons and chose to learn rumba, swing, and the hustle. Each week became a new adventure. When we walked to the car after our seventh lesson, we turned to each other and said simultaneously, "I don't want it to end." Our laughter rang out across the dark parking lot. We determined then to keep dancing.

Six months later, we dance two or three nights a week. The mambo and cha cha have brought new energy into our relationship. But the best is when Loren turns to me and says, "May I have this dance?" He takes my hand, slips his arm around my shoulder as we waltz across the floor doing an under-arm turn, and I know even forgotten dreams can come true.

— Kathleen Kohler —

Alone Together

There is no more lovely, friendly, and charming
relationship, communion or company
than a good marriage.
~Martin Luther

"**D**o you want to go on a date tonight?" my husband Eric asked. "We haven't spent much time alone lately." I sighed and looked down at what I was wearing. It was only 5:00 p.m. but I was already in my pajamas. We'd had company at our house for the past few days. Mere minutes after they'd left, I'd changed and grabbed a book. Playing hostess always wore me out, and I'd been looking forward to a quiet evening at home.

But I'd often complained that Eric wasn't romantic enough. Plus, he's my favorite person in the world, and I love spending time with him. How could I turn down his sweet offer, especially on one of those rare nights when our oldest could babysit? I smiled. "Let me get dressed," I said.

In the car, Eric reached for my hand. "Are you tired, honey?" he asked.

"Not tired exactly. Just… all peopled out."

He chuckled at my explanation.

"I love people, and I enjoyed visiting with our guests, but sometimes I just need time alone away from people and their expectations. I haven't had much of that lately."

"Would you have rather stayed home tonight?"

"No, because you don't count as people," I said. He chuckled again. "You know what I mean," I tried to explain. "Obviously, you're a person, but being with you doesn't wear me out."

"I know what you mean."

I squeezed his hand. "I meant it as a compliment."

He grinned. "'You're not a person' is a compliment?"

"Exactly. Because you're not *a* person. You're *my* person. And that means I can be myself around you. Like our time together still counts as 'me time.'"

He nodded, and this time I knew he really did understand.

We had dinner at our favorite restaurant. After we ate, Eric said, "I'm sorry to do this on our date, but I need to stop by Lowe's for a few things."

I scowled. Eric loved Lowe's, but I hated it. "Can you drop me off at the mall?" I asked. "I can look around there while you're at Lowe's."

He smiled. "That's a win-win because I can't stand going to the mall, and you can't stand Lowe's."

Eric dropped me off at the front door, promising to pick me up in an hour or so. I strolled around my favorite stores. I smelled the new lotions at Bath & Body Works, tried on a few pairs of shoes, and even purchased some adorable new sandals. It was a rare treat for me to shop without my younger kids in tow, and I enjoyed being able to take my time in the stores I wanted to visit.

When Eric texted me that he was on his way to pick me up, I sat on a bench at the mall entrance to wait for him. A lady stopped and asked if I needed any help.

"No, I'm just waiting for my husband. He had to go to Lowe's, so he dropped me off here. But he'll be back any time."

The lady sighed and nodded at the stroller she was pushing. "I haven't shopped by myself in years," she said. "I'm so envious."

I grinned. "It was definitely more relaxing."

When I got back in the car, Eric asked what I wanted to do next.

"Bookstore?" I suggested hopefully.

He grinned and turned the car in that direction. "I knew that's what you'd say."

"I know. It's my favorite place."

We went into the bookstore, each of us heading toward our favorite section. After each choosing a few books to peruse, we met back at a table in the coffee shop. Eric ordered a latte for each of us, and then we sat across from each other, reading and enjoying our coffee. We said very little to one another.

Two hours later, we checked out and headed back to the car.

I sighed, feeling refreshed, more content than I had in days. I thanked Eric for a great night.

"We didn't do much," he said.

"That was exactly what I needed, though," I said with a smile.

The next day, I was washing dishes, and Eric came into the kitchen. "I found a new study I think you'll be interested in," he said. He held up his phone so I could see it. "According to new research, having ample 'me time' is actually more important in maintaining a healthy marriage than going on date nights. I was really surprised by that."

I thought for a minute. "I'm not. Our lives are so busy, and we all need time to relax and not have to worry about taking care of anyone's needs but our own. We all need that, especially when we have children."

"But that's more important to you than going on a date?"

"I don't want to hurt your feelings, but sometimes it is. Having 'me time' makes me a better version of myself for everyone else. It makes me a better wife and mother."

"How do we balance this, though? There aren't enough hours in the day to make sure you get your time, but we still get time together. I think both are important, and I don't want to sacrifice one for the other."

I smiled. "We're balancing it better than you think, honey." At his confused look, I continued, "Last night, when I went to the mall during our date, that was me time. When we went to the bookstore, that was me time, too. That time was pulling double duty. It was good for our relationship, and it was good for me personally. It's me time and us time at the same time."

"It's like we're alone but together — but in a good way," he said with a smile.

"In a great way," I said.

In our marriage, Eric and I have found that including me time in our date nights is a great way to practice self-care while taking care of our marriage.

There's no doubt in my mind that Eric and I are better together. And sometimes, we're better alone but together, too.

— Diane Stark —

Love Notes on My Tree

What cannot letters inspire? They have souls; they can speak;
they have in them all that force which expresses
the transports of the heart....
~Héloïse to Abelard

"I wish I could find enough words to tell you how much I love you," said my tall, dark and handsome husband, holding me tight.

He worried about not being able to buy me a present. Emmitt had just finished his tenure in the Army and had enrolled in college on the GI Bill. We had been married only a few months, and he wanted our first Christmas to be special.

"You're my present and always will be," I answered. He smiled with relief. "Come on," I said. "Let's go shopping for a tree. Maybe we'll find one we can afford."

I think the salesman guessed our financial condition. "The trees have been picked over, but believe it or not, I have just the tree for you. I'll sell it for one dollar."

We thanked him and hurried home with the tree. We had nothing to decorate it with so we just sat and looked at it, listening to "White Christmas" playing on our little radio.

"Let's dance," Emmitt said, pulling me close. I thought I was in heaven.

Before he went to class the next day, he wrote me a love note. Telling me not to look at it until Christmas, he folded the paper carefully and tied it to the tree.

I decided to do the same thing. I would write a love note and hang it on the tree, too!

Emmitt noticed my creation and wrote another of his own the next day, and so did I. By the time Christmas Eve came, our "love note" ornaments "dressed" the tree in beauty.

Emmitt was still worried that I would be disappointed at not receiving a gift for Christmas.

Christmas Day arrived. Sitting together on the floor, we opened our love notes, and read them aloud to each other, moving ever closer.

Finally, I folded my last precious note and looked into his big brown eyes. "You are God's gift to me," I said, "and that's the greatest gift I could ever receive!"

He pulled me up, swept me off my feet, and twirled me around. We danced to the kitchen where we had a Christmas dinner of tuna sandwiches. To us, that tuna was a feast.

After Christmas, I took the notes off the tree and put them in a box. Little did we know we were starting a tradition. The next Christmas, we added new notes, and I carefully placed them in another box.

By the time our boys came along, we had a lot of Christmas notes. Each holiday, we wrote notes to them, too. They, of course, wanted to scribble on paper and hang their notes on the tree. We called it our "love tree."

As our sons grew, their notes became priceless. "Mommy, will you marry me when I grow up?" "Mommy, I love you because you pillow fight with me." "Mommy, do you want a dog that I saw outside for Christmas?"

"Daddy can we go rock hunting for Christmas?" "Daddy, I like the way you throw balls." "Daddy, you're the best daddy!"

All too soon, the boys grew up and had babies of their own. Yet, even today, every Christmas season, our grandchildren write love notes to hang on our special tree.

Our granddaughters never become tired of hearing stories about our first Christmas. "Mawmaw, could we read some of the notes Granddad wrote to you a long time ago on your first tree?"

"Of course," I say. I want them to know the extravagant love their grandparents have for each other.

We gather around in a circle, and each person gets a turn to pick a love note. Each one goes to the tree, picks a note on which his or her name is written, and pausing for effect, reads it aloud.

Jody starts. Pulling the first note from the tree, he unties the ribbon and unfolds the paper on which it is written. Smoothing the paper, he reads it to his granddad: "Granddad, I'm so thankful that you passed on a name to be proud of to my father, who in turn, passed it on to me!" I look at my tall, dark, and handsome grandson, and I see in him the tall, dark, and handsome man I married so long ago. In my mind, I hear the words "I'm Dreaming of a White Christmas," and in my heart, I dance with him again.

Love notes on our tree have become a legacy that has now soared with wings of love for four generations.

— Joan Clayton —

The Twelve Dates of Christmas

A wise lover values not so much the gift
of the lover as the love of the giver.
~Thomas á Kempis

My husband Peter grinned at me with the enthusiasm of a little boy as I reached for the last present under the tree.

"Really?" I thought to myself. "What's he so excited about? It's obviously a wall calendar. He makes sure I get one every Christmas. Maybe he personalized it with family photos or something."

When I opened the wrapping I was confused. It was just an ordinary calendar with mountain scenes — beautiful but nothing exciting. I glanced over at Peter.

"Thanks! It's great," I stated with forced enthusiasm.

"Yes, it is great!" he grinned even wider. "Open it."

I flipped open to January and there, taped on the first Friday of the month, was a gift card for Starbucks.

"You complain I never plan anything! Now I'm good for the next twelve months, and paid in full up front too! Our first date in the new year will be coffee and scones at Starbucks," he announced proudly.

I grinned back at him, very impressed with my groom of twenty-five years. He and I have firmly believed in the necessity of a date night at least once a month, when the two of us go out for an evening without any of our four kids tagging along. As romantic as that sounds, lately that had been reduced to meeting for an hour at our local diner and had basically become just another obligatory appointment.

Peter's excitement on this Christmas morning was contagious. I flipped to February and saw a gift card for our favorite seafood place taped to the 13th. After our reservation had gotten "lost" at a horrifically busy restaurant on our very first Valentine's Day together, I swore to always celebrate the day before. It was sweet of him to take my vow into account.

I looked at March and on the 4th was a gift card for my favorite Mexican restaurant. My eyes started to tear up. That was our middle son's birthday and since he had just moved away from home for his first real job, I wouldn't be able to celebrate it with him in person. How considerate of Peter to keep me busy that evening.

April 23rd was Administrative Professionals Day and since I work as an Executive Assistant, on the 23rd was taped a gift card for our favorite steakhouse. May 14th is our wedding anniversary, and on that date was taped a gift card for my favorite buffet.

For June we had been planning a road trip to visit my mom who lives 1,000 miles north of us, and on the departure date he had taped a gift card for our favorite road-stop restaurant. July 29th is my birthday and on that date he had taped a gift card for McDonald's and had written "Big Macs and Sundaes on the Beach!" which is my very favorite kind of picnic.

And the rest of the year was every bit as romantic, sweet and thoughtful. Peter brought a whole new meaning to "Personalized Calendar." When I looked up from the most perfect gift ever to stare at my amazing, if not always perfect, husband, I definitely planned to renew my lease on him for another twenty-five years.

—Jayne Thurber-Smith—

45

Love Him Unconditionally

Love is patient; love is kind. It bears all things, hopes all things, endures all things. Love never fails.
~1 Corinthians 13:4-8

My husband and I were returning home from taking our daughter, Chelsea, to college. We had been through this three years earlier when we took our son to college, but then we still had Chelsea at home. Now the house would be quiet; no more kids around.

I asked myself: *What's next in our lives? Where do we go from here?*

As the weeks passed, Chuck and I became moody. I cried easily when reminded of Chelsea, and I purposely avoided her bedroom — too many girly things around. Chelsea was a daddy's girl and it was obvious my husband was sorely missing his little buddy, his sidekick, too.

The pain seemed to be getting worse. Yet, I thought, *Shouldn't we be finding comfort in each other over our mutual loss? Shouldn't it be easy now to turn to each other?*

I had thought the same thing after my stepson died when he was seventeen. As we struggled through that nightmare, I could understand how couples divorced following the loss of a child. Our current situation was similar, but the grief was on a much smaller scale. Still, when both parties are hurting deeply, it is hard to be there for one another, to show interest in the other person.

One day when Chuck came home from work, I greeted him with a perfunctory kiss and asked halfheartedly, "How was your day?"

"Good, how was yours?" he asked, feigning interest.

"It was okay, except the dishwasher's still not working right. And, thankfully, there weren't any phone calls, so I got some writing done. That was nice — no interruptions."

"Hmm," was his only response.

That's it, a "hmm?"

Gone were the days of announcing to our kids, "Daddy's home!" and watching them run to greet him at the door, jumping up and down, begging for him to scoop them up and throw them on the waterbed, one at a time. How they loved that! And how he must've enjoyed that, too....

Now he came home to a wife who talked about the dishwasher and the telephone. Hmm.

Suddenly, I recalled how short I'd been with him the other night and the hurt I'd seen on his face. He'd been looking more tired lately, too.

In my own grief, I had been focusing on how moody he had been. I had not considered what I might be like to come home to. Quickly, I prayed one of those intensely painful prayers, asking God to show me how I come across to others. I knew, for the sake of my marriage, that I had to face the painful truth: How had I changed over the years? What was I like to live with?

Suddenly, a short conversation from years ago was crystal clear in my mind. When our kids were preschoolers, Chuck and I were going through a tough time in our marriage. I knew we needed help, but I thought people who sought counseling were weak. So, instead of personal counseling, I chose to go to church, hoping a sermon would give me the answer. And, wouldn't you know it, that Sunday the pastor said, "We all need counseling at times from wise people. It is usually pride, though, that keeps us from seeking the help we need."

Ugh.

I called the church the next day for an appointment with the pastor. When I arrived, I was certain that, once he heard my story, he would readily agree with me — divorce was the only answer. I was sure of it.

Imagine my surprise then, after pouring out my heart to this kind man, when he responded with: "You need to love him unconditionally."

I stared at him. What?

The pastor continued, "Love him the way *you* want to be loved — with no strings attached."

That was it. Three words: "Love him unconditionally." Three words that changed the course of our marriage. Three words I have never forgotten. Three words that still have the power to change hearts.

Suddenly, I remembered something else I'd heard years ago: "If you want to be treated like a queen, you need to treat your man like a king."

I had not been treating my man like a king. I'd been pouting over not being needed as a mother on a daily basis. I had not been showing my husband the love that *I* had been craving.

What could I do to improve this next chapter of our lives? How could I get us out of this rut?

The answers came daily. First, I began my mornings reading about the love God has for us and wants us to have for others. I saturated my mind and heart with it. Then, I purposely began hugging Chuck more. Judging by his shocked reaction, I realized just how far apart we had grown. I started listening to him more intently, and he reciprocated. As I did more things to please him, such as make his favorite foods and choose his favorite movies, he voluntarily helped with the housework. I even began watching some of his favorite shows with him instead of staying on the computer in the evenings, and he began handing me the remote, willing to watch the shows that *I* liked.

Gradually, our marriage became better than ever. A spark had been rekindled. We started talking about the future. Our twenty-fifth wedding anniversary was around the corner. We decided to splurge and take a cruise to Hawaii. After all, we had reached a milestone — it was time to focus on ourselves. And from the moment we boarded the ship, we were like two kids in a candy store, having the time of our lives!

That old principle once again held true: When we show love to another, especially when we don't feel like it, our feelings will catch up. It's a mystery, but when we love those who seem hard to love, we are actually teaching them to love us back. Here's to the next twenty-five years of loving unconditionally.

— Connie Cameron Smith —

46

Ten Times a Day

To love is nothing. To be loved is something.
But to love and be loved, that's everything.
~T. Tolis

n February 2003, I was moving to Hawaii to marry my boyfriend of four months. At only nineteen years old, I got quite a lot of advice before I made this huge life decision.

Most of the advice could be summed up in three words: "Don't do it." This was said to me in various ways, "You're too young…" "You haven't dated long enough…" "It's been long distance, so you don't really know each other…" But I was headstrong. Determined. Young and in love. So, I went through with my plan.

My boyfriend Matt was a Marine. He had been put on "stop loss," which is a military term meaning that his unit was under the possibility of deploying, and no one was allowed to leave their duty station. Because of this, we could only get married if I moved to Hawaii. It wasn't a terribly hard decision to make. On February 12, 2003, Matt asked me to marry him. On February 13, 2003, I put in my notice at work. Two weeks later, I was saying goodbye to a job and people I loved.

Most of the advice I had received about this marriage came unsolicited. And much of it was rather condescending. Despite this, the people I worked with at the sheriff's office were truly wonderful people. On that last night of work, they presented me with a few gifts, a card and a collection of cash they had pooled together. I *oohed* and *aahed* over the presents, pocketed the money, and glanced at the card. The messages were fairly standard — "Good luck" or "Best wishes" — but one person, one of my sergeants, wrote out a really thoughtful, detailed message. The message, in a nutshell, said that despite our young age, our brief dating time and our short engagement, our marriage could work if we worked for our marriage. She went on to say that during her marriage, she had come to find "these ten pieces of advice the most useful." Then she went on to list those ten pieces of advice.

Now, I don't remember all ten, and since I'm not a terribly sentimental person, I didn't save the card, so I can't go back and reread them. I only remember one of them, and it was the best advice I have ever been given. It was number seven in her list of ten, which I remember only because seven is my favorite number. It said, "#7: Say 'I love you' to each other no less than ten times a day."

Matt and I put this advice to use immediately in our short engagement and our marriage. In the beginning, we would make a joke of it. "How many times did I tell you that I love you today? Only seven? Here are three more." But over time, saying "I love you" became a habit — a lovely, endearing habit. We tend to say it far more than ten times a day. We say it when either of us leaves the house. We say it when we hang up the phone. We say it in texts more times than I can count. We say it randomly when nothing else is going on. We say it in intimate moments and public moments. We say it in a teasing, playful manner, and in a serious, romantic manner. We say it before we go to sleep. Sometimes, we say it at what we think is the end of a conversation, and then we continue the conversation and say it again a few minutes later.

We say it so much that our youngest son once bragged that he knows we are happily married because "you are *always* saying you love each other." We say it frequently, not only to each other, but to our three children who, having picked up on the habit, say it frequently to us as well as to other important family members. However, it is not just something we say; it is something we act on and feel deeply about. While it has become somewhat routine, it is never said lightly.

Those many "I love yous" — too many to count over fifteen years — have carried us through so much. Through dumb fights and through fits of laughter, through difficult times in our life, through triumphant times, through deployments and welcome homes, through births and through loss, through mundane days and through exciting moments. When my husband can't be home because the military calls him away, when he can't call, when he can't get online, when he isn't there to say "I love you," I have a thousand memories of him saying it to hold in my heart.

That simple piece of advice in that card was the best advice I have ever received. There is nothing more important than letting the people that we love *know* that we love them. Whether it is with words or not, say "I love you." Say it and mean it, and don't wait for a "perfect" moment.

— Jacqueline Chovan —

47

Nurture It Tenderly

*In the enriching of marriage the big things are the little
things. It is a constant appreciation for each other and
a thoughtful demonstration of gratitude.*
~James E. Faust

When I was growing up, my best friend lived across the
street from me. I was at her house so often that I was like
a member of the family. I loved my friend's mom almost
as much as I loved my own. Mrs. Shepard was a cake-
baking, cigarette-smoking, romance-novel-reading, stay-at-home
mom. I especially loved her spectacular flower garden. My friend had
no interest in the garden, but I was enchanted by it.

I spent hours — ultimately, years — helping Mrs. Shepard tend
her flowers. Her back yard was a delight to my senses. The vibrant
colors, the floral scents sitting heavy upon the air, and the buzz of the
pollen-drunk bees made the garden feel alive; it was a heartbeat I felt
inside my chest. I treasured my time in her garden and dreamed of
the day I would have my own.

I will never forget the morning my friend's father packed his bags
and left home for a "new life." I found Mrs. Shepard on the bench
swing in the middle of her beloved blooms. She gave me a tremulous
smile as I approached, wiped the tears from her cheeks, and made
room for me to sit beside her.

As we swung together, I said, "Maybe he'll come back."

"No, he won't," she said sadly. "He's gone. He made it pretty clear that he doesn't love me anymore."

"How can that be?" I asked with an aching heart. "How could he just stop loving you?"

She sighed. "He didn't 'just stop' loving me. Love's been slipping away from us for a long time. I was sitting here thinking that marriage really is a lot like a garden; you know better than anyone how much energy it takes to care for it. For all the hours I spent keeping things alive out here, I never acknowledged the fact that my marriage was dying in there," she said, nodding toward the house.

"Let me give you a piece of advice," she continued. "When you get married — not only at the beginning, but when you're deep into the years — treat your relationship like a garden. Nurture it tenderly every day." I sensed the wisdom of those words and tucked them into my heart for safekeeping.

My husband and I invest a lot of time and energy in coaxing beauty from the land around our mountain home. We cherish the time we spend with our flowers, shrubs and vegetables. Throughout our marriage, we have tried to stay mindful of the fact that our garden is the perfect metaphor for our marriage. While others have compared the two, we have tried to live it with intention by applying the basic tenets of successful gardening to our lives together.

Start with Good Soil: Because the root of any living thing is dependent upon a strong foundation to thrive, good soil is our most important purchase each spring. Before we committed to marriage, we planted our roots in a friendship based on mutual respect. We made sure that we had the same values and priorities. We laugh often, fight fairly and accept each other's imperfections.

Create a Plan: Before we put anything in the ground, we map out a blueprint to give each individual plant the optimal amount of sun, shade, rain and drainage that it needs. This gives it the best chance for success. In the same way, we took steps to pre-plan the most important aspects of our lives. We defined our career, financial, parenting, fitness and leisure goals before we walked down the aisle. We even had to figure out how to handle the inevitable conflict. We believed that our plans didn't take the spontaneity out of a marriage, just the unwelcome surprises that could tear it apart.

Nurture: Planting the seedlings is the fun part. It's the fancy dress, champagne toast, first dance, and exotic honeymoon phase of marriage. But the real commitment to those seedlings begins later — often under a hot sun — and continues. It's in the day-in, day-out grind that a marriage finds success, as well. My husband and I think of ourselves as a team. We run errands, work on household projects and volunteer our time to good causes together. We nurse each other through the inevitable illnesses. Our devotion to each other in the moments that aren't glamorous fortify our commitment to each other.

Sunshine: Few flowers will thrive without the benefit of the sun. My husband and I believe that a marriage must also be rooted in prayer, faith and trust.

Pruning: Deadheading is essential for preventing spent blooms from robbing a plant of much-needed energy. It also helps make way for new flowers to grow. In our home, we "prune" to check in and see how we're doing. We take time to listen, express concerns or get rid of hurt feelings before they can rob us of our energy. It's amazing how the removal of old distractions clears the air and renews our marriage.

Spice It Up: My husband and I spiced up our property with soft lighting, quirky ornaments and Adirondack chairs around a fire pit. We go hiking every week. We go on adventures and we share the excitement — and renewed love — when we kayak a rapid, horseback ride in the desert, hike in grizzly country, or dog-sled over snowy terrain. Of course, it doesn't have to be "death-defying." It just has to be fun!

Vase Arrangements: The best part of gardening is the beautiful finished product. An artfully arranged vase of flowers on our dining room table gives us a wonderful sense of accomplishment, as well as great joy. For our marriage, this means we set aside time to celebrate our love. Like a stunning bouquet, it's a gift to be treasured. We pack a picnic on a sunny day, hold hands at the theater, watch a sunset on a sandy beach or linger with our novels on a rainy morning. Most importantly, we express our love in a dozen different ways each day.

Mrs. Shepard and I remained close until her death several years ago. I think of her fondly when I'm tending my flowers in the cool of a summer morning. On my wedding day, she gave me a basket of gardening tools and an assortment of flower seeds with a note that read: "Nurture your gardens tenderly; the one that grows under the sun, as well as the one that grows inside your hearts." I keep her wise words of advice framed on my bedside table so I can always stay mindful of them.

My husband and I will celebrate our thirtieth anniversary in a few months. We have tended to our marriage as lovingly as we have tended our garden. I believe Mrs. Shepard would approve!

—Vicki Kitchner—

48

The Un-Love Letter

Simply love your spouse better today
than you did yesterday.
~Aaron and April Jacob

As I opened the door, my two little girls squeezed past me, dropped their backpacks on the kitchen floor, and hit the fridge for their after-school snack. A tote full of research papers begging to be graded slumped from my shoulder onto the table. I was ready for my own pick-me-up, a cup of leftover morning coffee, before making dinner.

I turned toward the coffeepot. The morning dishes weren't in the sink, and the floor had been mopped. The pile of junk mail that usually cluttered the counter had been replaced by a single envelope with my name printed in my husband's familiar scrawl.

My heart fluttered. He hadn't written a love letter to me since he was in the police academy before we were married. Then I replayed the casual comment I had made on my way out the door that morning: "Since you're working evenings this week, it would be nice if you'd do something to help out around the house while you're home."

Instead of reaching for a coffee mug, I picked up the letter, anticipating an apology and his gratitude for everything I did as a wife and mother. But when I read the first line, my heart sank. It was not a love letter.

"I'm tired of being accused of not helping around the house. Yesterday, I washed the windows and cleaned the gutters. I serviced the lawnmower and sharpened the blades to get ready for summer. Did you notice? I also picked up your car from school and took it for an oil change. I bet you didn't notice that either, did you?"

I glanced through our now pristine windows at the mountain covered with spring green. No, I hadn't noticed the windows had been washed. Did he really take my car to the garage so I didn't have to waste a precious Saturday morning on vehicle maintenance?

The letter continued in the same tone — a little anger, a lot of hurt — and I deserved every word. It wasn't only what I'd said that morning that prompted his protest. It was a culmination of comments I'd mumbled over the past months: "I wish you would… You never… Can't you just…"

I wasn't completely oblivious to his household contributions, but instead of giving him credit for the tasks he did, I nagged him about the tasks he didn't do. The truth was, when he worked evening shift, I envied the solitude he enjoyed by day. He spent hours alone in a quiet house while I took on the parenting role for both of us at night — dinner, homework, baths, bedtime. Then I graded papers or made lesson plans before I collapsed into bed. Who had time for laundry? For dirty floors? For solitude? Not me.

But I also didn't have time to wash windows or mow the lawn, and I didn't have to — because my husband did.

I folded the letter and slid it inside the envelope to hide his words and my shame. I walked to my bedroom, opened my top dresser drawer, and tucked the envelope in the front corner so every time I opened that drawer, I would see it and remember.

I returned to the kitchen, pushed aside the research papers on the table, and snatched a pen and notebook from the tote. My hand paused above a blank page. Careless, hurtful words had tumbled so easily from my mouth, but these new words must be deliberate and meaningful, worthy of forgiveness. I wrote, "I'm sorry."

Our younger daughter, Randi, skipped to the table and leaned against me. "What are you writing, Momma?"

"A love letter to your daddy." *Filled with gratitude for all the energy he spends taking care of our family,* I added silently.

She covered her mouth and giggled. "Kelli!" she called to her big sister. "Mom is writing a love letter!"

She put her hands on her hips and looked straight at me. "Do you love my daddy?"

"Yes." I smiled. "I do."

— Karen Sargent —

49

Second Chance

*The concept of two people living together for 25 years
without a serious dispute suggests a lack
of spirit only to be admired in sheep.*
~A. P. Herbert

t was a strange experience. Married twenty-five years, divorced two. Our ostensible reason was the empty nest syndrome when our son went away to college. Idiosyncratic words and gestures crossed the threshold from cute to dumb. Silences hung from the ceiling, cocoons of sighing air.

Anger came easily, particularly the self-righteous, enabling anger without a filter.

One night, I stormed upstairs following a number of directed remarks to sleep in the guest room. My parting words were "I'm not going to live like this." That weekend, a temporary hotel stay. A one-year apartment came next, followed by the purchase of a home for me.

We spoke to each other twice — division of property, no argument there, and also to sign the divorce agreement. Our son was not a direct part of anything, being away at college. Of course, this simplifies the story, but it was about us. He knew he was loved by both of us and would not have to make any choices.

A couple of years later, I got a letter with familiar handwriting. I was surprised, but not unpleasantly. I waited for about an hour to open it. I didn't think there were any legal or family issues to resolve. It fell from my hand once, and I nearly tore it in half when I opened it. She had apparently written the letter in installments, as there were two different colors of ink.

My uncle had passed away two weeks earlier, and our son told her. "I know how important family is to you. I'm sorry Uncle Ed died. I've found out that doing things just to please myself doesn't. Maybe we were too hasty. If you ever want to just sit down and talk about what we did and could do, we can have a beer or two and…"

Knowing she hated the taste and smell of beer, calling it "piss in a glass," I could see the sour look. While reading, I heard the sound of water falling from a large block of translucent ice, held by both of us.

I finished the letter. The second part of the letter became the conventional catch-up with the news, closing with a reminder to call if I wanted to. I reached for the telephone, sat on the couch and dialed. She used her professional voice to answer, and I giggled, "Boy, you know how to get a guy's attention. Needless to say, you have my interest. How about going to Fairchild Gardens?" This had long been a sore spot. She wanted to go there, and I resisted. I was pleased with myself for remembering that, but brought back down to Earth when she disclosed she and a girlfriend had gone down there three months earlier.

She must have sensed my disappointment, "Oh, but I'd love to go again. It's even better than I expected. How does Sunday sound? Look, I've got to get back to work. See you at noon."

Our son was home for spring break, and his total reaction to my announcement of our first date was "Cool."

When I picked her up, he admonished us to take it easy. One might say he was unimpressed with everything.

It was a perfect spring Florida day. We talked about what each of us had done over the last couple of years. Of course, our son had passed on any interesting tidbits to each of us anyway. The sunroof let us bake in the sun, and when we arrived, the breeze off the water was welcome. The Gardens looked like the paint chip counter at Home Depot.

After the Garden, we went to a Mediterranean restaurant for lunch. I had lamb shanks, while she had a gyro. I saw her looking longingly at the wine list and told her I wouldn't hold her to a beer. After we ate, she wanted to see my house.

The drive home was fairly comfortable. We spoke of our son and the immediate past and future, but did not refer to our former married life. The sun was setting when we arrived. I poured two glasses of wine, and we sat on the patio watching lights go on in the homes around the lake. Her warm hand grabbed my arm, and she pulled me to her for a kiss. I think it surprised her as much as it did me. We both sat speechless and smiling.

"Do you want to stay for dinner? I'm sure I can find something to eat." (I had nothing in the refrigerator.)

"No, thanks. I have to go home and prepare for work. Maybe next time."

"Sounds good to me."

The unspoken words hung like a Calder mobile. We both had enjoyed ourselves, but didn't want a couple of glasses of wine to rush that which must wait. I drove her home, the evening being as encouraging as the daytime. Just before leaving her house, I said, "I'll call you later."

"Okay." A friendly and chaste kiss on the cheek and a hug.

We had several more dates and began to travel together again. I had forgotten what a pleasure it was to go somewhere I hadn't been before, and how much we both enjoyed that. Mount Dora, New York City, and the Keys, even Epcot.

I found out later that she didn't date. Neither did I during the time we were apart.

The summer air was waning, fall slowly cooling the air, but not the ardor. I once again asked her to marry me. "Yes." The ceremony was the three of us and a clerk of the court, who read from a small tattered book in a government garden. We got into three cars and drove back to work.

I don't recommend getting a divorce to save a marriage, but it worked for us, an unintended consequence. We needed a separation to find a reason to be married.

— Timothy A. Setterlund —

50

Forty-Nine Perfect Hearts

A hundred hearts would be too few to carry
all my love for you.
~Author Unknown

I pulled back the dining room chair and saw a small, wrapped present sitting atop my seat. Dinner plate in hand, I stopped short, thinking of the unwrapped gift that lay hidden away in my dresser upstairs. "Oh," I said to my husband. "Are we doing this now? Yours isn't ready yet."

"Open it," he said.

I knew what lay inside, even though I didn't know the color, or the size, or even the material it was made of. I knew, however, that when I untied the bow, lifted the lid, and unwrapped the tissue I would find a perfect heart. An ornament for our Christmas tree.

My first heart arrived when we were newlyweds decorating a tree we had chopped down ourselves from a nearby farm. We had finished hanging the few ornaments from our blended households on its branches when Randy placed a small box in front of me.

"A present?" I squealed. "But it isn't even Christmas yet." He just smiled and nudged the box a little closer. I lifted the lid and gasped. A blown-glass, heart-shaped ornament with swirling colors lay inside.

"A heart for my sweetheart," said Randy. I kissed him and found a place on the tree where we could admire the heart all season long.

The next year I decided to surprise Randy with a heart bought especially for him. Weeks in advance I started looking for the perfect ornament to take its place beside the one he gave me. Finally I chose one made of wood, something pretty yet sturdy, to last through the years. We finished decorating our tree, and I pulled the package from my pocket.

"I got something for you," I said with a grin.

"I got something for you, too," he answered, pushing another package my way. And so a tradition was born. Much like our new marriage, in the beginning giving the hearts was easy. With no kids, few possessions, and time on our hands, we could shop until we found the perfect heart to add to our growing collection. Then our daughters came along.

Within a few years Christmas became a whirlwind of things we had to do with shrinking amounts of time to do them in. We hit the ground running the weekend after Thanksgiving and didn't stop until we sprawled exhausted beside a mountain of discarded wrapping paper on Christmas morning.

As our daughters grew, the rest of the year seemed to pass in a blur as well. We ferried the girls to art classes, soccer games, piano lessons, and set aside evenings to help with homework. There hardly seemed time for us as a couple; we were a family, a team of four, united in the purpose of raising girls who could take on the world.

Even so, every year Randy and I still gave each other a heart, despite feeling at times as though shopping for it was just another chore. Some years all the hearts we found looked like ones we had already given. Some years, heart-shaped ornaments were hard to find. Some years, we fought on tree-cutting day, hurling angry words at each other as we crammed one more event into our overbooked holiday schedule.

Those years, the hearts helped us put our anger aside. For how could we nurse a grudge when a tissue-wrapped heart lay waiting, a symbolic olive branch to put things in perspective?

Year after year, heart after heart, we filled our tree with ornaments of porcelain, glass, wire, raku, and wood, in colors of blue, red, green, purple, gold, silver, and swirling mixes. Each delicate piece is a reminder that though our relationship is fragile, it is also sturdy, and like the ornaments, with careful tending it will last.

Now, with our daughters in college, Randy and I once again decorate the tree on our own. We hang our favorite ornaments in prominent places, but every piece in our two-and-a-half decade collection is precious in some way, for they remind us that at the core, at the heart of things, we started out as two. And with any luck, we will face the world together as two once again long after our children go off to make lives of their own.

"You know," I say, as I unwrap this year's heart, a vibrant blue, blown-glass piece with a beauty separate from any that have come before it, "we're up to forty-nine hearts. At some point, we're going to have to quit this."

Randy looked at me as a quiet smile made its way from his eyes to his lips. "Never," he said. "Never."

— Cindy Hudson —

51

How Love Works

*Life appears to me too short to be spent in nursing
animosity or registering wrongs.*
~*Charlotte Brontë*, Jane Eyre

I was seventeen and had just gotten in a huge fight with my boyfriend. I was crying in my room when my dad came in and sat
down next to me.

"What are you going to do?" he asked.

I shrugged. "I'm not sure."

"If you're going to forgive him eventually, you may as well do it
now. After all, it's Christmas Eve."

"But I'm really, really mad at him."

"I understand that. But if you know you're going to get back
together with him eventually it's mean to wait and ruin his Christmas."

I sighed. "I do still care about him. I really don't want to end our
relationship over this stupid fight. But I want to stay mad at him for
a few days."

"Why?"

"To teach him a lesson."

My dad shook his head. "That's not how healthy relationships
work. If you value the relationship, you need to make things right
between you and the other person as soon as possible."

"But if I forgive him right away, he won't be as sorry as if I wait
a few days."

Dad shook his head again. "Nope. You can't hold a grudge to

teach him a lesson. That's not how love works. You need to decide if the relationship is worth holding on to. If it is, you need to offer forgiveness immediately."

After my dad left my room, I called my boyfriend and offered him my forgiveness. We made up and enjoyed a lovely Christmas.

Less than a year later, we broke up for good. In hindsight, forgiving him wasn't the best move for my life. I should have seen the fight as the red flag it was and ended the relationship sooner.

Although getting back with him wasn't the best decision, I've never forgotten my dad's advice. I've carried it into every relationship I've had since.

My husband Eric and I have been married for twelve years. While we have a close relationship, we do argue occasionally.

One of our biggest arguments was on the day of our fifth wedding anniversary. It was on a Saturday, and by noon, when he still hadn't said anything about our special day, I knew he'd forgotten.

I was hurt and angry. A part of me wanted to pout and make Eric feel really bad for forgetting. I wanted to punish him to make sure he never forgot again.

But then I remembered my dad's words. *If you know you're going to forgive him eventually, you might as well forgive him now.*

Eric hadn't hurt me on purpose. He'd made a mistake, and it caused me pain. But he hadn't set out to do something hurtful.

I was upset, but forgetting an anniversary is obviously not a reason to end an otherwise-great relationship. I knew I would forgive him eventually.

So I had two choices. I could pout all day, ruin our anniversary, and forgive my husband a few days later. Or I could offer forgiveness right away and make the best of what was left of our special day.

It was tempting to hold the grudge, to make sure my husband realized that he'd messed up. But Dad's advice rang in my ears: *You can't hold a grudge. That's not how love works.*

We ended up having a pretty nice day. And Eric has remembered every anniversary since then.

In life, we all have to decide if our relationships — both romantic and platonic — are worth the effort we put into them. If someone is hurting us on purpose and they never seem truly sorry for the pain they've caused, maybe forgiveness isn't the best course of action.

But if we value the relationship and know that forgiving past hurts is the right move for us, we should never wait to offer it. Holding grudges isn't good for them. Or us.

My dad taught me to be quick to forgive when the hurt is accidental and the relationship is important to me.

Time with loved ones is valuable, and we don't want to waste it being angry.

Forgive quickly. It's how love works.

— Diane Stark —

Never Too Late

A Single Yellow Rose

The best thing to hold onto in life is each other.
~Audrey Hepburn

Do you believe a single yellow rose can change someone's life? I do. On a cold November night, I flew into the Denver International Airport after spending a week in my hometown. I always knew I'd go home again someday, but I just had not been ready. It was the place where Richard and I grew up. We had met in first grade, started dating as teenagers, married, raised three children, and lived the company-transfer-lifestyle of the 1970s. We eventually settled in Colorado.

Richard's untimely death the previous year changed my life, and revisiting our hometown by myself was a frightening idea. However, the members of my grief support group encouraged me to take the big step, so I called my daughter and asked, "Would you get me reservations for a week in Iowa in November?"

Before I left Denver, I arranged for my daughter to pick me up at the Denver Airport on Saturday evening. When I called to confirm the time of my arrival, she announced, "Bob D. wants to meet you outside Door 4 by the baggage claim area thirty minutes after you land."

Hmm, that's a surprise, I thought. *I wonder why Bob wants to pick me up.* Bob had been a good friend. In fact, he and his wife had participated in a Bible study group with us, and Richard and Bob had been golfing buddies. Richard had often commented, "Bob is a really nice guy. You should get to know him better."

And I did get to know him better. After our spouses had died within two months of each other, we joined the same grief support group. I discovered why Richard had admired Bob, and because of his kindness, generosity and gentle spirit, he became a good friend and a fellow griever. The week before I left for Iowa, Bob had called and asked, "Since I lost my golfing buddy, would you join me for eighteen holes of golf this afternoon?" He and I discovered laughing and teasing each other was something new for two people who were used to crying together. "Sometimes, I just go to the mall and walk around to be with other people," Bob had told me.

Because of his comments, I wasn't totally surprised about his phone call to my daughter. He could kill some time on a lonely Saturday evening and meet a friend at the airport.

That's when more life-changing events began. On Saturday evening, I stepped out of Door 4, pulling my suitcase. Bob gave me a quick hug, grabbed the case with one hand, and opened the passenger door with the other. While he walked to the back of the car to deposit my luggage, I turned to get into the car. There, lying on the passenger's seat, was a single yellow rose.

"Bob, you brought this for me?" I asked in surprise.

"I thought it was appropriate to bring a rose for my friend," he answered. Then he looked at me and smiled. "I missed you."

I was at a loss for words. *Hmm, is something different here? Do I want something to be different between us? What do I say?*

"How about stopping and getting something to eat?" Bob asked before I could comment.

"Okay," I said, thinking we'd probably stop at a fast-food restaurant on the way to my house.

"Would you like to go to that little café in Parker? It's a nice place with good food," he suggested.

Uh-oh, I thought. *And very appropriate for private conversations. What's wrong with me? It's my friend Bob.* All the while, I was holding my single yellow rose. Still a bit dazed by the turn of events, I inadvertently carried it into the restaurant.

During the previous year in our support group, Bob and I had shared our honest feelings about everything connected with the loss of a spouse, including our anger and disappointment in unanswered prayer. After we settled into a cozy booth, we spent two hours talking about our families, our desire to follow God's will, and our anxiety regarding the future. We were both in our mid-sixties, and we didn't want to stop living. We each had a bucket list of adventures to experience and places we wanted to see.

Wow, are we talking about us? I wondered. *This is Bob, my friend, my buddy.* But there was the single yellow rose in my lap. "We've both suffered tremendous loss this past year. Whatever the future holds, I hope neither of us gets hurt," I commented.

We had always greeted each other and said goodbye with a hug. That night, we hugged a little longer than usual, and it felt good.

"How would you like to go to a movie?" Bob asked me the following weekend.

"Is this called a date?" I asked. "You need to know you're talking a foreign language," I added.

"The same goes for me," Bob laughed. "Wow, I'm going on a date in my sixties!"

Yes, that night was the beginning of a new life for Bob and me. During the next several months, we became a couple. Bob's sons lived miles away. However, Bob kept them apprised of our new "dating" relationship. "We are so happy for you two," was the constant reaction from family and friends.

Since we were very aware of our new motto, "treasure the moment," seven months later, we chose to get married with our children and grandchildren surrounding us. I carried a small bouquet of yellow roses.

"Do you ever regret remarrying when you were in your sixties?" my friend Linda asked me four years ago.

"Never!" I answered. "There are still times of adjustment and compromise, but it's all worth it. We've discovered new hobbies like traveling in a motorhome, spending time at Bob's cabin on the lake in upstate New York, and rounds of golf in new places. We even played at St Andrews in Scotland. Now that we've moved into our seventies, we've learned sitting side by side in our recliners is also a good way to spend an evening."

And it was, until September 2017. Fatigue and weakness in his legs, arms and hands had plagued Bob for over a year. Finally, a neurologist gave us the bad news: "We have ruled out all other possibilities. You have ALS, commonly known as Lou Gehrig's Disease, and it is fatal."

Our love for each other, our faith in God, the prayers and support from our families and friends sustained us during Bob's last months. We often told each other, "I'm glad we decided to get married. It's been a wonderful fourteen years."

Yes, a single yellow rose changed my life when I was in my sixties. However, my life has changed once more. Several months ago, our families and friends gathered to celebrate Bob's life. Once again, I carried a single yellow rose.

— Betty Johnson Dalrymple —

53

Love Online

Grow old with me! The best is yet to be.
~Robert Browning

L ove at eighty-two? Highly unlikely! But two years ago, I found it on the Internet.

I had been widowed two years when a friend urged me to give a dating service a try. "Are you kidding?" I asked. "Who's looking for an eighty-two-year-old woman?"

"You'd be surprised," she responded. "They say there's someone for everyone. Why don't you try eHarmony or Match.com?"

"Don't be silly," I scoffed. "I'm not that desperate!"

But I was.

One night I secretly got on my computer and entered my profile on a dating service: "Looking for someone who enjoys candlelight, soft music and good conversation. Must be between the ages of 75-85 and live within 50 miles of Clearwater Beach, FL."

A few days later, my computer signaled that I had received photos of twelve men between the ages of sixty-five and eighty-five, living in Denver, Tucson and Seattle.

"You must be working from the Sarah Palin book of geography," I complained to the Internet service. "I live in Florida!"

Within a day, I had a new page of Florida men, from both the East and West Coast. I gave them my best, but I struck out on all counts.

A few weeks slipped by, and I was losing heart, when suddenly... There He Was! "Harvey1926." His profile matched mine exactly. He was born in March, 1926... I was born in February, same year.

Harvey's picture showed that he was tall and good-looking, with a mane of white hair and a smile that hinted at a sense of humor.

We had both lived in Massapequa, Long Island, and both worked for CBS in Manhattan. Harvey was the director of music royalties... I was a songwriter for Fred Waring and His Pennsylvanians on CBS television. Yet our paths never crossed.

He had a player piano... I had a Steinway. We had both read *Bomba, the Jungle Boy* as children. (I even had a pet monkey named Bomba.)

There was just one problem. "Too bad," I wrote. "We would have been perfect for each other, but you live in New York, and I live in Florida."

Harvey wrote back, "We'll meet in Paris!"

Hmm, he had definite possibilities!

He had received responses from other hopefuls and actually had dates with three women in the New York area. In fact, his granddaughter commented, "Grandpa, you had more dates this week than I did!" But none clicked.

"Tell me more," I wrote.

He had been a widower for six months, had two married children and three grandchildren, had traveled the world, and now was looking for someone who enjoyed Broadway shows and sing-alongs with friends around his player piano. The Paris trip would come later.

I painted as dazzling a picture of myself as I could. But then, on second thought... "I have a confession to make," I wrote. "I walk with a cane."

"In which hand?" he asked.

"The left."

"That's good," he answered. "I walk with one in my right hand. We'll fit together perfectly."

After a week, e-mails weren't enough. We exchanged phone numbers and with 164 years of living between us, we had plenty to talk about.

His children had already made reservations to fly him to Sanibel for the Christmas holidays. Two days before they left New York, he learned that they would be renting a car in Tampa and driving south.

A quick call to me determined that, yes, he would be welcome to visit me for a few days when he got off the plane.

His family was stoic.

"Can she cook?" queried his daughter.

"An octogenarian Lolita!" sniffed his cousin.

"Get a pre-nup!" counseled his lawyer son.

My family was equally supportive.

"Don't cook for him, Mom," advised my older daughter.

"How do you know he's not an axe murderer?" fretted my younger daughter.

"Get a pre-nup!" warned my son.

So much for the children! We were in love, and we hadn't even met.

A somewhat disgruntled family parted with Harvey at the airport gate.

"Maybe we should wait until you're picked up," they suggested, but Harvey was adamant... they should drive to Sanibel, and he would join them in a few days.

We almost missed each other at the exit. He waited at one door, I waited at another. After forty-five minutes, he was beginning to think he might have to take a bus to Sanibel. At that moment, I realized my mistake and drove a few feet to where he was sitting. We were equally excited to find each other and fell into each other's arms before driving to my condo.

Between moonlit walks on the beach and candlelight suppers in local bistros, our four days together went far too quickly. Every word, every nuance, every touch brought us closer together.

While Harvey spent the holidays with his children, I joined my daughter in Washington, D.C. We were out shopping in her car when her cell phone rang. On the other end, a rinky-tink piano played and an off-key voice sang, "I just called to say I love you."

"He's a keeper, Mom," she laughed. And sure enough, he took a train to Washington for New Year's Eve.

It only took a little time to convince me to return to New York with him to see how I'd feel about living there again.

Once there, I knew I'd found my new home. To suit our grandchildren's college schedules, we selected August for our wedding date. Friends suggested we call an interfaith center to locate an officiant who would marry us in Harvey's Greenwich Village apartment.

We were somewhat taken aback when a young yogi, recently ordained, answered the phone, but he was available on our chosen date, so we moved ahead with plans. He apologized that he had never performed a wedding before. "No problem," we assured him happily. "Between us we've been married six times. We'll walk you through the ceremony."

Harvey's apartment on the fifteenth floor, with a view of the Empire State Building in the background, couldn't have been more romantic for our wedding. My son escorted me to the flower-laden altar in the living room where Harvey awaited us with his son, the best man. Then our minister shared the ceremony with my two daughters, who read my favorite verse from First Corinthians.

In attendance were our five children and their spouses, six grandchildren and three great grandchildren.

And Harvey delivered on his promise of Paris for a two-week honeymoon, followed by a ten-day river cruise on the same rivers where he had fought in WWII during the Battle of the Bulge.

The climax, though certainly not the ending of this fairy tale, is that Harvey and I celebrated our first wedding anniversary at the wedding of one of my granddaughters in a little New England church. This time it was Grandma who read First Corinthians in the ceremony. As I looked across the congregation at Harvey, the words had new meaning... "If I have a faith that can move mountains, but have not love, I am nothing... And now these three remain — faith, hope and love. But the greatest of these is love."

— Phyllis W. Zeno —

54

One Text at a Time

Technology is best when it brings people together.
~Matt Mullenweg

I resisted at first, but my son persisted and I learned to text. Little did I know the huge role my new communications "skill" would play in my future.

Not long after I learned to text, my husband Phil suffered a massive stroke. After he spent a year in a nursing facility, I brought him home and became his full-time caregiver. It was a heartbreaking and exhausting time, but I never regretted giving him the comfort of home and family as he fought for recovery. Sadly, it was a battle won in heaven rather than earth as he received his final healing almost five years following the stroke.

I had actually met Phil at an online site for Christian singles. It had been a good experience, and we were blessed with a loving marriage. And I knew I wanted to find love again. I decided to look online to see if I might discover some Christian widowers who shared my faith, lived close by, and loved the outdoors (and hiking) as much as I did. Because my faith was a big priority, I listed that in my profile.

I made several friends and had a few interesting dates, but nothing serious developed until the day I spotted a profile that seemed to match my desire for a strong faith and my need to be outside. He lived in a city nearby, so I sent a brief comment that we seemed to share similar interests.

Shortly afterward, I received a reply. "I would like to get to know you better. I am impressed with your faith." After a few private e-mails, we arranged to meet at a nearby river park to walk. We exchanged phone numbers… and began texting!

Our first meeting went well. We talked and walked non-stop, and I gave Jim a book I had written containing stories about my life. Jim's wife had died suddenly after over forty years of marriage. Between us, there were seven children and nine grandchildren! As we parted for the evening, we made plans to meet again soon for another hike.

Let the texting begin! In the days that followed, I discovered that Jim's preferred method of communication was text messages. He texted comments and questions in response to my book. As we continued meeting to walk, hike and talk, we considered whether our relationship might have a future. Jim began texting me good morning and goodnight messages to start and close my day. I looked forward to the little "ding" that would tell me he was thinking of me.

Even the first "I love you" came in the form of a text! The morning messages became "Good morning, Sweetheart," and the evenings ended with "I love you most." We connected occasionally throughout the day and "discussed" our plans the same way. Jim owned a goat farm and a part-time shipping business. Our busy schedules required pre-arranging our time together, and texting made it possible to interact at our own convenience without the disruption of a phone call.

As we grew closer and began including our families in our friendship and plans, we used texting to exchange family photos and even the sports schedules of grandchildren. A truly special event was celebrated together by text as we welcomed an additional grandson into my family. Jim awaited the birth announcement via text updates and then rejoiced with us as photos of Josiah Keller Kirkpatrick arrived also by text.

When we are separated and I am traveling, Jim gets "treated" to my experiences on wooded trails or waterfalls and sometimes even my food as I text pictures of my adventures. We have even enjoyed the fun of multi-family texts filled with emojis and sibling banter.

While my marriage proposal actually took place on a mountaintop at a beautiful state park in Alabama (with no cellphone service), many of our wedding plans continue to be made by text. And I recently sent a text picture to Jim of the beautiful wedding bands we had designed after I had just picked them up.

Jim and I will soon begin life together... and there seems no reason to believe the texting will slow down even then. But I cannot even imagine what I could have missed if I had refused to learn how to text! I owe a huge thank you to that persistent son of mine for both his perseverance and his capable tutoring... via text, of course!

—Lettie Kirkpatrick Whisman—

55

A Clear Connection

Love is our true destiny. We do not find the meaning of
life by ourselves alone — we find it with another.
~Thomas Merton, Love and Living

My wife and I dated in high school, then went our separate ways. Several years later, we reconnected with some help. What God gave Theresa and me, in my view, was a very clear message — a message that we both understood and trusted.

Theresa and I both grew up in Louisville, Kentucky. She attended an all-girls Catholic high school, Mercy Academy. I attended an all-boys Catholic high school, St. Xavier. Theresa became friends with my older sister, who also attended Mercy. Several weeks after we met, I got up the nerve to call Theresa on the phone and ask her out on a date. We were both in our junior year of high school. We continued to date and became very close over the next two years.

We discovered that we had similar core values and morals. Our strengths and weaknesses were such that we could tackle just about any project together. We were an example of "opposites attract" in the best possible way. We complemented each other. Completed each other. Everyone told us that we were destined to be married to each other. But we were still very young.

After high school, I started at the J.B. Speed School of Engineering at the University of Louisville, which also meant alternating semesters in Middletown, Ohio during my last two years. Theresa began taking classes at Jefferson Community and Technical College in Louisville and then transferred to Western Kentucky University in Bowling Green. We went our separate ways and started dating other people, but we still kept in touch.

Sometime during my junior year of college, I started hearing a kind, gentle voice in my head. It kept saying, "You are going to marry Theresa." I found myself getting into these mental conversations. *How can I possibly marry Theresa? We are not seeing each other. She is dating some guy who keeps asking me to help him fix his Ford Pinto, and I have been seeing a young lady in Ohio and another in Louisville.* But I kept hearing that voice. "You are going to marry Theresa." I prayed and thought about it, wondering why I was feeling like this.

Finally, one night, about four months since I had talked to or seen Theresa, I heard it again: "You are going to marry Theresa." I thought to myself, *Okay, I give up. I will call her up and talk to her.* I wasn't even sure if she was in town.

So I picked up the old rotary phone in my parents' kitchen to call Theresa, but I did not hear a dial tone. You see, I had picked up the phone at that split second between when an incoming call is connected and the phone actually rings. It was Theresa on the phone.

It seems she had been hearing a similar nudging voice for some time and decided to call me at the exact same time I had decided to call her!

Six months later, we were engaged. A year after that, we both finished college and got married. God had a plan for us and I am so happy we both said, "Yes."

— Mark J. Thieman —

56

Finding Love Later in Life

Life can be strange — a person who once was a
stranger across the room is now the love of your life.
~Andy Atticus

By the time I reached my sixtieth birthday, I had led a successful, exciting and fulfilling life by most standards. I had worked as an occupational psychologist, a market research consultant, and a helicopter instructor. I had walked round the whole coast of Britain, visited more than eighty countries, and flown almost all types of flying machine. Bucket list? Mine had been completed long ago. There was nothing left that I desperately wanted to do. I lived in a gorgeous country cottage with great views, along with my much-loved cats, and I now earned my living writing about all the things I'd done in the past. I was quite content. After all, what more could I ask for?

However, there was one area of life in which I had been less successful. I had never married, nor really even had a long-term relationship. For many years, I had been too busy with careers and travelling to care about such things. After that... Well, it just hadn't happened, and I hadn't worried that much. But now, as I found myself getting older, things changed. I started to envy those people I knew who had a lifelong companion. I had good friends, but no one really close to me.

Now that I wasn't going out to work, for the first time in my life I started to feel lonely by myself in my little cottage. The idea of sharing my life with someone other than the cats gradually became more attractive. But how could I do that? Surely, it was far too late. Whoever heard of someone meeting their soulmate over the age of sixty? And I knew I couldn't settle for just anyone.

However, I decided to make a last try to meet someone. On the advice of friends, I joined a couple of dating websites. But by 2010, when I was sixty-one, I realised that this was unlikely to work. Most men wanted someone far younger, and I had little in common with the few I met. Many found my background intimidating, and almost nobody could cope with my multi-cat household! It seemed I was doomed to grow old as a lonely, mad cat lady with exciting memories.

Then, just as I was about to let all my subscriptions lapse and give up altogether, I came upon a profile written by a cat-loving man who lived on a canal boat. He wrote well, and he sounded interesting and, well, quite a lot like me. He was a few years younger than I was, but that wasn't a problem from my point of view, although I realised it might be from his. I ignored the profile for a while, but I kept coming back to it, and wondering, just wondering... Should I have one final try?

I decided it could do no harm as I was pretty immune to disappointment by then. So, I wrote to David, telling him about my cats and my life. And he wrote back. We corresponded a bit more, and then we talked on the phone. We seemed to get on well. But that was all that happened for a couple of months as he carried on boating and showed no inclination to meet. I recall saying to a friend that I'd heard from a nice man, but he didn't seem to want to take the friendship any further.

Then fate took a hand. I acquired a new Maine Coon kitten, and David really wanted to see her. So, he came to my house, mainly to meet nine-week-old Xena! But we got on really well and couldn't stop talking to each other. After that, we started seeing each other regularly. I've always joked that it was Xena who really brought us together!

Soon, winter came, and living on the boat became hard, so David accepted my invitation to move in for a while, bringing his cat Cookie with him. After that, he never really left. True, he went back to the boat from time to time for short periods, but that was all. We gradually went from being good friends to being very much more. Eventually, David sold the boat and moved in with me permanently.

We have now been together for ten years. Two years ago, we bought a house together in a nearby town that we both liked and enjoyed fixing up together. We have travelled extensively, and I found out how much more fun it is going to new places with someone to share things with. He introduced me to his children and most recently to his new granddaughter. He took me boating, and I introduced him to cat showing and yoga. We took up ballroom dancing, both of us learning it for the first time. Life together is fun! But, most importantly, we share the same ideas and values, and are still growing closer and closer. He tells me several times a day that he loves me, and I tell him the same thing.

I still can't believe that, at the age of sixty-one, I finally found my soulmate. I am now seventy-one, and life just gets better and better. I consider myself to be very fortunate. So, I always tell people in their forties, fifties and older who lament being alone and say it is too late, my life is proof that this is not the case. You are never too old to find love!

— Helen Krasner —

57

Love Lids

When you forgive, you in no way change the
past — but you sure do change the future.
~Bernard Meltzer

t was early fall and the kids and I were looking for a new house, closer to the city where we drove almost an hour every day for school, church, shopping… everything. We had found the perfect house in the perfect location at the perfect price. And then I got the phone call.

It was my husband, from whom I was separated. "What would you think about you and the kids moving into my house and then I could get a smaller place?" His place was big and roomy and way too large for a man living alone. And it had land: my secret heart-of-heart desires. A place in the country with acreage.

A deal was struck — he would stay a couple of months in the lower level of the house and the kids and I would have the main floor. We would make the best of things, pool our finances, and put our differences aside until he found an apartment.

At first it was weird. We hadn't shared a home in years. We hadn't shared more than an argument in years. The months stretched out and he stayed. Financial burdens became a financial crisis and stressed us both to our limit. We had no choice but to learn to share.

Over time, we adjusted to living under the same roof and the kids had their dad with them to say goodnight and good morning and to join us for Family Night and family prayer. We all worked together in the yard and jumped together on the trampoline. We planted a garden and took pictures of every new vegetable as if it were a new baby in our family. One day it hit me: the kids were happier having both their parents with them. My own fog of worry and frustration at the situation lifted as I marveled in this blessing. We began to feel like a family again. Except for the tiny little detail of Mom and Dad not being together and not really even liking each other.

The financial struggles worsened and it seemed as if no end was in sight. Strangely though, this tremendous stressor began to create in me a compassion for my husband that I hadn't felt in years. There was no way we would ever get back together, but a new sort of friendship and kindness began to blossom. My heart softened; his heart softened.

After two years of learning and struggling and changing, one summer evening my husband came to me. He was humble and gentle and I could see his heart was truly hurting. He entered my room and asked if we could talk. I immediately felt nervous. It's never a good thing when someone says that. He perched on the edge of my bed, the pine canopy bed with the cutout hearts he surprised me with fifteen years ago when I was carrying Noah.

"I think we should try to see if we can fix our marriage."

My mouth dropped open. I never saw this coming and refused to open my own heart.

"No."

The conversation deepened and the pros and cons were discussed, but inside I was terrified to trust this man again. The conversation continued for days but I couldn't bear to crack my heart open to him, not even to let the teeniest ray of hope in. I had wanted this change and now that it was here, it was too late. Years too late.

About a week later, Marty suggested that we begin praying together. Just the two of us, like we used to back when we were happy. Eons ago. I agreed that this would be a good idea. What was the harm in prayer? I kept my heart firmly clamped shut and that night we prayed together.

I listened to my husband's humble words, felt his good, strong spirit and something inside me thawed. Each night we prayed and each night I felt something shift more and more between us. I started to believe that maybe we could be a family again. I prayed hard in private for guidance. If this was God's will for us, then He would have to help me find the faith. I needed proof.

The proof came in small, unexpected ways. Ways that showed me two stubborn people really can change. Each of us began to make changes within ourselves, not putting pressure on the other to change, just focusing on what we needed to improve on our own. Marty wasn't the only one who needed to change, I knew that. I began to be kinder to him, letting go of years of hurt. I felt peace inside at this change in myself. The change affected him, but it healed me. As I let go of my hurt, the walls I put up between us began to come down. Little, everyday things helped pave the way for big changes.

Marty stopped doing little hurtful things and replaced them with loving, thoughtful gestures. Flowers arrived from him weekly. Also gone were the snide remarks about my daily Diet Coke. In their place arrived a giant Diet Coke in our fridge every morning, the lids decorated with little love notes. The first one shocked me. I opened the fridge and couldn't believe my eyes. Not only had he bought me a soda that morning, but he wrote "I love you" on the lid in bright colors with little hearts. The second one surprised me and the third one had me eagerly anticipating what was on his next "love lid." His little notes made me smile all day. I secreted the lids away in a drawer and pored over them again and again. My husband is not a demonstrative man, so this was a tangible change that showed me he really was trying. I needed to try too. My faith began to grow with each "love lid."

As part of our self-assigned "marriage homework," we watched the movie *Fireproof*. It opened my eyes to the realization that the sacred vow of marriage is not about how much the other person deserves love, or how happy he makes you. My vow was to love unconditionally.

We had decided to attend any conference or marriage retreat we could find. Marty searched far and wide, but they were all too far away and we had no one to take the boys overnight. Finally he gave up, frustrated. One night on a whim, I thought maybe I should try too. The little seed of faith was growing in me. I scoured the Internet and I found an all-day Saturday conference called "The Marriage You've

Always Wanted" taught by none other than Dr. Gary Chapman, author of *The Five Love Languages*. It was only an hour away and tickets were not too expensive. I felt my heart speed up at this stroke of luck.

I surprised Marty with the tickets, excited and nervous and proud of my find. It ended up being the turning point for our marriage and one of the best days of my life. We took notes and listened raptly, soaking in a million lessons and reminders about how to be married and how to be good at it. Sitting next to my husband, watching the tears slide down his handsome face, I realized I was head over heels in love with him again. He was a strong, beautiful, loving man and a truly wonderful father. I felt so very, very blessed. My eyes filled and my heart overflowed at this gift of a second chance. Leaning on him, I knew we could actually put our marriage back together. And my fear evaporated.

I have a drawer full of love lids and it's still growing every day. We are renewing our wedding vows on the weekend of our anniversary next month. The road is still bumpy at times. Like a delicate flower, it needs care and attention. We nurture it with nightly devotionals geared for couples and supported by scripture and prayer. We have actual dates where I shave my legs, wear jewelry and he opens doors for me and makes me feel like a teenager again. We play question-and-answer games that help us learn about each other's dreams, hopes, fears and the things that make us feel happy. The nurturing part is new for us and takes work. But the reward is greater than I ever imagined. My heart is full again and our children are happy.

I know that without the financial crisis we faced, we never would have healed our marriage and our family. We were forced to depend upon each other and learn to work as a team to get through that crisis. The financial stress itself was horrible. But without it, we would still be a broken family.

Sometimes it takes a crisis to create a miracle. But it is worth every moment of pain, of worry, of fear. You just have to have the faith to walk through the fire, look for the path God wants you to be on, and get to the other side. Where the miracle is waiting.

— Susan Farr Fahncke —

58

The Bet

A ship in harbor is safe, but that is not
what ships are built for.
~John A. Shedd

At sixty-two I didn't expect to find love. But on New Year's Eve, 1998, when online dating still was considered more risky than routine, I resolved to try Socialnet.com. Long divorced and just returned from a decade overseas with the Peace Corps, I worked in Little Rock, far from my California origins. Dateless for eons, I pictured casual Saturday outings to view Renoirs at the Arts Center or to share fried chicken and a hike at Pinnacle Mountain State Park. Love was for others. I'd settle for companionship.

So masquerading as "Dumpling," I posted my online bio and personal preferences, and prepared to review my matches. My inbox promptly began to fill with a list of potential dates' screen names and the distance they lived from my Arkansas home. To learn more, I'd have to click on the profile. Sometimes I sighed at the quirkiness of the computer matchmaker. One match, Bettor, I left unopened… the man lived two thousand miles away. Not a good bet for Saturdays in the park.

Those nearby didn't always prove to be good bets, either. A Kentucky widower wrote that if I helped him raise his four teenage sons he'd provide me with a new washing machine. I passed. A Wichita Falls adventurer invited me on a rafting excursion on the notoriously challenging Cossatot River. We'd have to wait, though, until he convinced his wife that he deserved a weekend away. I declined. An Oklahoman declared he loved my moniker, Dumpling. He bet that I was one enticing fat mama. I didn't respond.

I finally agreed to meet one local widower for supper at Cajun's Wharf. The riverside setting, though, reminded him of the seafood dishes his late wife had prepared. Soon he was sobbing into his devilled crab as he recounted her prowess with halibut, trout and flounder. By the time he began to wail about her bouillabaisse, I'd finished with my barbecued shrimp… and our date.

Then one day at work my administrative assistant, Bev, asked how Social.net worked. I pulled up my list, which for months had been headed by Bettor's unopened profile.

I ran my cursor over his name. "I've never written this guy because he's too far away," I explained. "And with a name like Bettor, I suspect he's a gambler. But let's peek."

I clicked on his profile and quickly scanned it. Hmmm. Like me, he appreciated jazz, art, books, dogs, cooking, and travel. What's more… he sounded sane.

I glanced up at Bev. "I've been to the ends of the earth with the Peace Corps, so what's two thousand miles?" I pounded out a quick paragraph introducing myself.

Bev eyed me. "What if he turns out to be The One?"

The next morning I had a response in my inbox.

"My name's Ken and I think I'm in love," I read. "I value a coherent message. Bettor is my Nissan's vanity plate, which amuses friends here in Reno. I deal poker at Circus Circus, but don't gamble myself, as my three boys will attest." He added a link to his domain page, dubbed Sunflower.

I hesitated before clicking on it. I didn't want any kinky surprises. So I was delighted to find that he'd filled his webpage with photos of his three grown sons and assorted grandkids.

"You and your sons each are more handsome than the other," I wrote back.

We corresponded with caution, gradually building trust, and

then shared our private e-mail addresses. Eventually we traded phone numbers. Friends warned about axe murderers, but I believed in Ken's sincerity. "I don't even own a tiny hatchet," he'd assured me.

Sunday mornings, home from his graveyard shift, Ken would phone. He e-mailed jokes to start my day, and sent gifts, a wooden car, a casino chip, framed photos. Then one day I opened a small box to find a ring with a diamond sunflower. It had belonged to his mother, he wrote.

In turn, I mailed cards with sunflower motifs and a motion-activated potted sunflower that played "You Are My Sunshine," one of the only songs he claimed he knew the words to. We debated how and where we could meet in person, beginning to realize we were falling in love. "I've never had a doubt," Ken swore.

I decided to attend my high school reunion in California and then visit my father's widow in Napa. Ken drove from Reno to her place to meet me, and we toured the nearby wineries. When we paused for supper that first evening, the waiters all buzzed around after we described our long Internet romance. They produced a bottle of Chardonnay on the house, gazing at us with sappy smiles. We billed and cooed like aging lovebirds.

Weeks later I flew back to Reno for his son's annual mystery party. I sported a feather boa and toted a stuffed wirehaired terrier, and Ken looked dapper in his rented tuxedo, as we impersonated detectives Nick and Nora Charles from the *Thin Man* movies.

I returned for the holidays, suitcase stuffed with Christmas gifts and decorations, and Ken provided a little tree. His son joined us for Christmas dinner and presented us with a mouse pad that featured us in our *Thin Man* costumes.

On New Year's Eve afternoon Ken taught me some poker basics so that I could accompany him to work that night. Because of the Y2K fright, though, the card room crowd was sparser than anticipated so he got a phone call from the manager offering him the night off. We rushed out to rent videos, grabbed a bottle of champagne and ordered a pizza.

At midnight we toasted the millennium and made a joint resolution to marry. On July 1, 2000, we wed at his son's home in Reno. Socialnet. com sent us a Waterford crystal photo frame. It holds a picture of us cutting our cake and sits today on the top shelf of a china cabinet in the living room.

Together Ken and I cruised the Mediterranean, the Baltic, and the Alaska Inner Passage. We hoisted steins in Munich at Oktoberfest. We searched for Nessie in Inverness, and pub-crawled in Dublin. We gardened, played a running gin game, watched *Jeopardy!* and spoiled our two dogs and three cats. I never quite mastered Texas Hold 'Em. For nine years Ken e-mailed me those daily jokes. We survived surgeries, spats, falls and fractures. We wandered those art galleries and picnicked on fried chicken, just as I had envisioned. I confess that Ken sauntered, rather than hiked.

After a lingering illness, my sweet Bettor died last spring. But opening his profile proved to be my best bet ever. He indeed turned out to be The One, my sunshine, my love. He's left me with a myriad of precious memories.

You can bet that I adore technology. Who knew that it would lead me to companionship... and to love?

— Terri Elders —

59

Take a Chance

In the shaping of a life, chance and the ability to
respond to chance are everything.
~Eric Hoffer

"Mom, just give it a try."

"I don't know, Danny. I'm fifty-five. Fifty-five-year-olds don't do Internet dating. We meet people the old-fashioned way."

My son snorted. "Of course, they do! Besides, how's the old-fashioned way working for you so far?"

"Ummmm…," I mumbled.

"Exactly. Alexa's mom met Rich on the Internet, and now they're engaged." Alexa is my daughter-in-law. Her father had passed away from cancer seven years after I lost my husband to the same disease.

Danny continued, "They met on an 'Over 50' website. You would be meeting men who have some of the same life experiences and values you do."

"I have Walter. We share the same values." Walter is my rescue dog.

"Sure, Mom," he chuckled. "It's just something to think about. Dad's been gone almost twelve years. It would be nice if you weren't alone."

After hanging up, I did think about it. I thought about the life I had built over the four years I had lived in Taos, New Mexico, since moving from Colorado. I was teaching at a local charter school, going out with friends, and meeting with my book group every month. My younger son, Ben, had recently moved to Taos from Colorado to help start a new CrossFit gym, so I even had family nearby. Danny and his family were only about five hours away in Denver, so I was able to see my granddaughters pretty often. For the first time since losing my husband, I was feeling stable and happy in my "aloneness." Why should I mess with something that didn't feel broken? Other dating experiences had not been exactly successful. Sure, "alone" morphed into "lonely" from time to time, but much less often than before. I decided to pass on Danny's suggestion.

Not long after my conversation with Danny, my stable, comfortable life began unraveling at an alarming rate. My landlord of three years called to tell me she wanted to sell the condo I was renting. Did I want to buy it? If not, my lease would not be renewed, and I should consider this my forty-five-day notice to vacate so she could get it ready to put on the market. While looking into my finances to see if purchasing was an option, my principal called me into her office to tell me my position was being cut and my contract would not be renewed the following year. My head swimming, I called my landlord to tell her I wouldn't be buying the condo and set about searching for new employment and a place to live.

While searching online for jobs and housing one day, an advertisement popped up for the "Over 50" dating site Danny had told me about. Thinking it might be a sign, I decided to fill out the profile and check it out. Everything else in my life was off-kilter; why not add one more thing?

Over the next couple of weeks, I ran around packing up my classroom and condo, putting things into storage, and moving into an efficiency condo I had leased for the summer. While updating my résumé and looking for teaching positions, I would get notices from the dating site telling me someone had looked at my profile and sent me a "flirt" or a message. The site would also send suggestions for profiles I might want to look at. Curiosity always got the better of me, and I couldn't help looking at the notices.

One day, a notice popped up telling me that someone had checked my profile, but had not sent any notice of interest. I opened up his profile to take a look. Steve was my age, recently widowed, and had lived in the Denver area for about twenty years. He was in the process of selling his Denver home and moving to a mountain home he owned about an hour north of Taos. One of the photos in his profile was of a vintage Volkswagen bus — the kind with the pop-up camper top. On a whim, I commented, "This looks fun!" on that photo and went back to my job search, a little disappointed that he wasn't interested in even chatting in the website's chat room. A couple of days later, a notice popped up that I had an e-mail from a potential date. Surprisingly, it was from the man with the VW bus. He liked that I had responded to his picture of the bus and decided to take another look.

We began writing back and forth, sharing more about our lives and experiences as we got more comfortable. Both being widowed was something that mattered very much. It was so nice to be able to talk to someone about that kind of loss and have him understand. Because his loss was much more recent than mine, he had a lot of questions about the grieving process. As I shared my story with him, I felt even more healing myself.

Finally, we decided to take the big step of meeting. We agreed to meet for lunch at Orlando's, a New Mexican food restaurant in Taos. I was so nervous about meeting him. I would stop and laugh at how worried I was about what to wear, what I would say, and how it would go. When I got to the restaurant, I looked around, but didn't see anyone who matched the pictures in the profile.

Oh, no! What if he stands me up? I worried.

Not long after I sat down, I saw Steve walk into the outdoor seating area. As I stood up to greet him, I felt a rush of recognition beyond just matching a face to a photo. I felt like I knew him, even though we had never met before and had only talked online.

After we ordered, he told me how nervous he had been getting ready for our date. We laughed about feeling like teens and how strange it was to be dating at this time of our lives. As lunch was winding down, we were both wondering what came next.

Suddenly, Steve grinned and said, "I drove the bus here. Would you like to go for a ride?"

"Of course!" I answered. "Can Walter come, too? He's waiting in the car."

That first ride in the bus called Buttercup was the first of many adventures Steve, Walter, and I have shared.

Sure enough, Danny had been right. As dating quickly evolved into an exclusive relationship, followed by an engagement and plans to marry, our common experiences and shared values have formed the foundation of a surprising and wonderful second chance that neither one of us expected, but are so grateful for. Sometimes, it's a good idea to listen to our kids.

— Lynne Nichols —

60

The Box

Fate laughs at probabilities.
~Edward George Earle Bulwer-Lytton

'm not sure how long I sat there staring at the e-mail. It may have been a minute, it may have been an hour. It was a short message — only three sentences, fewer than fifty words, but I knew it would change everything for me. I was suddenly hearing a voice that had been silent in my life for seventeen years. Until now. Somehow, I had my Amy back.

Even after nearly two decades apart, I could hear her laugh, smell her hair, feel her presence. As the shock and surprise eventually yielded enough to allow rational thinking, the words and wisdom of my late father inexplicably came to mind — sometimes things don't turn out the way you plan.

For the last year my life had been changing at lightning speed. An unexpected phone call on an ordinary Friday led to the abrupt end of my twelve-year marriage. This was merely the opening act of weeks of pain, frustration, and arguments. Children, family, and friends were notified, and I found myself packing for the move that would usher in the rest of my life, whatever it held. That's when I found the box.

It was a square cardboard box, which had apparently been pushed to the back of my now-empty closet. I opened it to discover remnants of my childhood and college days — old awards and certificates, cards, letters, photos, and a small ring.

The ring. I held it in my hand and stared at it for several minutes.

It was familiar, but why? Finally, a long-closed door in my memory opened, and I remembered. I gasped out loud — not an exclamation, but a name — "Amy." Yes, the ring belonged to Amy.

I suppose nearly everyone has a memory of "the one that got away," and Amy was mine. After meeting in junior high, we became best friends in high school, spending our days and nights talking about life and fate. A few years later, we decided to risk the friendship for a chance at love, and we began dating. By college, we were engaged, with a wedding and a lifetime of happiness within reach. But fate had different plans, and we eventually parted ways. As Dad always said, sometimes things just don't turn out the way you plan.

I continued to stare at the ring and reveled in the unexpected trip down memory lane. As I began to repack the contents of the box, I realized I couldn't simply pack the ring away. It belonged to Amy and I needed to return it to her. I had not heard anything about her for years, but the last information I had put her thousands of miles away — and married. Suspecting that the re-emergence of a former fiancé after so many years might be disruptive, I reached out to a mutual friend to ask if I could simply mail her the ring and let her handle getting it back to Amy. So I e-mailed the friend to get her address, and briefly explained my circumstances. She immediately replied, and assured me that I could contact Amy without disrupting her life.

And that's when it happened. In a blink of an eye, I had my best friend back.

A brief e-mail led to another, then another. Within a day, pages of e-mails were exchanged, as we caught up on our seventeen years apart. I learned that Amy was also going through a divorce, having just filed the paperwork a few days before. I learned that we were both in the same line of work. I learned that she was living about 2,000 miles away from me, but ironically, she was minutes away from a town I'd be visiting in a few weeks. I learned about the winding path her life had taken over the years. I learned I was still in love with her.

E-mails gave way to texts, which turned to daily phone calls, leading to a surreal reunion a few weeks later. I don't remember much of the conversation from that night. I remember laughing. I remember trying to keep my heart from bursting out of my chest. I remember feeling at home again.

Over the following weeks and months, we marveled at the miraculous timing of all of it. How could both of us, with zero contact for almost two decades, come back together as we did? How could we be going through simultaneous divorces after we'd each been married for more than a decade? What were the chances of finding the box at that precise moment in time, along with the ring, forgotten dreams, and a mutual friend to connect the final missing piece?

A little while later, I found myself at a secret lunch with Amy's parents. For the second time, I asked for their permission to marry their only daughter. For the second time, they agreed. As I left the lunch, I assured them there would not be a third time. I was being given a second chance that few ever receive, and I wouldn't waste it. Not today, not tomorrow. Not ever.

Several months later I stood in front of family and friends exchanging vows of marriage with the love of my life. She was no longer my ex-fiancée or "the one that got away." She was now simply my wife. My best friend. My soul mate. My Amy.

Life can be a puzzle. At times, it can seem cruel and unyielding. But then there are the moments when the wonder and magic of it are almost too miraculous to fathom. Whether guided by luck, fate, or divine intervention, somehow we find our way to the place we belong.

And as it turns out, Dad was right. Sometimes things don't turn out the way you plan.

Sometimes, they turn out even better.

— Rob L. Berry —

61

Another Chance

Without forgiveness, life is governed by... an endless
cycle of resentment and retaliation.
~Roberto Assagioli

M y husband David and I loved our new son-in-law. We liked his sense of humor and his kindness toward others, and we accepted him as our own. But within months of the honeymoon, Jerry resumed acting like a bachelor with his old friends; gambling and other behaviors began to surface. Now we wondered if Shelley and Jerry could indeed live "happily ever after."

After two years, the birth of our first grandson brought joy into both families. We hoped this responsibility would improve our son-in-law's conduct. But deception, broken promises, and treatment programs became part of the marriage. Household items disappeared, and large gambling debts mounted.

When the marriage ended, I went to court with Shelley and watched her sit with a stoic face on the witness stand. While the judge decreed six years of marriage terminated, I cried silent tears in the back row.

Afterwards, we stopped at a coffee shop to "celebrate" Shelley's new freedom.

Over our treats, I said, "I thought you would be crying and upset."

"Mom, I don't have any tears left. I have cried and grieved for years. Now it's time to move on with my life."

And life did continue. Shelley began graduate school that very day. We participated in our four-year-old grandson's activities with special camera moments. Within the year, our son was married in a beautiful wedding, and Jerry brought our grandson into the back of the church for family pictures. While he stood across the room watching, I felt such sadness as I thought about Jerry and Shelley's own "perfect" wedding pictures.

Our ex-son-in-law's lifestyle spiraled downward with changed jobs and broken promises for visitations. His erratic emotional behavior became a concern for both families. One afternoon, I felt that I should pray for Jerry's safety and state of mind, but my prayers seemed insincere. How could I pray for Jerry without love and forgiveness in my heart? I didn't want to love him or have him back in the family. I just wanted him changed into a responsible father.

That day, I sobbed as I released the resentment that had wrapped around my heart. I chose to forgive Jerry. Silently, a divine alteration occurred. Suddenly I felt at peace, and for the first time in years, I prayed for his wellbeing without any bitterness. A few months later, he began a faith-based treatment program out of town, which lasted over two years.

Shelley raised her son and received no child support during this time, but we witnessed miraculous provisions for her school and living expenses. Our daughter also worked a full week, juggled graduate-school studies, stayed active in church, attended support groups, and ran a small home-based business. She ministered to other hurting women in painful relationships. Over the next months, Jerry apologized for many wrongs to her during their son's visitations. Through honest letters, deep emotional wounds began to heal. Seeds of love began to grow.

One fall day, David and I decided to drive the two-hour distance for Jerry's graduation ceremony and sit alongside his family and our daughter. We wondered how long this change of behavior would last as he publicly testified of his recovery. When he thanked Shelley with a verbal acknowledgment, we could see sparks flying between them. David and I looked at each other.

Driving home, my husband commented, "We didn't sign up for this again."

After Jerry's return to the city, the two attended an intensive marriage seminar for broken marriages with follow-up sessions. Our daughter learned to trust again and forgive her ex for the years of addictive behaviors and back child support she never received. The four of us met on several occasions, and a shallow foundation of trust began to form. But when we took our family picture for the annual Christmas card at Thanksgiving, we did not include Jerry. After all, he had not officially rejoined our family, and maybe their relationship would crumble again.

After Christmas, my husband and I were out of town when Shelley called us with the news. They had gotten engaged and wanted to remarry on their original wedding day in February. They wanted our blessings. Before returning home, David and I searched our hearts to release any residual bitterness we held. We decided to give Jerry another chance.

Five years after their divorce, my daughter and son-in-law remarried before friends and family who had been a part of their tumultuous journey. Our ten-year-old grandson escorted his mother down the aisle as the only attendant in the service. The wedding ceremony included marriage vows, but they also made a covenant promise to their son to never separate again.

When I thought back on it, I realized that eleven years earlier we had participated in a lavish *wedding*. On this afternoon, through prevailing love, we witnessed a *marriage*. Sniffles could be heard throughout the room.

Afterward, David and I, my elderly parents, and our son and daughter-in-law embraced Jerry as he re-entered our family circle. We took photos of the reunited family during the short reception. The couple drove away for their honeymoon, and a big bundle of joy arrived nine months later — a baby boy of restoration.

I often tell people, "I have two grandsons from two marriages and one set of parents."

Fourteen years later, their love continues to flourish. We have helped Jerry in his successful estate-sale business, and people stare in amazement after hearing our stories. Since their remarriage, many other couples in anguish have listened to Jerry and Shelley share about their divorce of despair and their remarriage through forgiveness. Forgiveness made room for love and another chance.

— Sharilynn Hunt —

62

Mom on Match

In the end, we only regret the chances we didn't take.
~Author Unknown

Me? On the Internet? My three daughters were crazy. They knew I hated the computer. Each of them had tried to teach me how to use it and failed. I didn't care if I was Internet illiterate. I had my typewriter and telephone, so I could communicate just fine.

Two of them even came up with the idea of "Mom on Match," which I immediately rejected. Did they really think I, at age eighty-seven, was going to find a date with some old man that way? Never mind that one of the girls had told me earlier about the scammers and criminals out there who prey on older women like me. I wanted no part of that nonsense.

But they wouldn't give up. So, one night, when I felt very tired and wanted to shut them up, I reluctantly agreed to let them put me on Match.com. I didn't have to do anything. They did it all and then instructed me on how to use it. (I didn't take a single note.)

About a month later, all three girls wanted to see the results I'd received from Match.com. None existed! They found out then that I hadn't used it; I didn't even know how. So the one who lived closest took over. She got on the computer, found a gentleman who hadn't given up when I didn't reply on Match earlier, and answered him. Like me, he was a former educator, loved to dance, and enjoyed watching football. After talking on the phone for two weeks, I reluctantly agreed to meet him for lunch. We had much in common, so we continued to meet, had dinner dates (he always brought flowers), enjoyed ballroom dancing (something I hadn't done in years), saw musicals, and went to Indianapolis Colts football games with his season tickets. Spending time together was very comfortable, and we began seeing each other more as the months passed.

Then, one evening, a surprise proposal came in the middle of a dance floor. I love surprises, but I wasn't ready for that one. It did, however, spark some serious discussions about a possible future together. Later, we met with our pastor to examine things further and prepare for a marriage that would bring both of us happiness. We knew we each had a few old habits that should be discussed, and at our age we also had to address possible challenges for the future.

Time passed. We grew even closer together as we explored housing possibilities. My fiancé had a home about twenty miles from my apartment that he would sell. (I had sold my home earlier.) We decided to live in a cottage on the grounds of a senior community that offered all levels of care for the future, if necessary, and a large apartment building with dining, fitness, and ongoing activities we liked. And it was in a perfect central location.

Our small wedding took place a year and a half later, with a reception afterward for family and friends. Then, on our honeymoon cruise, we even won "The Newlywed Game!"

Now, almost two years later, we still feel like newlyweds and have recommended Match.com to others, some of whom have connected. And, yes, I use the computer constantly these days, often to write down such stories as this — which, I admit to my daughters, is a lot of fun.

— Queen Lori —

Take the Risk

And Always One More Time

*Have enough courage to trust love one more time
and always one more time.*
~Maya Angelou

I have a framed quote from Maya Angelou sitting on my desk that became my mantra after I was suddenly widowed. It was that quote that gave me the courage to try online dating. I had to admit that my fear of being alone outweighed my fear of online dating. So, with a little nudge from my persistent friends, I began weeding through profiles.

The process was interesting. It wasn't difficult to meet men — several showed interest. But at this phase of my life, it proved nearly impossible to make a lasting connection. I had a few relationships that were a little more than casual, but nothing ever felt right. It always felt like I was trying to force a piece of a puzzle that did not fit. Now, later in life, I wasn't willing to settle or, worse yet, change. As I endured these missteps, I would go through periods of feeling hopeless, believing that I was destined to be alone for the rest of my life. Then, hearing Maya's voice say, "Have enough courage to trust love one more time and always one more time," I'd become hopeful.

Near the end of my three-month subscription on a senior dating website, I finally read a man's profile that intrigued me. "I enjoy indie music and indie movies," it read. I drafted a short e-mail to him and as pleasantly surprised when he responded.

We met for dinner soon after that. There was an unpretentious calmness about him that was very appealing to me. As we talked, I didn't feel the need to sell myself. He laughed and smiled at appropriate times and asked thoughtful questions. Midway through the meal, I remember thinking, *I could spend a lot of time with this guy*. Dinner led to frozen yogurt afterward. I didn't want the date to end. When the date was over, I texted him to say I had a great time and breathed a sigh of relief when he immediately texted the same back to me.

And then I didn't hear from him for another week. Trusting Maya, I summoned the courage to send him another text: "Hey, you want to do something this weekend?" His response indicated he had plans, but that he'd be back in touch.

And then I didn't hear from him for two more weeks. I had heard the "I'll be in touch" line before. It's usually a nice way to brush someone off. So, I deleted his contact information.

Two weeks after that, I received a text. He explained that he had been in China on business and wanted to know if I was free the following weekend. On our first date after he returned from his trip, he held me in his arms as we danced at an outside concert. Hearing Maya's words in my head, I allowed myself to start to fall.

More than five years later, my heart still races at the sound of his voice, and I get a warm feeling at the touch of his hand. Today, as we build a life and future together, it feels so right. We have such a strong bond and a true partnership that is supportive and caring. The puzzle pieces of my life finally fit together.

Dating later in life isn't for the faint of heart. Sometimes, it can feel like a never-ending gauntlet of rejection and avoidance. As we age, the baggage we carry sometimes gets heavier. But the baggage we carry makes us who we are.

From my vantage point, falling in love at this stage has been a fulfilling and wonderful process. There's something so serene yet invigorating about finding love now. We have created a relationship grounded in love and respect that feels different from any other I have experienced.

We aren't in a rush to get married and start a family, and we aren't distracted by material things or overly focused on moving up the corporate ladder. We are seasoned at life and can prioritize what's important. We have the maturity that comes with living a long life that had several bumps in the road. Neither of us needs to be right all the time, and both of us listen to what the other has to say. And, taking nothing for granted, both of us appreciate each other and the "we" that we have become.

People often comment how happy I look. I must admit that my happiness is hard to contain. I feel so blessed that life's journey has led me to a place of such joy. I am grateful every day for what we have, knowing it was a lesson in perseverance to get to where we are. And I am grateful that I never gave up hope.

The advice I give my single friends is the same advice I took from Maya: "Have enough courage to trust love one more time and always one more time."

Thank you, Maya.

— Michelle Paris —

64

Deploying Intuition

*One of the most important relationships we have is the
relationship we have with our mother.*
~Iyanla Vanzant

I was fidgeting and nervous before entering the restaurant to celebrate my twenty-fourth birthday. My family would be meeting my new boyfriend.

Dinner went smoothly and at the end my boyfriend surprised us when the bill arrived. "I hope it's okay with everyone, but seeing as I won't be able to take Sarah out or buy her dinner for a long time, I would like to pick up the check tonight."

Randal was leaving the next day to finish his one-year deployment in Afghanistan.

I had always told my parents that I would never fall in love with a soldier. I didn't think I was strong enough to survive that kind of relationship, with all that time apart and so much danger.

We went back to my parents' house after dinner and my mother managed to steal Randal away from the group for a few minutes. I watched them share a private conversation and a hug.

The next day I watched the man I loved walk toward the plane that would take him thousands of miles away from me for eight months.

I knew that I wanted to be with him. To me, he was worth the wait and the pain that I would endure while he was away.

My mom comforted me. "That boy is so in love with you," she said. "I could tell from the first moment I saw him."

"Really?" I asked, giddy but unsure.

"Oh, yeah. Without a doubt. Don't be surprised if things progress quicker than you think."

"What do you mean?" I said.

"I can see him wanting to marry you. He told me last night how much you mean to him and I can tell you feel the same way."

I trusted my mother's judgment more than anyone else's and hearing her words gave me the reassurance I needed to go into this deployment confidently.

My mom was right! Randal and I fell deeper in love from opposite sides of the world. With nothing but a telephone and letters between us, we embarked on an adventure neither one of us was prepared for. Weeks later, Randal shocked me by proposing.

I needed the opinion of the person I knew would always be honest with me. "Mom, Randal asked me to marry him. Be honest; do you think it's too soon?"

"Sarah, love doesn't have a rule book," she told me.

Months later, after our wedding, my dad reminded me that I had once declared that I would never marry a soldier. It was my mother who helped me see the truth. She has always known what is best for me.

— S.L. Blake —

65

Writing My Way to Love

Why not go out on a limb? Isn't that where the fruit is?
~Frank Scully

My friend Gail was the one who convinced me that I could write fiction. I met her when we were both working on a healthcare project for a government contractor. We became friendly, and one day she showed me a story she had written. Although I had been an editor for my high-school newspaper and majored in English and History in college, I had never been able to write fiction. I was entranced.

Gail invited me to join her writers' group and encouraged me in my efforts. Soon, I found myself bringing forth a story and creating characters who became very real to me. My protagonist was a troubled lawman embroiled in a mystery from his past. He returns to his North Georgia roots and meets a woman who helps him find his way. I didn't know whether I wanted to love him or to be him, but I felt very close to him. Maybe all new writers are infatuated with the heroes they create.

I came down with a bad case of bronchitis that winter that had me down for almost three weeks. As I lay on the sofa recuperating and channel surfing, I stumbled upon reruns of *The Waltons* and started watching. I happened to see a few episodes that featured the sheriff, Ep Bridges, and I could see qualities in him that dovetailed with those of the lawman I was conjuring up in my story. I became intrigued with the actor portraying the sheriff because he was clearly the one who had breathed life into this role and made it his own. The actor's name was John Crawford.

Sitting at my computer, I searched for him on the Internet and found to my genuine surprise that he had appeared in many other shows and movies that I had enjoyed throughout my life. There was a quality and depth to his acting that touched me, and I found him very endearing. I sensed from watching him perform that there was much more to him than met the eye.

After a fan site came up in my search, giving an address for him and reporting that he responded positively to fan mail, sometimes with a phone call, I made up my mind to write to him. Mind you, I had never done anything like this in my life, but I felt my guardian angel sitting on my shoulder, nudging me along. Here's what I wrote.

> Dear Mr. Crawford,
>
> I am a huge fan of yours for your compelling portrayal of Sheriff Ep Bridges on The Waltons. When I did a web search on you, however, I was amazed to discover that you were also one of the stars of my very favorite episode of The Twilight Zone, titled "A Hundred Yards over the Rim." I'm sure that without my realizing it, that was one of the reasons why I loved the episode so much. When I watched it again online, I knew for sure. It was a great story, and you were wonderful as Joe, the café owner. I would love to know if that show was as much fun to make as it was to watch, and where it was filmed.
>
> On the Internet, I found your contact information and a lot of positive comments from fans who had written to you, so I thought I'd take a chance. I'm 53, and I've never written a fan letter to anyone in my life! I just wanted to let you know that I think you are a very gifted and talented actor; you made the character of Ep Bridges real, and I found myself wanting to know him better. I really liked the episode where Ep proposed to Sarah; your sensitive, subtle portrayal of Ep as a man beyond the role of sheriff was right on the mark. The restraint that you exercise

in your acting makes your performances all the more powerful.

When I originally watched The Waltons, *I was the same age as the kids on the show, so I had a completely different take on it. Now that I am watching the reruns on the Hallmark Channel as an adult, I see your character as a peer, and I find him very attractive; I definitely see Ep as a romantic character, mostly because he doesn't try to be one. It's interesting how a role that you played thirty years ago can continue to impact people throughout and even beyond your lifetime, so your art lives on forever to touch many more people than just the original viewers. I just wanted to share that with you and thank you for enriching so many lives like mine with your fine acting. If you want to write me back, I would love to hear from you and hear any interesting stories or comments you might want to share about your work on* The Waltons *or* The Twilight Zone.

I signed it, "With all good wishes," and included my name, address, telephone number and e-mail, to cover all my bases.

I waited a day before I mailed it, and even then, as I stood in front of my mailbox debating my decision, I had the strangest feeling that I was setting something in motion that would change my life. I finally opened the mailbox door, set the letter carefully inside, closed the door and put up the red flag. My heart was pounding as I walked back to the house, but I felt compelled to reach out to this stranger who felt so familiar to me.

Three days later and three thousand miles away in California, John Crawford received my letter and called me that same evening to thank me. I actually missed the call because I had company and it went to voicemail, but I called him back at midnight and we talked until almost 2:00 A.M.

Soon we were talking every day, sharing each other's lives and racking up enormous phone bills. He made me laugh. He made me think. He touched my heart. I was a widow with two school-aged children who had lost my husband to cancer nine years earlier and had never so much as gone out on a date since then. He was much older and had been married and divorced, in true Hollywood style, six times. Neither of us was looking for love or thinking that romance would ever come into our lives again, but we were wrong.

What followed were the sweetest eighteen months of my life, falling in love with John Crawford and getting to know him, visiting him in California and learning about the life of this remarkable and accomplished man.

John was a writer as well as an actor, with an award-winning screenplay and a book to his credit. I confessed to him that I had named my main character "Ep" in honor of him. Without hesitation, he told me to change it; the protagonist had to be my own, not an imitation of someone else. John listened to me, supported me in my writing and allowed me to index his book that was about to be published. He always gave me good advice. I was honored that he shared his triumphs and tragedies and so many wonderful stories with me until his death in 2010.

As for that first novel, I'm still working on it. I've published several short stories and have embarked upon other projects, but I'll always have a soft spot in my heart for my first protagonist, the one who came to life from my imagination and revealed himself to me through my writing.

That troubled North Georgia lawman led me to the greatest love of my life.

— Elizabeth S. Kline —

Because of Barkley

*You enter into a certain amount of madness
when you marry a person with pets.*
~Nora Ephron

To be honest, I wasn't much of a dog person when I first met Barkley, Jim's four-year-old black Lab. Jim and I had barely been dating a week when he brought me to his house for the first time. We were coming home from a nice dinner and were greeted by the competing smells of I-better-clean-my-house-to-impress-this-girl Lysol and diarrhea because Barkley had had a tummy ache. Normally, I would have plugged my nose and waited outside until the mess was cleaned up, but the look on both of their faces somehow convinced me to stay and help. Jim was horrified, and Barkley was ears-back, tail-between-his-legs embarrassed. He slithered away to hide in the next room, and Jim and I threw first impression etiquette to the wind and picked up our mops.

It was putrid and disgusting, but as we dry heaved and plugged our noses together, I got a glimpse into the special bond between the man I was falling for and the dog he loved so much. Jim knelt down to pet Barkley's face, and told him he wasn't mad. He kissed him on the nose, and then turned to me, smiled sheepishly and said, "Well, welcome to our home!"

That was the beginning of my crossover into becoming more of a dog person. It wasn't easy though. For the first four months, I couldn't be around Barkley for more than a few hours before the itchy, watery eyes and incessant sneezing started. I hated the shedding, and one day he drooled a puddle into my favorite running shoes.

I thought the dark floors and black couches, sheets and towels were a bachelor thing, but when I tried to brighten up the place once we started talking marriage, Jim refused to let me get a beige rug because Barkley would shed on it. It was a bit trying when we couldn't go on long trips because Barkley couldn't be left for too long. We couldn't walk on certain "no dogs allowed" paths because Barkley couldn't come along, and we couldn't stay out late because Barkley had to be let out. Literally, everything Jim did considered Barkley. Though it was frustrating, and I didn't always understand it, I knew that I was falling in love with Jim partly because of the way Jim and Barkley loved each other.

The first time I saw Jim cry was because a conversation somehow moved in the direction of discussing a time when Barkley might not be around anymore, and our first domestic fight happened when I tried to clean a little clutter off Jim's kitchen counter by putting Barkley's treat canister up in the cupboard.

"That has to stay on the counter," Jim pleaded. "That's Barkley on the front of it."

"No it's not, babe. It's a picture of a dog that looks like Barkley," I said, trying not to hurt his feelings, and genuinely believing that a thirty-three-year-old man wouldn't know that sometimes companies use pictures of black Labs for marketing material.

"Yes, it is, I promise you! Look, he has the same collar and tags," he explained, pointing. "It took me a long time to save up the UPCs so I could get a tin with his picture on it!"

Before I came along, Barkley and Jim had traveled the country as a physical therapist and therapy dog team. Most of the time, they were each other's only companions. They had been through endless adventures and incredible challenges together, and had formed an incredibly close bond. Barkley was a best friend, cohort, and coworker. They were a team, a package deal, and a dynamic duo, and I was beginning to see that the only way I was going to make it into the family was if I found acceptance through Barkley too.

Jim was gracious and let us gently warm up to each other. When I had the flu, he left Barkley with me so I would have someone to watch movies and take naps with. When I was sad, Jim and Barkley cuddled with me on the couch, and when Jim had to go out of town, I got to watch Barkley so that he could keep me safe and make me feel protected. Little by little, Barkley and I accepted each other.

Nearly one year after the night we mopped the floors, Jim asked me to marry him. The three of us were hiking one fall afternoon and Jim called Barkley over to his side. He reached into a little backpack Barkley was wearing and got down on one knee. As Jim popped the question, Barkley sat by his side, staring up at me, and wagging his tail. At that moment, I knew that Barkley was asking too, and I was joyfully saying, "Yes!" to both of them.

Looking back, I can see that I had fallen in love with Jim because Barkley had, in his own special way, taught me that he was a man worth falling for. That first night that I decided to stay and clean, Barkley showed me that Jim had a heart of gold and did not get mad easily. He demonstrated that he would stick around when things got messy, and would love and console us when we didn't feel well. When Jim and I argued about the treat canister, Barkley taught me that Jim wanted to display his love for us to the world instead of hide it behind a cabinet door. I knew that I could trust Jim because Barkley trusted him, and I knew that I would always be taken care of because Barkley was taken care of. The adoration in Barkley's eyes confirmed that Jim was a man of character, strength, and kindness, and I can see now that life is so much better because of Barkley.

— Kara Johnson —

Green Card for Sale

Vive la Canada. This country is not for sale.
~Don Sweet

irst of all, let's be clear. I am not a Canadian. While it is true that I was born just five miles from the Canadian border, in the Upper Peninsula of Michigan, I never in my wildest imagination thought that I'd ever marry a Canadian. I mean, come on. They say "eh" at the end of every phrase, they sit on Chesterfields and they are so irritatingly... polite. Who can live with that?

Once I graduated from Michigan Tech, I headed west and eventually found myself in Salt Lake City, Utah, out of money and in need of a job. I was fortunate to find employment, and began dating and looking for Miss Right. Who could have imagined that I would find a Canadian girl? I mean, I had Idaho, Wyoming and Montana in between Canada and me, and those are very large states!

It started one Saturday with my joining several young men and women for a day of cross-country skiing. Out of nowhere, this little fireball plowed into me and knocked me down in the snow. "Are you are alright, eh?" she said. Did she say, "eh?" I must have had too much snow in my ears. As I brushed myself off and stood up, I found myself looking at her startling blue eyes and crooked smile. I was a dead man!

When I got up on Monday morning for work, and found my apartment door and my whole car bound in plastic wrap, I'll admit I was intrigued. This girl was enticing, even if she was nationally challenged.

I found out that she was teaching elementary school in one of the rough parts of town, and that she had a tremendous love for her students. Wow, I thought. Depth and those blue eyes. Did I say I was a dead man?

I'll admit that I was very interested, but I wasn't ready to get too serious with any girl at that particular time. That is, until I found out that she was about to walk out of my life forever. As it turned out, she had a work visa to teach school that never should have been granted to her. About the same time that I found her, Uncle Sam also found her, and decided it was time to send her back across the border. That is, unless she could get her hands on one of those green cards.

I'll be honest — I had to do a lot of soul searching in a big hurry. Should I take a leap of faith with this girl I had only know a few months? And a Canadian at that? My head was swimming... don't rush things... but those blue eyes... there are plenty of other girls... what a sweet smile... she's older than me... what a caring heart... but... but... she's a Canadian!

So we made a deal. She would give me $10,000 to marry her. Then she would get her green card, allowing her the ability to live in the USA, we would get the marriage annulled, and I could use the money to buy a really nice new car. Perfect plan, eh?

So here we are twenty-nine years later in Boise, Idaho. She's got her green card, but I'm still waiting to get my $10,000! I'm not letting her go until I get every penny! Through the years I've grown to truly love this wild Canadian woman, with her pretty eyes, big heart, and her patriotism — for Canada! She refuses to take out American citizenship, because, of course, she's Canadian.

However, there are some perks. I'm one of the few people who get to celebrate two Thanksgivings each year, and she makes a great stuffed turkey! Our two children have dual citizenship, and hey, she's still so darn... polite!

So a few years ago, I quit fighting it. I bought a large Canadian flag to fly from our house for those holidays from up North. I've learned to love vacations in beautiful British Columbia, and we love the traditional music of Cape Breton. I'm still not convinced that Smarties are better than M&Ms, but she is.

So hey, Blue Eyes. Slide on over next to me on the Chesterfield and I'll put on some Celine Dion, eh?

— Bruce Mills —

Leaving the Swamp

Inaction breeds doubt and fear. Action breeds
confidence and courage. If you want to
conquer fear, do not sit home and
think about it. Go out and get busy.
~Dale Carnegie

When my wife died of kidney failure in 2006, I withdrew socially. Other than dealing with people at my job as a newspaper reporter, I spent most of my time alone at my Arkansas home. I had been married for eleven-and-a-half years and had settled comfortably into the role of married life. I didn't want to meet new people. I feared any connection I might make with someone new would only end again.

The grieving process was a lonely journey. I adopted a shelter cat, and I was content spending my evenings watching television or reading books while the cat vied for my attention.

That contentment was reinforced when I tried dating. Two old girlfriends found me within a year or two after my wife's passing. Each relationship was dysfunctional, mostly because of my fear of losing again. These relationships ended amicably, and I returned to my lone ways.

Then my cat died. I was tired of loss. Venturing out was pointless because it would only result in meeting someone, becoming attached emotionally, and then experiencing more abandonment. So I accepted my solitary lifestyle.

The only social connections I really made were with "friends" on

Facebook. It was the perfect medium. It was a fitting way to get a hint of personal socialization without getting too close.

But the very medium I used to avoid the outside world led me to an entirely new world. And my concept of infrequent contact was shattered when I found myself craving more interaction with one person.

One of my "friends" was a Boston law professor who had another friend, Holly, who lived north of Chicago. She would join in during some of our posted "conversations" about sports or news or just life in general. One of us would come up with some spirited, fun discussion that the others would join in on. Holly and I began sending chat messages on occasion. The frequency increased, and we would spend several hours in the evening chatting back and forth. Surprisingly, I found myself looking forward to the evenings so I could resume chatting with Holly.

Our chats were deep at times; we'd talk about our childhoods and family lives. At other times, they were light and jovial. We developed our own inside jokes and referred to them often.

The chats evolved into a phone call one evening that lasted over three hours. The more I talked with Holly, the more I realized she was a special person.

I learned she was selling her home, and I blurted out one evening that I would help her with cleaning her yard in preparation for the sale if she wanted. It was totally out of character for me. Since my wife died, the furthest venture I had made was a 250-mile round trip to St. Louis to watch a Cardinals baseball game alone. Now, I was offering to drive 554 miles to northern Illinois to rake leaves.

Weird.

I think Holly thought it was weird as well. A guy offering to drive that far to do yard work sounded more like the makings of a murder story that appears on *Dateline NBC*. Reporter Keith Morrison would stroll down the street, saying pensively, "If only she hadn't worried about those leaves...."

Holly told me she'd think about it. When I looked at it from her point of view, I realized how odd my offer was and understood her hesitancy.

But a few days later, she messaged me, saying if I really wanted to come up and help, she'd appreciate it.

That led me to gassing up the car and driving the 554 miles to meet her in September 2015. Seeing her in person, obviously, was much better than talking on the phone. As the week progressed, I found that getting to know her was rekindling feelings I hadn't experienced since my wife passed away. I was fifty-five then, but this had me bumbling around like a seventeen-year-old kid on prom night.

On the second night of my visit, we watched for a lunar eclipse that most of the country was waiting for. It was cloudy, and we never saw it, but that didn't matter to me. I was star-struck just being in her presence. And later, when I drove her home and made the four-mile trek back to my hotel, I got lost both in bliss and along the road. The trip was a straight line from her house to the hotel. A three-year-old who could do dot-to-dot puzzles could easily figure out the path. But I failed and forgot where the turn was. When I did find it, I pulled into the wrong lane and, when seeing a car headed for me, I drove over the median helter-skelter, thumping over curbs and drawing the wrath of those who knew how to drive. I embarrassed myself all while wearing a goofy grin.

I stayed there a week, and it was blissful. We visited a lighthouse and beach park on Lake Michigan. We bought groceries like a married couple and walked her dog in her neighborhood at nights. I raked her yard and bagged the leaves. We also hooked up a DVD player in the hotel and watched movies.

The last night I was there, we watched *Shrek*. Those of you who have kids know the film; I had never seen it. The premise of the 2001 movie is an ogre who lives alone in a swamp and enjoys his reclusiveness. His solitude is interrupted when he and a talking donkey are enlisted to rescue a princess. In the end, Shrek wins the princess and finds friends, all by leaving his swamp.

Later, as we talked about the week we had, Holly noted that I, like Shrek, had "left my swamp" after I told her I broke from the routine of my own world and ventured out.

Six weeks later, I returned to see Holly. Then in January, she took a train to visit me in Arkansas. I made seventeen more trips to see her in 2016. Sixteen times, I drove back alone. On my seventeenth trip back, I wasn't alone. Holly had sold her house, and she, her two cats and a dog came back with me.

She's been with me now for eleven months, and we've created a life of our own. Two years ago, I was afraid to step out of the box I had created, the protective shell I developed so I would no longer feel loss. One Internet message, one phone call, and one trip changed all that. I shed the shackles of loneliness and despair, and found true love by leaving my swamp.

— Kenneth Heard —

69

What Would You Do If You Weren't Afraid?

Your life does not get better by chance.
It gets better by change.
~Jim Rohn

ost of my life, I let fear stop me from doing the things I wanted to do. I was always stopped by the "what ifs." I don't know how I managed to scratch my way out of a bad marriage. Blind determination, I suppose, driven by a desire to just get out.

My two best friends were always there for me through it all, each supporting me in different ways. One of them was my "girls' night out" gal, and we would go out for dinner and cocktails every other Friday night.

One night, we were trying a new restaurant. As we chatted, my friend leaned in to me and whispered, "The bartender keeps staring at you." I very discreetly looked over at the bar, and I practically fell out of my chair. The bartender was the most gorgeous man I'd ever seen! "We have to have a drink at the bar," I said. I was surprised these words came out of my mouth, as it was unusual for me to be so bold.

We proceeded to the bar, and the exchange of energy between the bartender and me was undeniable. He was so good-looking and emitted such good energy that I felt as though he was out of my league. Quite honestly, I didn't think I'd see him again, so when he messaged me a day later, I was floored. Throughout that week, he and I messaged back and forth. He invited me to come down while he was working, and said he'd buy me a drink. But then, the communication just dropped off. I assumed he had lost interest, but that invitation still gnawed at me.

That weekend, my other best friend, who never gets a chance to go out, made a once-in-a-blue-moon plan to meet me for drinks. I told her I really wanted to go back to where that bartender worked. Just as I was about to leave my house, she texted me. A snag had come up, and she wasn't sure she'd get there.

I really wanted to go to the restaurant, but by myself? My internal thoughts were not helpful. *What if she never shows? I can't walk into a bar alone. I'm afraid to do it. I don't even know if he's interested. I'll look like a fool.* I sat there paralyzed with fear, swaying radically between taking off my make-up and going to bed or standing up and getting in the car. I started scrolling through pictures on my phone, mostly screenshots of social-media memes I had saved for one reason or another. Then I landed on the meme that would change my life forever. It said, "What would you do if you weren't afraid?"

It was a simple question really, but extremely profound. *If I eliminate all my fears from the situation,* I asked myself, *what will I do?* The answer was exactly what I did. I got in the car and drove straight to the restaurant. I cast fear aside and did exactly what I wanted to do, despite the negative possibilities.

The result? He and I have been together for two years and share a wonderful home together. His love is beyond anything I could have dreamed of.

If I hadn't cast fear aside that night, I would have missed out on the love of my life. So now, when opportunities arise and I'm apprehensive or don't know quite what to do, I ask myself that one question: "What would you do if you weren't afraid?" Whatever the outcome, at least I can say I didn't let fear hold me back.

— Sarafina Drake —

70

It All Started with an Open Door

*When you meet the one who changes the way your
heart beats, dance with them to that rhythm
for as long as the song lasts.*
~Kirk Diedrich

was fifty-four years old. I had been divorced for ten years after
a twenty-five year marriage. I was lonely but I was afraid to try
online dating, even though everyone told me I should. I wanted
to fall in love again, but I figured it would just happen. I didn't
want to deliberately go after it.

And then I was invited to a pig roast by my long-time friend
Carol. There I was again, alone in a crowd. Weaving in and out of
people, making conversation here and there. On the deck, going into
the house, I reached to open the door, but suddenly it was opened for
me. I looked up from the arm that was holding open the door, and
there he was, a tall man, looking directly at me with his big, brown,
beautiful eyes.

He said, "I don't believe we've been introduced."

I told him, "I'm Carol's friend Nancy."

He answered, "I'm Tim, but I suppose you've already heard all
the bad things about me."

It took me a moment to realize that he was Carol's ex-brother-
in-law. I knew of him, of his character and continued good standing

with the family, even through the divorce. To my relief, I was able to answer him honestly. "I've only heard good things about you." He smiled, and we parted.

That was the extent of our conversation. Over the next few months, that short conversation and those brown eyes came into my mind a lot. I could recreate the whole thing, frame by frame. A few months later, on Christmas Day, I called Carol. To my surprise, she told me that my name had come up the evening before at a family gathering. Tim was asking Carol about the woman at the pig roast. He was describing me! He said he would like to meet me again sometime.

To my chagrin, nothing came of it at that time. I later learned that Carol felt awkward setting up her sister-in-law's ex-husband with one of her friends. Tim now tells me that he assumed Carol had assessed the situation and found him not good enough for me. Poor guy.

Obviously, our story wasn't done. In May, Carol's mother died. A group e-mail was sent out to family and friends about the service. Reading it, I noticed Tim's name and e-mail address. It was as if it was flashing in bright neon yellow! I saved the e-mail. The next few days I attended viewings, the church service, and the wake. I was filled with anxiety about potentially seeing him, making sure my hair was just right and my clothes just so. I felt guilty about my distracted focus. Carol's mom was a dear woman to me! Here I was at her funeral, hoping to see Tim. How crazy is that?

He did show up to the funeral, and we spoke very briefly at the entrance of the church. He remembered my name!

At that point, it had been eleven months since he opened the door for me at the pig roast. After explaining the whole story to my hairdresser (isn't that why we go there?) she encouraged me to figure out an excuse to send him an e-mail. "You gotta take matters into your own hands." She's a very wise woman.

I happened to know that his daughter was expecting a baby. It took me two days to write one paragraph wishing him well on his future role as a grandpa. I was terrified hitting the Send button and shocked that I actually did it! I was never this forward, and this was totally out of character for me.

The next afternoon, I got a reply. He was surprised. "I didn't even think you knew who I was. We never really had an opportunity to chat. I'm flattered by your letter. Let me know if you would like to meet sometime. If not, I understand."

Well, we did meet, at a local brewery. I found out he had just bought a boat. He found out I loved to fish. I even baited my own hook and took the fish off, too.

How nervous I was. I had not had a "first date" in thirty-nine years.

That brewery date was two years ago. My wish to be in love again is officially checked off my bucket list. I'm sharing all the love in my heart with a man who is sharing his love, too. I feel like a teenager. People tell me I'm a new person and have come out of my shell. I glow and giggle. I'm so grateful that I found the boldness to contact him. It all started with an open door, but I'm so glad I had the courage to walk through it.

— Nancy Beaufait —

Conquering My Mountain

Leave the beaten track occasionally and dive into the woods.
Every time you do so you will be certain to find something
that you have never seen before.
~Alexander Graham Bell

At age fifty, I found myself on a rocky path. I had just gone through a divorce, and I lacked self-confidence. I realized that I had consistently put other people's needs and expectations ahead of my own. I remember looking in a mirror one rainy afternoon and seeing a tear-soaked, puffy-eyed shell of a person who no longer recalled who she was, what she loved to do, and what she was capable of doing.

Back when I was in my early twenties, I looked forward to a life of adventure. I thought I might hitchhike across the country like my brothers did, scale mountains and swim in ice-cold streams in the stunning landscapes of the western United States. But when the time came to feed my soul like my brothers did, I shriveled in fear. Instead, I fed myself preemptive rhetoric like, *I'm a girl, and girls shouldn't be so adventurous. Something bad could happen to me.* This went on throughout my adult years, when my adventures were confined to car camping.

Not only did I avoid adventure, but I also held back from pursuing just about anything else I had yearned for in my youth. By age fifty, I still hadn't pursued my interest in art, playing the guitar, and singing.

I hadn't become a forest ranger, geologist, or paleontologist. Instead, I played it safe.

Then a new man entered my life. He picked up on my soul's unspoken desires. "How about backpacking for five days in Yosemite National Park?" he asked.

"Sure!" I said, wanting to impress him with who I wanted to be, not who I had become. And then I thought, *Backpacking? I can't go backpacking! I'm a girl. Backpacking's dangerous!*

Because I liked this guy so much, though, I worked through my fears and trained like mad for a month so I could go backpacking with him. I had never felt so full of self-doubt, but I kept reminding myself, *Isn't this what I always wanted? Isn't this supposed to be who I am, or who I think I am, or who I claim I am?*

For an entire month, I scaled local hills with an increasing number of water jugs in my backpack until it matched in pounds what I had to carry on the trip. My heart pounded out of my chest. My legs trembled, even with the aid of trekking poles. My back ached in as many places as there are vertebrae in a spine. And then the day finally came when my Adventure Man shot the deadweight cannonball that was me from its chamber and thrust me out with him into the wilderness at Yosemite.

Day One's hike proved to be the shortest trek, but the biggest reality check. I couldn't have been more relieved to drop the forty-pound backpack to the ground when we got to a clearing that would serve as our campsite for the night. When Adventure Man reminded me we would squeeze in a two-mile satellite hike to the North Dome vista before dinner, I forced a smile and replied, "Wouldn't dream of missing it."

All thoughts aside, when I first caught the view from North Dome across to Half Dome, where ants climbing along its uppermost ridge turned out to be people hiking to the top, or the view down into Yosemite Valley where meadows and trees rolled out before me like a lush, emerald green carpet, the views took my breath away... in a very good way.

Day Two proved better than Day One and had me thinking, *Maybe I can do this after all.* The trek was longer, but my body hung in there.

At the end of the day, I traversed a long tree trunk that had fallen across a wide stream, so we could camp at a desolate location on the other side. Sweating and shaking, I barely kept my balance with the weight of the backpack nearly tipping me over into the water on several occasions, but I made it and let out a deep sigh of relief when I reached the other side. I turned around, and after realizing what I'd done, smiled broadly and said, "Wow, that was all me. I did that." Soon, as we dumped our backpacks in the clearing of our campsite, we stripped down to nearly nothing and swam in the deep stream, losing the feeling in our bodies after ten seconds in the ice-cold water that had made its way from the snowier elevations upstream.

On the morning of Day Three, just as we settled into a breakfast of reconstituted eggs and sausage, I panicked when a young cinnamon-colored bear came way too close to our campsite in search of food. Adventure Man yelled at the bear, but it wouldn't go away. We waved our trekking poles over our heads to make us look bigger than the bear, but it wouldn't go away. When Adventure Man threw several rocks at the bear, I smacked him in the arm. "Throwing rocks? At a bear? Are you freakin' kidding me?" But Adventure Man knew better than I did. The bear decided it wasn't worth the effort and instead made its way over the stream on the same log we had crossed the night before — the same one we would have to cross within the next hour to get back on the trail. The next several hours, while trekking along heavily forested trails, I looked over my shoulder more than I looked ahead of me.

Later in Day Three, I had a major meltdown, when after eight miles my body decided it'd had enough. I could not walk one more step. As soon as my body decided to shut down, my rational brain decided to shut down with it. The only thing that didn't shut down was the waterworks coming from my eyes. Adventure Man missed the meltdown because he had gotten ahead of me on the trail. Eventually, I thought to blow the whistle that dangled from my backpack, after which he doubled back to find me slumped across a rock, unable to even lift myself or stop crying. He let me have my cry, and then announced, "Well, I guess this is a good time for having lunch." He injected as much humor as he could into the moment. He snapped a photo of me, after which I flipped him the bird. He snapped another photo of me, catching me flipping him the bird. He snapped one more photo of me twenty minutes later, and I managed a smirk.

The rest of the trip was harsh. My feet, full of blisters, stung with every step. When we took a wrong turn somewhere near the end, the final five-mile hike on the highway turned into eight miles—all uphill. It got so I had to take off my hiking boots the last two miles and walk in my socks, which felt marginally better than with the boots. But I made it. When we reached the car and dropped the backpacks to the ground for the last time, I felt an immense weight fall off not only my shoulders, but also my soul. I felt lighter than air.

After Adventure Man loaded my backpack in the car, I sank into the passenger seat and pulled down the sun visor to make use of its mirror. There in the mirror, I saw the reflection of that monumental mountain I once feared now fading like a phantom into the twilight sky. And I also saw someone I hadn't seen in a while—a bright-eyed, glass-full-to-the-brim me. Someone full of adventure, gratitude, and newly found wisdom. And I knew from that moment forward, I'd never lose myself again.

— Susan Maddy Jones —

Your Sweater Is Awesome

A desire to be in charge of our own lives, a need for
control, is born in each of us. It is essential to our
mental health, and our success, that we take control.
~Robert F. Bennett

A s a young child, I understood that my mother, from the moment I was born, had laid out my path. My path was straight, forged from steel and lined with barbed wire. I was not to deviate from nor question my path.

Make-up, short shorts, tight jeans, high heels or low-cut tops were not part of the approved ensemble. Boys were most definitely not allowed. On this path I would be an obedient daughter, student and member of the church. I would go to college, marry a good boy from the church, have children and settle down in some nameless Midwestern town.

For eleven and a half years I followed these rules and met all expectations. I was an excellent student, I practiced hard for my piano lessons, I visited my two approved friends, and I went to church, where I had to stifle my questions. At my church, we were taught the following:

1. Science was false.
2. The Bible was truth verbatim.

3. Premarital sex was an abominable sin.
4. The end of the world was imminent and preparation was required by all.

Outwardly, I accepted these teachings. I tried to fit into the awkward youth group gatherings and become an active, productive member of the congregation by serving lukewarm coffee in the food kitchen. Inwardly, I was confused because the rest of the world seemed to be doing just fine believing in modern science, engaging in premarital sex and not waiting around for the world to end. I felt I was hovering on the fringes of fully living.

On the cusp of my graduation from high school, I met a boy. It happened at my part-time job, amid harsh fluorescent lights, surrounded by racks of clothing and the scents of mingled perfumes from the cosmetic counter.

"Your sweater is awesome."

My eyes lifted to meet the blue stare of a tall, handsome boy with long, straight pale blond hair. He was dressed in a dark suit and colorful socks.

"Thanks."

He dipped his head in acknowledgment, grinned and walked confidently into the break room. With that seemingly trivial first exchange, I felt a sense of possibility and optimism. I was not sure what would happen, but I knew I had come to a bend in my otherwise straight path.

We began dating immediately, almost without conscious thought or spoken agreement. Being with him felt dangerous, freeing and exciting. He was confident, sophisticated, well educated, and intelligent. We took breaks together at the mall food court, laughing over limp Taco Bell and sticky tabletops. On his days off work, he dressed in black T-shirts with ripped jeans, drank alcohol, cursed and played electric bass. His friends were down-to-earth, non-judgmental and genuinely friendly, a far cry from the people I grew up with at church. He introduced me to new genres of music, such as the surprisingly lyrical metal band Tool and the experimental ramblings of Michael Gira. He taught me to appreciate the metaphysical art of Salvador

Dali, showed me indie films like *Garden State* and racy comedies like *Super Troopers*, and helped me enjoy new experiences. I was eighteen, he was twenty-one, and we were inseparable.

I brought him to meet my parents after a month of dating. They hated him on sight. The tension was palpable. I felt waves of judgment radiating from my mother as she questioned him the way a detective might interrogate a criminal. My throat was dry and my hands were slick with sweat as I contemplated the results of this disastrous meeting. In the aftermath, I was forbidden to see him again based on the sole fact that he was a treacherous speed bump in my carefully paved future. It was during this first meeting that I believe I made the unconscious choice to go against my rigid upbringing and make my own decisions.

Secretly, Andrew and I continued to date. With each lie and fabrication, I felt my protective bubble disintegrate and allow me to glimpse the freedom that every teenager longs for. I went to loud, outrageous parties, the bass pumping through my body. I stayed out past 9 p.m., driving around in his huge baby blue Buick LeSabre, feeling the cool night air snake through my hair and give me a shivering thrill. I made new friends, went to my first non-Christian rock concert and drank my first alcoholic beverage. I even committed the aforementioned abominable sin. I reveled in the feeling of truly belonging to someone and something.

Eventually, one hasty lie caused the entire house of cards to crumble around us. I can still feel the punch glancing off the side of my head as I sat at the dining room table in front of my mother, forced to disclose my intimate experiences in front of my family and youth pastor. Time slowed to a crawl as I was immobilized by shame, anger, hurt and final disillusionment. As if through a fog, I heard my brother call me a whore and saw my youth pastor convulsively clutch his worn brown leather Bible as he looked at me with disappointment and disgust. I will never forget the moment I saw my mother decide that I was tainted by my relationship with Andrew. In her eyes, I was ruined. My life as a sheltered, supported dependent ended that day. My parents turned me out of the house into the proverbial unknown. My car was taken and sold, my college funding stopped. I had nowhere to go but into the arms of the boy who had showed me a glimpse of how rich life could be.

Perhaps I was immature in how I chose to handle that fortuitous summer after graduation, or perhaps it needed to happen for me to realize that the weight of my predetermined future was slowly crushing me. On some level, I understood my need for rebellion and experimentation. I felt fleeting flutters of guilt as my previous "good girl" persona made herself known. But deep down, I yearned for the ability to be my own person and make my own choices, for good or bad, without fear of judgment from those professing to love me unconditionally. Andrew showed me that it was okay to fail and that it was okay to have my own opinions and ask questions.

For many years, I could not recall certain events of this time. The confused feelings of guilt, shame, freedom, and love were like tangled threads, too intertwined for me to examine them individually. Later, I was able to separate them and grow to understand how each thread was important to my personal development.

I keep the "awesome sweater" in the back of my closet as a memento of the quirky pick-up line that was the beginning of a new future. Sometimes I take it out, put it on and become the oppressed eighteen-year-old girl I once was. As I look in the mirror and see the moth holes and unraveling hem that belies its age, I wonder how different my life would be if I had chosen to wear something else that day. Meeting that boy eight years ago was the catalyst that changed me as a person and gave me the strength and ability to deviate from my path.

That boy has now been my husband of six years, and because of him, I am able to see how different the world is outside of the bubble made from religious judgment, rigid rules and fear. To this day, I still struggle with my personal views on religion and reconciliation with my family. As a new mother, I can only hope that my daughter grows up free to believe and experience what she wants. May she find acceptance in being herself, formulate her own beliefs, and love whomever she chooses.

— Emily Oman —

The Glory of Love

Friendship involves many things but, above all the
power of going outside oneself and appreciating
what is noble and loving in another.
~Thomas Huxley

am an introvert. I have a small circle of friends, and I generally do not make friends easily because being with most people takes so much energy.

Twenty-nine years ago, I started working at a new school. The English Department had an empty classroom that we used as a lounge. We gathered there every morning and afternoon, and I really enjoyed the people I worked with. I thought one woman in particular, Cheryl, was fascinating. I really enjoyed talking to her and looked forward to seeing her every day.

What I didn't know was that Cheryl was even more of an introvert than I was. I don't know what possessed me, but one day I announced to her, "You and I are going to be friends." She later told me that my forwardness had startled her. I could see she was reticent, so I said a few weeks later, "You can try to hide, but it won't work. We are going to be friends." And as the year went on, we did become friends. The more time we spent together, the more we discovered how much we liked one another.

My husband had a very close friend named Jerry. Jerry was more like a brother than a friend to us. In fact, to this day we refer to each other as brother and sister. My husband was not much of a handyman, so Jerry did most of the small projects around our house, and he ate dinner with us three to four times a week. He is my oldest son's godfather. Whenever I needed him, he was only a phone call and ten minutes away.

Jerry very much wanted a special lady in his life, but he worked in a male-dominated field and was shy around women. Previously, I had set him up on a date with a friend, and although the date went fairly well, it took him so far out of his comfort zone that he did not ask her out again. He was intimidated by the fact that she had a master's degree, and he only had a high-school education. After the date, he told me, "You are trying to make a silk purse out of a sow's ear."

Jerry would talk about his idea of the perfect woman. He wanted a woman who had the poise and bearing of a lady, but who was zaftig and high-spirited. I realized that I knew that woman: Cheryl. But, like my other friend, she had an advanced degree, and Jerry would immediately feel uncomfortable around her. Also, she is nine years older than he is, and I worried that they would see the age difference as an impediment. Similarly, when Cheryl would describe her perfect man, I knew who he was. She wanted a big, strong, affectionate, teddy bear of a man, one whom she could lean on, and who would take care of her and her house. Jerry fit that image perfectly. But I knew if I tried to set them up on a date, they would both freeze, and it would be a disaster. I was afraid that if I invited them both to dinner at the same time, they would see through what I was trying to do. I resigned myself to the notion that although they were ideal for each other, there was no way to bring them together.

But it was meant to be, so karma intervened for me. One day, Cheryl asked me if I knew a handyman who could do some small repairs around her house. Immediately, I thought of Jerry, but I knew I had to tread cautiously. I told her I knew someone, but I would have to get his permission to give her his number. That night when I got home from school, I called Jerry and explained the situation. I asked him if he was interested in helping her out. He said "yes," so I gave her his number.

The first time he went to her house, he worked for four hours.

The second time, he worked for two hours, and they sat on her couch and talked for an additional two hours. The third time, no work was accomplished, but much talking took place. Soon, every time I called him, he was with Cheryl. One night, my husband and I were headed for Denny's, and I called Jerry and asked if he wanted to join us. He came and brought Cheryl along. They were so comfortable with each other, sharing private jokes and just glowing. I looked at them and asked, "So, when are you two getting married?"

Cheryl looked at Jerry and said, "I don't know. Are we in love?"

Jerry replied, "I think so."

The wedding was wonderful, and my oldest, who was only four or five at the time, was Jerry's best man, although my husband was at the altar, too.

Now, they have been married for twenty-six years. All three of my boys call them Aunt Cheryl and Uncle Jerry. They truly are my brother and sister. After my divorce, they helped me raise my sons. We spend nearly every holiday together. We cook together and for each other. The family joke is that it is not a true family celebration without Aunt Cheryl's Jell-O, so she made spider and ghost Jell-O Jigglers for my middle son's rehearsal dinner before his Halloween wedding. We have cleaned each other's houses in emergencies. When my nineteen-year-old cat died, we were all there together in the vet's office crying and holding him. We share a lifetime of memories together. In recent years, both Jerry and Cheryl have had serious health issues, and now my sons try to rotate on a weekly basis, checking on them and doing small repairs for them.

All of this happened because I somehow found the courage to step out of my comfort zone and try to make a new friend. In doing so, I found a new family.

— Sandy A. Reid —

That's Amore

74

We Have It All

Behind every happy couple lie two people who have
fought hard to overcome all obstacles and interferences
to be that way. Why? Because it's what they wanted.
~Kim George

We thought we had it all — a beautiful house, three healthy children and one more on the way, two cars, a couple of four-wheelers for entertainment — and we loved it. We spent money like it was going out of style. Then, the market turned and my husband's job as a bigwig at a construction company was gone. The company had declared bankruptcy and was closing down for good.

We both started looking for jobs right away, but there weren't any to be found. With each passing day our panic increased and we continued to work together in order to pull our family through. The more we pulled together, the closer we got. I felt feelings of adoration for my husband that I hadn't felt in years.

That's why it was so hard for me to watch him blame himself for our current situation. I knew that he had no control over the economy, however, he constantly degraded himself and his spirits sunk lower with each snide comment. I continually asked him to stop, but he seemed to want to punish himself for not having a job.

Finally, one afternoon I pulled him aside and said, "We have four healthy children and each other. That's what's important. That makes you a rich man."

"But what if we lose the house? They'll hate me — you'll hate me," he replied.

I smiled at him and put my hands on both sides of his face to make him look me in the eye. "If we live in a cardboard box on the empty lot across the street I will be happy — as long as I have you." I smiled again as I realized that I wasn't just saying it. Somehow, in all the struggling together I had found that deep abiding love for him that I had on the day we said "I do."

I could see relief wash through him as his shoulders and neck relaxed and the tension left his body. He held me close and we were able to talk and plan and dream together in a way that we hadn't in quite some time. It was a turning point for us as a couple and a family.

We are still struggling financially, but I consider us well-off because we have something that money can't buy and no one can take away from us.

— Christina Dymock —

75

A Taste of the Past

Animals are my friends... and I don't eat my friends.
~George Bernard Shaw

Occasionally, I yearn to indulge in a "memory meal," biting into one of the nostalgic foods I adored as a child. As a lactose-intolerant Vegetarian-American, some of the most luscious, tasty treats, such as fried pork rinds, Mrs. Smith's Lemon Ice Box pies, and macaroni and cheese casserole are, alas, no longer options. Nibbling my way across an ear of corn is the closest I am ever going to get to gnawing blissfully on a juicy T-bone. Dabbing my spoon into fruit juice-sweetened frozen rice milk is my new ice cream binge.

But old cravings die hard. One day, after a particularly virtuous meal of locally grown organic broccoli, eggplant, onion and tomato, sautéed in organic virgin first cold pressed olive oil, and accented with organic brown rice, I found myself yearning for something toxic, fatty, crisp and crunchy, something that even back in my meat-eating and milk-drinking 1950s childhood people suspected simply couldn't be good for them — bacon.

Bacon came rarely into our household — but when it did, it was an event. I stood in the kitchen, watching my mother lay the lithesome lengths across the iron skillet. I watched the grease accumulate and bubble and I breathed in the pungent woody aroma that soon permeated every room. I was allowed to carefully pat the bacon free of grease. Then I waited eagerly for the four luscious porcine strips that would surround the obligatory egg. I ate the egg first. Then slowly, I took a bite of bacon, letting the crunchy meat lavish my tongue. I ate every morsel of the crisp strip and devoured every bit of the little fatty curl. I always wanted more and I always had to wait months before the next rasher entered our household.

I had not tasted bacon in years, but the moment I mentioned my craving, my partner Ron, who had also given up red meat and pork, began combing the grocery stores for the best "fake bacon." He brought home package after package of protein-textured strips, searching for the brand that could most nearly transport us back to the carefree eating of our childhoods.

But bringing home the bacon was only the first step. Ron then had to learn to cook the product just right, so it could evoke the crisp indulgence of the real thing. Putting the strips between paper towels in the microwave resulted in a desultory piece of vegetable protein that looked and tasted like, well, microwaved vegetable protein. The broiler produced a thin food the texture of cardboard with a smoky overlay. He laid it in a frying pan, without oil, and watched it grow warm but stay limp.

How could he cook that humble soy so it would resemble the heaven of our younger years? The answer came when Ron was sitting in one of his favorite diners, eating a fried fish sandwich and French fries: it was fat. He needed more fat.

The next morning, Ron found a large frying pan and laid the strips out one by one. He turned on a low flame and he added generous dollops of organic butter, our one exception to living dairy-free. Soon, each piece of bacon was surrounded by a bed of bubbling butter. The smell brought me to the kitchen and I watched as he lowered the heat, tenderly turning the bacon so it would brown evenly, cooking each piece until it had achieved the perfect crispness.

Ron laid out bread and piled on the bacon, adding tomatoes and slathering it all with mayonnaise. He presented the sandwich to me as if he were handing me a treasured old episode of the Ed Sullivan show.

I closed my eyes and took a big crunchy bite. The soy actually smelled and tasted like bacon. Ron and I sat next to each other at the table and reverently ate our sandwiches. I thought of my parents, both deceased. My mother was never a morning person, but she rose to the cooking occasion when bacon was on the menu. My father wanted to be a DJ but took a salesman's job so he could provide us with this occasional luxury. Ron and I shared our childhood bacon stories and I realized it didn't matter whether I was eating pork or soy: the memories themselves were just delicious.

— Deborah Shouse —

76

A Christmas Glove

The manner of giving is worth more than the gift.
~Pierre Corneille, Le Menteur

om didn't want much that first Christmas after she and Dad were married. Which was just as well. It was the end of America's Great Depression, and there wasn't much to be had.

"All I want," she told Dad, "is some nice black gloves."

"But you have black gloves," he protested. "Nice ones. I gave them to you last year."

"I sort of lost one," she said. "The left one. So I've just been wearing the right one."

"Those were expensive gloves," Dad sighed. "And I know how much you liked them."

"I did," Mom said. "So if you could get me some new ones, I don't need anything else."

"I don't know," Dad said with a slight smile. "If you're just going to lose them..."

Mom was pretty sure Dad was teasing. Still, she didn't know what to expect when at last the time came to exchange Christmas presents. She would have been pleased with anything, but she really did need the gloves — especially for her left hand. She carefully removed the ribbons and paper and opened the box. There they were! Beautiful new black gloves!

"Oh, Bud, they're perfect! Just exactly what I..." She paused.

"There's only one glove."

"Yes, that's right," Dad said, smiling proudly.

"But gloves usually come in pairs, don't they?"

"That's true. You'd be surprised how hard it is to find one glove. But there it is!"

"So where did you get it?" Mom wanted to know.

"I got it at Stanley's," he said forthrightly, almost proudly — and certainly stupidly.

"Stanley's!" Mom recoiled as she pulled the glove off her hand. "You bought my Christmas present at Stanley's?"

Immediately, Dad could see that he was in trouble.

"Well, I looked at some other places," he said, apologetically. "But that's the only place I could find the right glove. Er, left glove. Er..."

"That's my present — a glove from a second-hand store? What did it cost — a dime?"

"Twenty-five cents!" he blurted.

The fire shooting from Mom's eyes told Dad that revelation hadn't helped his situation.

The drive to Mom's parents' house for Christmas dinner passed without a word being spoken between them. When they arrived, Dad went with Mom's father and her little brother, Jack, to do some target shooting. Mom went straight to the kitchen to get some sympathy.

"Mother," she said, "you won't believe what Bud got me for Christmas."

Her mother smiled and nodded. "Wasn't that something?" she asked.

"You mean... you knew?" Mom asked.

"Darling, we've been immersed in it! He was here for hours, looking for your lost glove. Then he started going to every store in town looking for an exact copy. Whenever he found one that was close, he'd buy it and bring it to me to approve. He must've bought twenty left-hand gloves!"

"But that's... so..."

"Silly? Yes, I thought so, too," Mom's mother said, shaking her head. "And I told him so. But he said, 'Wanda loves these gloves. I'm sure I can find another left glove somewhere.'"

A lump began growing in Mom's throat.

"Now there's just one problem," Mom's mother said, picking up a stuffed pillow case. "What do we do with these?" Laughing, she emptied a pillow case full of black left-hand gloves.

The next hour passed slowly, as Mom awaited Dad's return. When at last he walked up the sidewalk she was standing at the door, her arms outstretched, a black glove on each hand.

Which, it turns out, was exactly what she wanted all along.

—Joseph Walker—

77

Knight in Shining Armor

To find someone who will love you for no reason,
and to shower that person with reasons,
that is the ultimate happiness.
~Robert Brault, www.robertbrault.com

T ed was a friend of my very best friend, Barb, who often told me hysterical stories about Ted's escapades. One day, I agreed to meet Barb at the establishment where Ted bartended on a part-time basis. Ted and I were introduced and shared many a laugh. That was not when I fell in love — although Ted would tell you that it was exactly the time that he did!

Since we had shared so many laughs and so much fun, Ted and I began dating. At that same time, I had just switched jobs. Unfortunately, after starting with my new employer, I came down with an atrocious head cold.

I got up for work one morning, feeling more like the walking dead than someone heading off to a workday full of challenges. I realized that having been at my new job less than a month it probably wouldn't be a brilliant decision to call in sick, so I persevered and forced my sneezing, feverish body into my office.

Ted was working the night shift at a local manufacturing firm. He would be finishing his workday as I was beginning mine. He called me before he went to sleep to see if I would like to meet him for dinner.

Ted immediately understood why I declined when he heard my voice, with my scratchy throat and tremendously congested nose, along with frequent coughing. I replied, "I'll be lucky to make it through this day and if I do, I'm planning to collapse under a warm blanket on my couch." I thanked him for the kind invitation and said I'd talk to him later.

I assumed that Ted would go to sleep while I continued my struggle to make it through my workday. But shortly after midday I received a call from our security downstairs. "Lil, you have a visitor." He didn't even give me the chance to question who my "visitor" might be. I had no idea if, in my clogged and muddled state, I had forgotten an appointment.

I dragged myself to the stairway to open the door, and as I walked onto the landing, I looked down and there was Ted, charging up the stairwell. I immediately envisioned the movie *Pretty Woman* when Miss Vivian speaks of dreaming of her knight charging up on a white stallion to save her from her imprisonment in a castle tower.

Okay, he was not riding to my rescue, but he did have a crock of homemade chicken noodle soup. He was taking every step ever so carefully so as not to spill a drop. It was somewhat difficult not to laugh aloud at the intense concentration on Ted's face.

Not only had Ted foregone his sleep, he had gone to the store, purchased groceries, and toiled in the kitchen making this soup from scratch. To make it even more incredible, my office was forty minutes from Ted's home through a fair amount of traffic. Yet, he made the journey balancing this hot soup in the car. He even brought crackers.

That was the moment I fell in love.

Over nearly twenty years of marriage, there have certainly been times when I have wanted to pour chicken soup over Ted's head, but then I think back and remember that special day in the stairwell. Homemade chicken noodle soup has become not only a comfort food, but also a dear symbol of my husband's love for me. I've made what seems like millions of meals for us over the years, from traditional mashed potatoes and meatloaf to glorious holiday feasts. Yet none can surpass my knight coming to my rescue with steaming hot chicken soup. That was truly a recipe made entirely with love.

—Lil Blosfield—

Past, Present, and Future

May no gift be too small to give, nor too simple to receive, which is wrapped in thoughtfulness and tied with love.
~L. O. Baird

When my husband asked me what I wanted for Christmas, I'm not sure if he was prepared for my reply: "The Famous Five series." His first response was, "What's that?"

I had to explain. He knew about my life as a missionary kid. He knew there was loss and grief associated with moving so many times and not really being able to go home again. He knew I had lost some material things along the way and would have loved to feel connected to a piece of each homeland I had known and loved. What I hadn't explained quite yet was my desire to connect with my past through the books I had enjoyed as a child.

During our elementary school years in Austria, my older brother and I would frequent the British bookshop in Vienna. During those visits and various book fairs at my heavily British-influenced school we acquired all twenty-one books in the Famous Five series by the British author Enid Blyton.

We were so proud to have the whole series, and enjoyed reading about the adventures of the "Five," which included siblings Julian, Dick, and Anne as well as their cousin Georgina (George) and her dog Timothy. Their adventures were akin to the Nancy Drew and Hardy Boys series; written in overlapping time periods, albeit set in England, with British perspective and vocabulary. The stories feature outlandish plots revolving around catching smugglers, counterfeiters and kidnappers — quite extraordinary, considering the heroes were mere teenagers! My brother and I loved them, though. The books were our passports to adventures we would never experience in our own lives.

Unfortunately, while my brother and I were at boarding school in Germany, our family had to return to the States quite abruptly from Turkey due to a health emergency. My parents had to make some difficult decisions about what to bring to America. Since books are heavy, my parents were unable to bring most of our books with them, including the Famous Five series. I was heartbroken when I found out, but with so many other adjustments to distract me, my loss was tucked in the back of my mind.

Fast forward to seven years into my marriage, some seventeen years after I'd left my treasured Famous Five series behind, and the Christmas I decided I wanted to acquire my books. I had been searching the Internet for the series and getting frustrated, because no American book publishers or websites had the books. We could have bought them on a foreign website, but we were nervous about using our credit card that way and having them shipped from overseas.

With all the distractions of the approaching holidays, I once again tucked the loss of my beloved books in the back of my mind, and focused on making the holiday memorable for my little girl. Christmas Eve arrived and my husband, daughter, and I sat around the decorated Christmas tree, which sparkled in the darkened living room. We traditionally opened one present on Christmas Eve and each of us picked a gift. My daughter opened hers first, then my husband. I eyed my chosen present, a colorfully wrapped box, and guessed what it might be. "An elephant?" my daughter giggled. "Oh, let's end the suspense!" I said, and began ripping off the wrapping.

It was a brown box, taped shut with clear packing tape. Could it be? I thought to myself. No way! As I picked at and pulled off the tape, my disbelief gave way to amazed joy as I beheld the title for the first book of the Famous Five series... and realized all twenty-one books in the series were nestled in the opened box! I looked up at my husband, with tears spilling over and dripping down my cheeks. "Thank you," I whispered, setting the box down and throwing my arms around his neck as he sat on the floor. "But," I stammered, "what American publisher was selling them? Where did you get them?"

My husband looked at me rather sheepishly and said, "India."

Apparently, he had scoured the Internet and found a British publisher that was reprinting the entire series in India, and paid the amount in British pounds. Never mind he had to break his rule and use our credit card in far-off India; my happiness was apparently more important. This gift did not just replace some of the many cherished items I had lost from my childhood, it signified the incredible love and devotion of my husband. His thoughtfulness gave me courage to believe I could heal, a little bit at a time, and reminded me that I was worth the effort.

Being a teacher, I had the entire Christmas break to read through all the books. It was wonderful. So many memories resurfaced as I read; my mother reading the suspenseful plots from the series to me and my brother, and times I had read by myself, treasuring my solitude in my cozy apartment bedroom. I laughed at how cheesy some of the plots seemed from the perspective of an adult. Throughout my marathon of reading, I felt like I was returning home.

Whether a gift revives the past, celebrates the present or looks toward the future, the way it makes you feel treasured as an individual is paramount. My husband gave me back a piece of my lost childhood, but I am even more grateful for what he did for my future.

— Kristina J. Adams —

The Rescue

Chains do not hold a marriage together.
It is threads, hundreds of tiny threads which
sew people together through the years.
~Simone Signoret

It had been one of those days. My three-month-old son, Tate, had not napped all day and now lay with his head on my shoulder, sobbing. Laundry waited by the washing machine, oatmeal was hardening in the breakfast bowls, and dirty diapers were emitting a smell from the trashcan. I surveyed my chaotic little world. Exhaustion washed over me, leaving me lightheaded. When would this day end?

For the last couple of weeks, I had managed to have the house cleaned and dinner well under way when my husband Jim got home from work at the end of the day. He worked all day and I got to stay home with the baby. It seemed like a fair trade. Jim had been very impressed, which made me very happy with myself.

This week, however, Tate was not his normal, happy self. He was getting his first tooth. Nothing seemed to relieve his pain for long.

Now Jim was on his way home during his short lunch break. I heated leftovers while holding my whining little guy. As Jim came in he surveyed the mess in the kitchen. "Not a good day?" When he turned to me he didn't need an answer. He could see I was still in the sweats I had slept in. When Tate let out an earsplitting cry, Jim picked him up. "I've got him. Take a break." I ran upstairs and cleaned up, got dressed, and did the minimum of my make-up routine so I felt more human.

Later that afternoon I managed to start the laundry and do some cleaning but then Tate started screaming again. Dinner would not be ready.

When Jim walked in, he took Tate from my arms, gave me a smile and threw his son playfully in the air. Tate squealed with delight. "Why don't you go up and take a break? Tate and I can handle things down here." He shooed me upstairs, telling me not to worry about anything. Lying on the bed, I briefly wondered what he was up to, but only for a minute. The next minute I was fast asleep.

I awoke two hours later. Jumping out of bed I ran downstairs. "Shhhhh." Jim pointed to Tate who was asleep. I walked into the kitchen and found that the love of my life had made one of my favorite meals. Coming from Italian roots, my husband knew how to create a very delicious spaghetti sauce. Before we met I had never been a huge spaghetti fan. But the combination of spices my husband used to make his sauce from scratch had me hooked from that first romantic meal he had made for me. It was all arranged — the meal, the light smell of vanilla candles, the soft music in the background. The oven even boasted dessert yet to come. Peeking in, I realized my husband had somehow made a trip to Applebee's and bought my favorite dessert ever — a Maple Butter Blondie.

"I thought you needed a night off." My husband smiled as he came into the kitchen. "You have been doing way too much around here. I can see you need a break." He escorted me to my seat and served me. We ate the savory spaghetti, tossed garden salad, mouthwatering, buttery garlic bread and enjoyed each other's company. As he served the blondie we grinned at each other. We shared it on one plate with two forks clinking together. And when Tate let out a loud cry from his crib upstairs, Jim said, "You stay right there. This will only take a moment and we will finish the rest of dessert."

The rest of the night consisted of foot rubs, long talks, and romance. Even to this day when we have spaghetti or blondies from Applebee's we always feel a little more romantic. My now six-year-old son knows when we have this meal we will act a little more "smooshy," as Tate puts it. And it always reminds me I am blessed to have such a thoughtful man who can turn a bad day into delicious perfection.

—Jami Perona—

80

Lessons in the Art of Love

Beauty is not in the face; beauty is a light in the heart.
~Kahlil Gibran

I t wasn't until he was in his early eighties that my father taught me about the depths of his love for my mother. I knew my parents had a fine relationship, but I never realized how much my father adored my mother. There was little hint of his admiration and passion in their visible everyday relationship. Only after my mother sank into Alzheimer's did my grief-worn father reveal his immeasurable love. He didn't talk about his feelings: He was, after all, a World War II veteran and a man taught to stoically endure for the sake of his family. But he showed me his devotion every day.

"Isn't she beautiful?" he said to me one day, as we sat with mom in the nursing home's private dining room, sharing a lunch I'd brought: my parents' favorite broccoli soup, half a tuna fish sandwich and a brownie. Mom had a little fleck of mayonnaise-laden tuna on her cheek and a blob of greenish soup on her bib. Her hair was greasy — she'd been resistant to taking a bath. To me, she looked like an old crone from the fairy tales, the kind of dirty, mysterious witch who might whisper a cryptic piece of wisdom that would save your life, but who certainly wouldn't win a beauty contest. I couldn't see what my father saw.

"Your mother looks so pretty in that sweatshirt," my father said a couple of weeks later. We were strolling the corridors of the memory care unit. Mom was shuffling along, holding each of our arms, her head bent. My mother's former wardrobe had gone the way of buttons and zippers and she now wore primarily sweats. I hadn't really noticed her outfit, but I stopped to look. Her pink sweatshirt highlighted the blush of color in her cheeks. When she looked at me and smiled, she might have been wearing a rose chiffon evening gown. Her face glowed. It took my father's observation for me to see my mother in a new light.

"I've discovered a sure-fire way to make your mother smile," my father said, later, when Mom was deep into the advanced stages. We were seated next to Mom's bed, watching her twist her sheet. I scooted forward, eager for my father's insights. My usual ways of making Mom smile were failing me and I felt bereft when she and I were unable to connect.

"Watch this," he said and he leaned forward and gave Mom a series of light kisses on her cheek. She smiled, then she giggled and her beauty shone so strongly that I fully understood what my father had always known: Beauty is there, if you're looking with your heart.

— Deborah Shouse —

81

How I Learned to Walk

Growth is an erratic forward movement:
two steps forward, one step back.
Remember that and be very
gentle with yourself.
~Julia Cameron

have always been lucky — very lucky. I was twenty-five, I had a great factory job, and I had won back my childhood sweetheart. Linda was beautiful, inside and out, with a quick and curious mind. She also had a great job working for the city. In 1988 we bought a house, got engaged, and had set our wedding date for June 24, 1989.

On January 26th of that same year, I pulled out in front of a semi-truck on my way home from work. I don't remember this; I don't really remember most of the 1980s. Everything I know about that day has been told to me by other people. The volunteer EMTs that responded to the call were all friends of mine from work, and what I know about what happened to me that day I gathered from them. Seeing the crumpled wreckage of my pick-up truck, they at first thought that I must surely be dead. Instead, they found me lying across the seat with barely a pulse. Luckily, the local volunteer rescue squad had received a pneumatic splint less than a month earlier. Without it, they would not have been able to keep my blood pressure sufficiently elevated to keep me alive for the twenty-five minute ambulance ride to the nearest level one trauma center, now called Regions Hospital.

I was diagnosed with a traumatic brain injury — a severe coup-contra-coup type — the equivalent of putting a delicate stereo component in a paint shaker and turning it on for a few minutes. I spent the next ten days in a coma. My body temperature had spiked to over 108 degrees on a couple of occasions and the doctors said it was likely that I had suffered further severe brain damage from that. They told my family to start looking into long-term care facilities or nursing homes. There really is no way to tell the effects of brain injury with any certainty ahead of time; it would be easier to tell what the weather was going to be like a few months out.

As I drifted out of my coma the collectively held breath of my friends and family was allowed to escape. I actually made pretty good progress over the next few weeks; I was starting to remember people's names and even regaining my sense of humor. Late in February, Linda asked me if I wanted to go through with the wedding. We were, after all, planning a big affair with 200 guests, and she needed to know if she should keep planning everything and reserving facilities and the caterer and so forth. I couldn't believe my luck! Here I was in the hospital. I couldn't walk. I could barely talk. I couldn't really dress or bathe myself. And yet the most beautiful and amazing woman I had ever known still wanted to marry me! I said, "Yes, of course."

Well, this was wonderful, but what could I bring to the table? I couldn't bear the thought of her burdening herself with me. I now felt a huge obligation; what could I do to shore up my end of the bargain? I decided that at the very least, I would walk my new wife up the aisle at the end of our ceremony. I would walk by Linda's side, as though she had an equal partner. I would learn to walk. She might have to work full-time, take care of a house, take care of me, and plan a wedding for 200 guests, but I was determined to walk side by side with my bride. I wanted to tell Linda how much I loved her, but my speech was so bad I was embarrassed to say it. I inwardly decided that I would express my love for her by walking. Each step was me saying, "I love you." This was my own resolve, I told no one of my plan.

It may sound simple, but achieving that goal was no small feat. Until that point, I had only taken a few steps, and even then, a nurse was holding me up. On my first day at rehab, a physical therapist wheeled me up to the parallel bars. I stood up and thought, "I love you." I wobbled, but I held my grip. White-knuckled and taking short rapid breaths, I felt like a ski jumper who had just left the ramp. I was only standing, but I felt like I was flying.

"You're doing well, Michael. If you need to sit, just let me know," encouraged the nurse.

I kept going. My legs felt full of water, dull and heavy. Center of balance was a misnomer to me; my balance was anywhere but center. I felt like there was a legion of Lilliputians pulling and tugging at their ropes drawing me to and fro. What I really needed to do was focus, but focus and brain injury are antonyms.

"Okay, shift your balance onto your right leg," I told myself. Then I began to draw my left foot forward. As soon as I raised it just a smidge, my balance swung wildly and I gripped the bars with both hands. I reset my feet and tried again. Weight to the right foot, lean forward, lift up the left foot. Think, "I love you." My foot came down heavy about three inches ahead of where it had been. My therapist grinned and congratulated me. People in the rehab room started to notice something happening over at the parallel bars. I smiled internally, but I knew this was only one step, and one step was not walking. Never one to be easy on myself, I had decided that two steps were required for it to be considered walking.

My legs were burning with fatigue, heavy lead exhaustion. I couldn't plant my feet squarely on the floor. My therapist saw my dilemma and again invited me to sit down but I declined. I swung my weight back and forth and caught the next forward motion and brought my right foot even with my left. "I love you."

I had walked. Everyone was looking as I leaned on the bar with my hip and raised one arm triumphantly. There was cheering and clapping. Then I collapsed back into my chair exhausted. "You did it, Michael. You walked!" said my physical therapist. I smiled. It wasn't me, it was Linda. I was only returning her love.

Five months later I did walk up that aisle with my new bride. I did it for Linda. I did it out of love. We have been married twenty-four years now.

My grandparents are ninety-six and have been married seventy-four years; I have coffee and cookies with them every week. Long lives and long marriages are traditions I intend to keep.

— Mike Strand —

82

From Opera to Hockey

The most important thing to remember is this:
to be ready at any moment to give up what
you are for what you might become.
~W. E. B. Du Bois

called my husband, Larry, at work. "I have good news, and I have bad." I said. "Which do you want to hear first?"

He played along like a good husband. "Give me the good news first."

"You can go to sleep early tonight."

"Okay. What's the bad?" he inquired.

"We're going to the opera!"

The joke was, the last time I made him go, he fell asleep. Even I had to admit it was a boring production. But when someone gave us tickets to the all-time favorite *Carmen*, I really thought he might enjoy it. When he nodded off again, I let him sleep. I only woke him when his snoring became louder than the performance.

Larry and I have always had our basic values in common, but our interests are as far apart as, well, opera and hockey. I love the arts, and he's a huge sports fan. His big passion is NHL hockey. He's shared season tickets with his buddies for years. I must admit there have been times I've been tempted to sell my ticket online or to a scalper. Tempted, but I'd never do that to my husband. Instead, if he wanted to go, we went.

I griped and complained, "Oh, not again!" but I went.

We attended the games with other couples. The rest of our group was enthusiastic about the game, even the women. They knew all the players and how to pronounce their four-syllable names.

We'd have a quick bite at the tavern next to the arena, after which I might half-jokingly blurt out, "Can we go home now?"

Our friends would give me a look as if I were from another planet.

I enjoyed participating in the National Anthem, but aside from the meal, that was the only thing I enjoyed about our hockey nights. Instead of appreciating the good seats we had, I'd complain: "It's cold in here!" My husband would offer me his jacket, but I wouldn't take it.

"I'll just sit here and suffer," I would say.

When the game started, my phone would be on my lap. Most of the time, I'd be texting or daydreaming. Sometimes, my texting would be interrupted when the home team scored. I knew they scored because everyone jumped up and exchanged high-fives and fist bumps.

What was so exciting about a bunch of grown men on ice hitting something called a puck with a stick? It was beyond me. When the team scored again, one of the women in our group turned to me and exclaimed enthusiastically, "Isn't this great?"

I shouldn't have said it, but I responded sarcastically, "Oh, yes! I'm thrilled!" Almost immediately, I regretted the snide remark.

I started to wonder. Why was I the only one NOT enjoying myself? Would I actually like this sport if I gave it a chance? What if I tried to change my attitude?

As I looked around at thousands of people cheering and getting increasingly excited, I decided to at least give it a try — for my husband's sake, if not for my own.

It took a few games, but soon I learned who the goalie was, who our latest player was, who had been traded and from where. When the other team scored, I eventually felt a jolt of disappointment with the rest of my crowd.

Soon I was asking, "What is icing?" "What's a hat trick?" and so on. I searched the program to see which part of the globe our players had come from.

My husband was surprised to see me getting involved. I was astonished myself! The cold no longer bothered me. I didn't keep glancing at the clock, counting the minutes until we got out. Time flew. The game was over before I knew it.

When our team won, I jumped up and down in a frenzy of my own. Leaving the arena on winning nights, I cheered with the rest of them.

"Are you coming to next week's game?" someone asked.

I turned to my husband. "Honey, can we? Can we?"

We did go to the next game and continued going often. I soon learned all the terms and expertly discussed all the game's particulars with my husband. Today, one would never guess I hadn't grown up with hockey.

Our friends couldn't believe their eyes when they first saw me sporting my team's really cool green jersey. "What happened to your designer jackets?" they teased.

Larry was so pleased. For our anniversary, he told me he wanted to reward me for being such a good sport, and he wanted just the two of us to do something special. I was delighted.

"I'm taking you to the opera," he announced, beaming.

A tiny twinge of regret went through me. I was hoping we'd go to hockey that night. But I didn't let him see my disappointment. I hugged and kissed him warmly.

The opera was enjoyable. Larry even stayed awake. But I must admit I couldn't resist a peek at my phone to check the hockey score. After all, we were in the playoffs.

Nowadays, it's so much more fun having the same things in common with my husband. Who knows? Maybe I'll even take up golf.

In the meantime, I can't wait 'til we win the Stanley Cup.

— Eva Carter —

Believe in Miracles

83

Mark and Maggie

It is not in the stars to hold our destiny
but in ourselves.
~William Shakespeare

Mark:

Everyone knew who I was in Italy — the hero of dozens of Spaghetti Westerns — but something was missing. I was surrounded by people and yet I was alone. I'd been with a lot of women but it never worked out, and no one made it all the way into my psyche. No one had been a true partner — my other half.

I worked all the time. After two decades of acting, I became a movie producer, partnering with my good friend Roger Corman. I had worked for him as an actor, but now we were producing a film together for the first time, making a female version of *Spartacus* with two women in the roles played by Tony Curtis and Kirk Douglas. Roger had cast Pam Grier and Julie Ward as the female gladiators, which was fine with me.

But then Roger called me one day and said that he had to replace Julie Ward because she had a scheduling conflict. He had found someone even better: Margaret Markov.

I had never heard of her but he said she was a beautiful, blue-eyed blond actress who had already co-starred with Pam in a film called *Black Mama, White Mama* that was a big hit in the U.S. That was fine, but I needed an actress who was known in Europe so that we could sell the foreign rights to help finance the film. And to make it worse

Roger said that this Margaret Markov was going to cost us $750 per week instead of $500 like Julie Ward. I tried to make Roger pay the whole $250 difference but he insisted that we split it. It was the first film I was producing with him so I decided to go along with it. But I wasn't happy.

Maggie:

I went over to Rome to shoot the film and I met Mark in the lobby of the hotel. He was a lot older than me but very attractive. He took Pam and me out to dinner and he was pretty annoying, flirting with Pam the whole time.

Mark:

I did it to get Maggie interested in me. I fell for her the moment I saw her. She was tall and stunning, with incredibly long blond hair. And she was so vivacious. That laugh! This girl sure had charisma. But she was only twenty-four and I had just turned forty, although I told her I was thirty-nine. I flirted with Pam to see if that would make me seem more desirable to Maggie, as if I was ignoring her.

Maggie:

That didn't work at all! He didn't realize that I hated that kind of game playing. I never planned to have dinner with Mark Damon again after that night. I would just act in the film and move on.

Mark:

I was fascinated. I went back to my apartment and read Margaret's bio. She was from Pasadena, California and the fifth of ten children. Wow! She had studied acting in Hollywood and had already been in several films, including two that my new partner Roger had produced.

I was already smitten and I couldn't wait to see her again. I was yearning for a simple, open relationship with somebody relatively sane. She seemed intelligent and sensitive, but refreshingly unsophisticated.

Maggie:

Pam and I started going out to dinner with Mark constantly. When it became clear there was something between us, Pam bowed out and Mark and I went out just the two of us. I guess you could say we were dating then, but when you're making a film it's all a bit unreal.

But then something happened that still gives me chills. We were telling each other about our favorite things—books, food, movies. I told Mark that when I was twelve years old I had seen an incredible scene in a movie. I couldn't remember the name of the movie but I remembered this scene vividly. A man with black hair, green eyes, and an old-fashioned white Victorian-era shirt was walking out of a burning mansion in a cloud of smoke. I had told my mother right then that someday I was going to marry that man.

Mark:

I was stunned. That was me in *House of Usher*, a film directed by Roger Corman. It was one of my best-known scenes, ever. When I got home after dinner I called Roger and told him about this eerie coincidence. He took full credit, reminding me that he was the one who directed *Usher*, who invited me to produce this new film with him, and who insisted we hire Margaret Markov.

Maggie:

I was already sold on this relationship. But then something else happened. It was a Sunday and we weren't shooting, so Mark and I were having a picnic in the countryside outside Rome. I was decked out in my "picnic" attire, wearing my hair in braids and a scarf tied around my head. We were walking along and all of a sudden Mark turned white as a ghost.

Mark:

I was speechless. "I swear to you this is not a line," I said to her. "It's the truth. I dreamed of you when I was a child. I was seven and

I dreamed that I was walking in a forest and a young blond woman appeared next to me with long blond hair in braids and a scarf tied around her head. In my dream, she said, 'Don't worry; one day we'll find each other.' I dreamed it a few times. It was really important."

I had never had coincidences like that occur with anyone. And I had never felt like this about a woman.

Maggie:

I was still recovering from my previous relationship so I was a little guarded with Mark, but over the next few weeks we figured things out. I put that relationship in the past where it belonged, and I was ready. Mark said, "Don't ever leave me," and I knew I wouldn't. After all this was the man I picked when I was twelve years old.

I told him, "Let's make a pact to always tell each other the truth."

And then Mark looked uncomfortable, and I thought *uh-oh*. And he said, "I told you I was thirty-nine but I'm really forty."

Mark:

Six weeks after we met, we flew back to L.A. together and even though my divorce from my previous wife had not come through yet, we declared ourselves married on the plane. And we've been together ever since — two children and more than forty years later. She's still the best thing that ever happened to me. We were clearly meant to find each other.

— Mark and Maggie Damon —

84

Trusting My Intuition

Do you think the universe fights for souls to be together?
Some things are too strange and strong to be coincidences.
~Emery Allen

've been an intuitive person all my life. To me, intuition is a palpable thing. On countless occasions, I've known what friends or acquaintances were going to say before they said it, and I've known who was calling before answering the phone. So who was I to argue when a low, calm voice informed me in a dream that I would find my new husband through a personal advertisement?

I turned thirty-nine in 1983. I'd been a divorced, single mom for nearly nine years, and although I'd made a good life for my teenage sons and myself, I had recently felt ready for love and commitment. But although I felt open to meeting the right man, my career as a jewelry designer wasn't conducive to finding him. I created my art alone in my studio. When I sold it at weekend art fairs, my customers were mostly women, with my few male customers buying gifts for wives and girlfriends.

And how would I meet a man anyway? I'm a non-drinker and don't frequent bars or singles' events. My women friends might have fixed me up with co-workers like in the movies, but no one did.

After the dream, the personal ads attracted my attention, although I resisted the idea of finding a man through the personals. Finally, I decided a personal ad was no stranger than any other way to meet a man — and my intuition confirmed that, crazy idea or not, it was going to work.

Searching for the right words to describe the man I envisioned forced me to consider what qualities he'd possess. A few false starts later, I came up with the following ad:

> *Single mom artist, 39, with heart, soul and desire for intimacy, seeks single man, 35-45, with same — must be gainfully employed, financially solvent, and capable of giving and receiving love. No wimps. No walking wounded. No pessimists.*

Finding the right man didn't happen immediately. I paid for the ad and two renewals during the following months. I received 165 responses in my newspaper post-office box. This was pre-Internet and e-mail. We got acquainted via "snail mail" and phone calls. I went on blind dates with eleven men: shop owners, teachers, businessmen, lawyers, a glass blower, and a carpenter. For the most part, they were polite, presentable and sincere in their desire for long-term partnership — but no one was the partner I was seeking.

Maybe I was making a mistake. My long-time faith in my intuition wavered. But then one last letter showed up in my mailbox. It was a small envelope, neatly addressed. The moment I touched it, I had a clear, strong feeling I'd found the right man.

We exchanged letters. Lee was forty-two, had been divorced for five years, was gainfully employed, and owned a home in a coastal community near San Francisco. I found him to be an intelligent, articulate, and liberal man, with grown children who were out on their own. We saw eye-to-eye on core issues like religion, politics, love of family, animals, and the environment.

I loved the sound of his voice. He made me laugh and feel like a girl again. We made a date for December 10th to meet at a café in my neighborhood. Since it was the Christmas season, the café's door and windows were covered with large Santa Claus images, obscuring the street outside. I arrived first and positioned myself at a table near the door where I could see each customer enter.

We hadn't exchanged photos. I knew I liked him, but didn't know what he looked like. But unless he had two heads and was actively insane, my intuition told me I was going to fall in love with him.

I held my breath each time the door opened. *No, not him,* I thought as an unkempt man entered the café. *Not him either.*

Then I saw Lee: wide shouldered, with thick, jet-black hair combed back from his high-cheekbones, wearing a black jacket and a red shirt as described. He saw me and smiled. I smiled, too.

What more can I say? We liked each other immediately. The rest is history. For me, the right thing to do was to trust my intuition. Had I not trusted the voice in my dream that told me I could meet the man of my dreams through a newspaper ad, I'd have missed out on my personal message that led to meeting the man I've been happily married to for more than thirty years.

— Lynn Sunday —

85

Recovering Together

You've gotta have hope. Without hope life is meaningless.
Without hope life is meaning less and less.
~Author Unknown

W e have learned that when life brings tragedy, you must search for that speck of light, that speck of hope within it. It may not always manifest itself right away; you may not be in a place immediately to see that light. Sometimes we need to let ourselves hurt, to grieve. And then sometimes that speck is more like a boulder when you come upon it.

Our story starts on January 3, 2010. Mike was on a routine patrol in Afghanistan. He and his Air Force teammate were assigned to an Army unit to call in air strikes. On this day they were ambushed and shrapnel from an improvised explosive device (IED) hit Mike. Four of his brothers lost their lives and many others suffered injuries. Mike was left completely blind. He faced an unknown future in a pitch-black world.

January 3rd was a hard day for me too. My whole world turned upside down when I was informed that my husband, Sgt. Joshua Lengstorf, would not be coming home. The grief was overwhelming and I prayed I would be strong enough for our fifteen-month-old daughter. I felt so lost and the world felt like such a dark place. I was struggling with my pain, my anger, and trying to understand. I learned that it was okay to just let go and feel all the emotions. It was okay to ask, "Why?" Letting it all out helped me to start healing. And then I learned that I had an inner strength I never knew existed.

I met another young widow at a memorial for our husbands. Her husband had lost his life in the same attack as mine, while helping with the chaos from the first explosion. He had been Senior Airman Mike Malarsie's teammate. And that's when I learned about Mike, whose family was chronicling his journey of recovery on a blog. I began to read it. A few times I felt that I should reach out to him, but quickly squashed those thoughts. He was probably coming to grips with his new life and I was trying to cope with Josh's passing. But one night I couldn't ignore the prompting and I contacted my friend about meeting Mike. A few weeks later my young daughter and I were on a plane.

Mike was in California learning to live his life blind. His dream growing up had been to serve in the military and now he was on a new adventure. Since learning of his four fallen brothers, he had dedicated his life to living with purpose. He had lived and they had not, so he was determined to avoid feeling sorry for himself. Mike pushed himself to get through blind rehabilitation so that he could give back and begin again. He remembers being a little lost. He didn't know what to expect. He didn't know anything about blindness.

Josh's outlook on life had been to just get out there and do it. I realized the best way to honor his memory was to be brave enough to live again. I know it sounds clichéd, but something happened when Mike Malarsie and I met. It was like soul recognized soul. We both felt it but were confused by it and a bit afraid. Eventually we had to discuss it. The timing wasn't the best, but we put our trust in Heavenly Father and took a leap of faith.

Fast-forward four years, and we are married and that young daughter is a big sister. We have moved several times, and most importantly, we have learned amazing lessons about life and ourselves. We have had ups and downs but we are strong. We have learned not to take life for granted and to live life to the fullest.

Mike has attracted a lot of media attention and has been interviewed on TV shows all around the country, spreading our message of hope and faith. He even became part of the Chicken Soup for the Soul family when his guide dog, Xxon, won the seeing and hearing guide dog category on the American Humane Association's Hero Dog Awards nationally broadcast TV show. Chicken Soup for the Soul's pet food business was one of the sponsors of the Hero Dog Awards and as a result Mike and Xxon have appeared at Chicken Soup for the Soul events and our family has expanded again to include those new friends.

Now Mike has a wife, children, a guide dog who has given him back his freedom of movement, a new career motivating other people, and friends all over the country. As a couple and as individuals, we have learned that there is always hope. Our whole story is about hope — hope that each of our futures could be good again, hope that we could continue to grow as people. We each had our dark moments, but we saw that speck of light. Hope is right around the corner for all of us. We sometimes have to put in some effort to get there, but there is always a light. Just keep looking for it!

— Jesse Malarsie —

86

Dream Date

To those who have given up on love:
I say, "Trust life a little bit."
~Maya Angelou

The wedding ceremony took place on a sunny August day, charming everyone in attendance. Blossoms filled each corner of the garden at the historic inn and a soft breeze rustled the leaves as we all waited for the bride to appear.

And then, she was there, moving with grace down the length of the aisle, a picture of simple beauty and style. Her dress and the estate grounds reflected a modest elegance in a silent nod to this, her second marriage.

I wiped away a stray tear. This wasn't her first time to recite the vows, but I was certain it would be her last.

She reached the podium and turned to gaze at her groom, his face beaming with an infectious joy.

I smiled as I watched this young man, once such a mystery, now as familiar as if he were my own God-chosen son. And in a way, he was.

***

It all started around a year earlier in the middle of the night. Was it too much pizza, or had I watched one too many romantic comedies? Or was it something more that caused my subconscious visitation?

The dream had felt so real.

I stared at the man, his tall, stocky frame filling the crowded kitchen's threshold. He looked about five or ten years younger than I, with curly salt and pepper hair topping a sensitive, intelligent face. Brown eyes shone behind wire-rimmed glasses, his grin exuding confidence.

Watching him from across the room, I felt an impulse to speak with the stranger. Somehow I sensed his kindness and knew he'd protect those he loved. In an instant, my thoughts flew to my twenty-something daughter. My single daughter.

I glanced away to scan the space, hoping to spot her long blond hair or hear her laughter nearby. I couldn't see her anywhere. A moment later the people overflowing the area vanished. When my gaze returned to the doorway where the figure had stood waiting, it was empty.

I jolted awake, the glow of the bedside clock my only witness in the midnight quiet. Darkness shrouded the bedroom, and the street lamp outside my window sent a solitary ribbon of light across my comforter.

What was that all about? The gentleman's visage burned into my mind like a brand, forever committed to memory, whether welcome or not. But why? What was so special about this dream figure? Questions riddled my rest until morning.

As sunlight brightened the sky, I headed downstairs to set some coffee to brewing. Sounds coming from my daughter's room alerted me she was awake. The door squeaked open and she joined me in the kitchen.

"Morning."

"Hi, honey. Did you sleep well?"

"Yes, fine." She poured some of the brew into our cups and passed one to me. I had waited a long time for "fine" to become the norm for her.

Our daughter had left an abusive marriage and accompanied my husband and me in a cross-state move. Three years had passed and for the most part the scars had healed. There were no more nightmares or flat, unemotional responses. No crippling self-esteem issues. Even her pets seemed secure sharing their lives in our home.

I sipped the coffee and gazed at my child, her blond hair flowing down her back in a silky stream, her dark brown eyes reflecting warmth from within. My heartstrings tugged a notch tighter. "Do you work tonight?"

"No. I'm getting together with one of my friends."

I glanced out the window. A blue jay perched in our old walnut tree, preening, its azure feathers catching the light like a blue flame. A few fleeting moments later it took flight and was gone. My throat tightened.

I refused to ask whether or not she had a date — I knew the answer. The men she'd met since her divorce had left her hurt and wary and she'd all but stopped pursuing romantic relationships. A couple of months earlier, she'd joined the online dating community, choosing a service that focused on our faith and offered a free trial period. Nothing lasting had developed from that venture. Over time, both her interest and participation waned.

I was worried. Would she never experience the blessings I'd found in marriage — laughter and tears born of time-tested love?

"Let's go upstairs and check out the dating site together."

"Mom." She rolled her eyes as well as any teenager.

"Come on. It'll be fun." Crossing the dining room, I turned my head to see if she would follow.

"Oh, all right."

Minutes later, we snuggled together in our pajamas in front of the computer. She scanned a few profiles, not settling on any one.

She opened another and there he was, the man from my dream! His smiling face seemed much younger and his hair darker than the fellow in my vision, but he was unmistakably, undeniably the individual who'd stood in my kitchen's entry, as if waiting for something... or someone.

I gasped. "That's him."

"Who?"

"That's the man I dreamt about." My heart skipped a beat. "I think he's the one."

"The one what? What are you talking about?" Her gaze remained on his photo.

And I knew. "The one you're going to marry."

Disbelief shadowed my daughter's expression, but she listened as I relayed my nighttime vision to her. "So you think I should meet this guy?" I could hear the excitement in her voice as her focus returned to the picture.

"I'm sure of it." I stretched an arm around her for a hug. "He's been waiting."

Her head rested on my shoulder for a moment and she sighed, long and slow, like a runner finally crossing the finish line.

As her gaze met mine, I smiled. "And so have we."

***

A blue jay zipped past, returning my thoughts to the present as the pastor spoke. "Will you promise to love, honor, cherish and protect her, forsaking all others and holding only to her forevermore?"

My dream son-in-law leaned a few inches closer to my child to answer, his voice lowered. "I will."

I believed it then and I believe it still. The wait is over. And this dream came true.

—Heidi Gaul—

87

Arranged Marriage

What's meant to be will always find a way.
~Trisha Yearwood

Breathing in the hot dry air of Botswana, I puffed on. I was out for my daily jog on the dusty roads, praying in my mind as I listened to the children shout *Lekgoa,* which was the local word for white lady. In this part of the world, seeing a white person was rare. People always stopped and stared.

After being a missionary for almost a year, I was used to it. I was here to minister to the people, but I thought I could never become one of them. Their life was too different from mine on so many levels! I still struggled to understand Setswana, their language. People used a community standpipe for water and had no indoor plumbing. Electricity was a luxury. I grew up so differently — going to our family's country club in South Georgia, spending summers vacationing in Europe.

Suddenly, as I trekked along, a distinct thought came to me: "You will marry Percy Thaba." That was weird. The thought came again stronger and clearer: "You will marry Percy Thaba." I had never even met Percy. He was the big brother to one of the youth in the local church I worked with. He was away at college.

"You will marry Percy Thaba!" Was this God speaking to me? Didn't He understand that an American like me wouldn't be compatible with a man from Botswana? What would we have in common? Could we ever understand each other? We were raised in such different cultures! How would we raise our children?

What would people say? I was here to reach out to the people, not marry one of them! That would be a distraction to my mission! My parents would never approve. What color would our kids be? And their hair... I didn't know how to take care of that! Reason after reason came to mind as I argued with the "voice" that was so clearly repeating over and over that I would marry Percy Thaba.

Physically exhausted from running under the hot African sun, I returned home. As I stretched my legs, I surrendered. I realized that the majority of my reasons for not wanting to marry an African man were because I worried about what people would think. Ultimately, I trusted God. I whispered, "God, if this is you speaking, prove it to me today!"

I showered and went to the Saturday youth group I led weekly at Francistown Baptist Church. After a few minutes, a taxi drove up and a young man got out. All the youth shouted, "Percy! You are home from university!"

My stomach dropped. My mouth grew dry. This was Percy? Today? I had been there more than ten months and had never met him. What were the odds that I would meet him today? I took a deep breath and calmly asked one of the youths, "Is that Percy Thaba?"

Excitedly, he responded, "Oh yeah! You have never met Percy? He is so cool!" It was too much to handle. I fled to the outhouse to gather my thoughts. Normally, I avoided that hot, smelly mud brick building, with its small hole dug into the ground, but today my heart was racing so fast that I barely noticed the awful stench!

I composed myself, walked out and almost bumped into Percy. He smiled and thrust out his hand confidently: "You must be Ashley! I have heard you are doing great work here in this church. It is nice to meet you. Actually, your supervisor called me and asked if I could help you while I am off university."

I mumbled something about needing to gather the youth and get started. I was too shocked to speak. He was supposed to partner with me?

After youth group, he casually sauntered over: "Wanna come by my house tonight so you can catch me up with what you are doing with the youth? I want to figure out where I can pitch in." I agreed. It was time to get to know my future husband.

Before heading over to his house, I called my friend and told her everything. "So," she said. "Did you walk up to him and say 'Hey, I had a vision today that I was going to marry you?'"

I gasped. "No! I don't even want to marry him!"

By the time I headed to bed that night, after spending three hours talking about our goals for the youth program, I had changed my mind. Would a guy so holy ever look at a girl like me? This guy was amazing! I had never met such a smart, kind, considerate, and godly young man.

Being the good Southern girl I was, I kept quiet about my developing feelings. I waited for him to make the first move. After two weeks of working side by side in ministry, I got a shock. Percy pulled me aside one day, asking if we could talk about something important. My heart raced. He took a deep breath and began to share his heart. "Ashley, when I became a Christian at age fifteen, I looked around my country. I saw the extremely high HIV rate and how easily people fall into temptation here. I made a vow to God that I would not even date a woman until she was the one I would marry. In order to do that, I must avoid any tempting situation. My feelings for you over the past two weeks have grown into more than friendship. Therefore, I am going to talk to your boss and ask her to find you a new partner."

"Wait!" I blurted out, desperate not to lose him. "I had a vision! God told me I would marry you!"

He responded, "But you are an American! It would never work!"

I laughed and said, "I know! I told God but He didn't seem to care!"

Three years later, I married Percy Thaba. We celebrated our tenth wedding anniversary this year. I still think he is the most amazing man on earth. I thank God every day for the clear premonition that Percy was the man for me. It made me look past my fears about color and make the best decision of my life!

— Ashley Thaba —

88

One Last Thing

Dreams are today's answers to tomorrow's questions.
~Edgar Cayce

When I was in high school, I was certain that I had my life figured out. I was going to graduate, go to college, and have a great career. None of my plans included marriage. I thought I would never find someone, mainly because no one had ever been interested in me. At least, that's what it seemed like. I had crushes, and had even asked a boy or two out, but I was always rejected.

This was something that I kept to myself. Nobody knew my deepest fear about my future. Then, one night in December 1997, I had a dream that changed my outlook.

I was walking aboard a Navy ship with my grandpa. He was showing me around and talking to me about my worries of being alone. He said I needed to let go of the idea that I would be alone because he knew I would have love in my life. We stopped in a room where a sailor was standing with his back toward us. All I could see of him was that he was tall and had dark hair.

"Here, sweetheart," my grandpa said. "This is the man you will marry. He will love you more than you know. Please do not worry anymore. You are going to be okay."

I woke up after that to the sound of my sister sobbing downstairs. A chill passed through me, and I knew something terrible had happened. I rushed downstairs, worried that something had happened to my sister's disabled son. I was relieved to see him lying in his crib, just fine, but I turned into the living room to see my family gathered. They all wore sad expressions. The grandfather I had just dreamt about had died.

I didn't want to believe it. I had just seen him a few days earlier. He was healthy and happy. He had just married a few months before, after a long time of being alone after my grandmother had passed away.

My dad told us that it seemed like Grandpa knew his time had come that morning. He had woken up, kissed his new wife, told her he loved her, retrieved his temple clothes from his closet, and laid them out. Then he lay back down and passed soon afterward.

I would also come to learn that I was not the only one who had dreamt of him the night before. I knew then that my dream was him saying goodbye.

Four years later, I was in a much better place. I had more confidence. I no longer worried about being alone, even though I thought marriage was a long way off. I had had a few relationships by then and knew I would find the right man when the time was right. I was preparing to attend school in California. I had also just started to speak regularly to a new guy friend on the phone. He had just re-enlisted in the Navy. Our conversations grew into a long-distance relationship.

In November 2002, I married that friend. Shortly after I did, I was telling him about how I wished he could have met my grandpa. Talking about him reminded me of the dream I had the morning he passed away. I cried, not because I was sad, but because I realized the dream was not just a goodbye. My grandpa had shown me my future husband after all.

— M.D. Krider —

89

It Begins with an "H"

Pay attention to the feelings, hunches, and intuitions
that flood your life each day. If you do, you will
see that premonitions are not rare,
but a natural part of our lives.
~Larry Dossey, The Power of Premonitions

was a widow with thirteen children. Seven of them still lived at home. It had been five years since my husband died, and I was still overwhelmed. I certainly did not want to be without a companion for the rest of my life.

One evening, I took a walk alone where I could pray. "Please, Lord, don't you have someone in mind for me?"

I was shocked when a voice immediately answered. "Yes, his name starts with an 'H,' but it's a name that is not too common to you."

For the next six months, I paid attention. *Who did I know whose name began with an "H"?* While having coffee with my friends or just anywhere, I began to doodle on napkins and receipts. I wrote Hank, Henry, Hubert, Hy, Herbert, Hilton, Hans, Heinrich, and Howard. Those names weren't too common to me, but worse yet, I knew no one by those names. As the months passed, I became impatient. *Whose name starts with an "H," and when will I meet him?*

I knew for sure that I had heard right. It was something that I could hold onto because I knew that it would eventually happen.

Four months later, my friend Jenny called. "Irene, I have an extra plane ticket to England. My son can't make it. Will you go with me?

We can stay at my mother's so it won't cost you a dime. You'll just need a little money for souvenirs."

Going to England was an answer to prayer. I'd visited there eleven years earlier. The fog, darkness, old buildings and castles intrigued me. At that time, I told my girls that I would return to England and stay a month so I could really enjoy all England had to offer. Now, that wish was coming true.

Jenny's only sibling, David, met us at Heathrow Airport. He was a tall, blond chap who was in the military. He and Jenny were óverjoyed to see one another.

It seemed we dined with old friends and acquaintances almost every night the first week. I had the opportunity to enjoy Indian cuisine, as well as many other fancy restaurants. But my recurring pangs of loneliness made me question what I was doing there. One lovely evening, while in a ritzy café, soft strains of romantic music were playing. Immediately, I recognized the piano pieces played by Richard Clayderman. I could barely contain myself as I listened to song after song during our meal. My heart was bursting with memories that I had shared with my late husband. We had played that very same music on many occasions.

"Irene looks tired," David said, motioning to the waiter. "Let's be going. I guess she's not used to the time change."

I laughed. I felt partied out. All I wanted was to go back to Jenny's mother's house and fall asleep.

Finally, in bed, I surprised myself when the floodgates of my heart broke forth. I sobbed so loudly that I hoped Jenny and her mother wouldn't hear me in the adjacent room. I'd always been strong, hiding my own fears and disappointments. I didn't know exactly why I was weeping uncontrollably, but I knew that I needed to share my life with someone. I lay in bed, praying through my tears that God would comfort me. "Lord," I prayed, "I want a companion, someone I can walk this path with, someone who really cares for me." The last words I recollect before falling to sleep were, "Lord, I thought about everyone I know, and there is no one whose name starts with an 'H.'"

My dream was shocking, yet clear as a bell.

An old friend I had known for more than thirty years, someone with whom I hadn't connected for quite some time, appeared. He had the biggest smile on his face. "You haven't thought of me," he said.

On that note, I awoke with a light peeking through the bedroom curtains. A joy I hadn't experienced for a long while surged through me. I knew that my dream was my answer. Not only was this man a gentleman, patient, kind, and giving, but he was available. And, the best part was, his name began with an "H."

"Hector Spencer," I said, as warm fuzzies accompanied me all morning. I repeated his name over and over in my mind.

All the while, Jenny and her mother commented, "You sure look happy today." I kept my dream to myself, tucked in my heart. I could hardly wait until my vacation was completed.

Upon my arrival back to the United States, home never looked so good. Every day, I would think about Hector and wonder what he was doing. I knew he lived in St. George, Utah, but I had absolutely no clue when or how we'd meet. Three days later, a dear friend, Rhonita, invited me to lunch. I felt we had not seen each other often enough, and it was a delight to spend the afternoon with her. No sooner had we seated ourselves at the table in Denny's when she presented me with a book. I read the title, *How to Fall Out of Love.*

"I brought this book for you, hoping you will read it. Maybe you will be able to move on with your life. You need to find someone to share your life with."

I laughed. "I don't need this book. I already know who I'm going to marry."

She looked shocked. "How can we be this close, yet you haven't shared this with me?"

"I just found out myself," I laughed, hoping she wouldn't think I was crazy.

"Who is it?"

"Sorry, I can't tell you because he doesn't even know yet."

We both cracked up.

"You're so funny," Rhonita exclaimed. "If he doesn't know about it, how do you think it will ever happen?"

After swearing her to secrecy, I cautiously revealed to her my earlier premonition about the "H" and my dream.

"Wow, you sure seem certain about this, don't you?" Skeptical, she asked, "Who is he?"

"All I will say is that we both know him."

"Don't do this to me," she said. "We're friends! If you can't share with me, then who can you share it with?"

"I understand, really I do, but it's not right. I would absolutely die if he ever heard about this. It would ruin me, for sure."

"When will you know?" she ventured.

"The problem is," I confessed, "I don't know how we'll ever meet. He lives so far away."

"Well, I may be able to help you if you'll tell me your secret. Please, Irene, I promise I will not tell a soul!"

Desperate as I was, and knowing I could believe her, I shared my anticipated destiny. "It's Hector Spencer."

"Oh my, I can see you guys together. Honestly, I can. Did you hear that Hector's youngest daughter, Amanda, won Miss Pre-Teen Utah?"

"No, when did you hear about that?" I asked.

"I heard about it last week. In fact," she advised, "I think this is a perfect time for you to call and congratulate him. Maybe something will come of it."

I called directory assistance that evening. Extremely nervous and not wanting to sound too forward, I dialed his number.

"Hello?" answered the familiar voice. "This is Hector Spencer speaking."

For the first time in my life, I was absolutely at a loss for words.

"Hello?" he repeated.

"Oh… hi… uh… this is Irene." I grasped for words, hoping to make sense. "I heard about your daughter Mandy being crowned. Congratulations!"

Hector was very cordial. In fact, I felt his excitement in just sharing memories of old times together. Before I realized it, we had caught up on one another's lives, not realizing forty-five minutes had passed.

"Are you going to be in San Diego long?" he asked.

I told him that I was visiting my daughter indefinitely.

"Every now and again, I travel there for business. Would you care to go to lunch sometime?"

The rest is history. We were happily married twenty-five years. I feel comforted knowing that God gave me something to hold onto in my loneliness—a hint, the letter "H," to help me make my way to Hector.

—Irene Spencer—

Love at First Flight

There is no surprise more magical than the surprise of
being loved. It is God's finger on man's shoulder.
~Charles Morgan

I felt good butterflies in my stomach instead of the dread of another lonely day. I fixed my bowl of cereal and fresh strawberries. I sipped my second cup of coffee and tried to recall his face. Two times around a dance floor wasn't enough time to get a mental picture of someone I had just met.

My life was defined by visits to doctors and so much fatigue it took my best effort to get out of bed. Going to a singles' dance the previous weekend was not my idea of fun, but my best friend Sue had dragged me to the Methodist Church event and convinced me to try the electric slide. I was catching my breath and tapping my toes on the sidelines when Charles had asked me to dance.

So why did I agree to meet Charles this day for lunch and a hike? I wasn't the hiking type. Just thinking about a hike made me tired. Since my husband's death, dates had been few and far between. Aren't women over fifty — especially a woman in my condition — more in danger of dying from a terrorist attack than finding another man? I often prayed, seeking God's will concerning a second marriage, but convinced myself that no man in his right mind would date a sick woman.

"Don't lead him on. Tell him the truth right away," Sue insisted on the phone.

"Can't I just have fun and forget about my disease for one day?" I responded.

"Be sure you tell him before it gets serious," were Sue's last words.

I laughed. "Don't worry. Getting serious about a man isn't on my radar screen."

The morning flew by as I showered and selected jeans and jacket, with a turquoise shirt. Native American earrings made the color pop. Nike walking shoes completed my ensemble. I was glad most people couldn't tell how bad I felt by looking at me.

I reread the directions I had scribbled down, then backed my car past the fading yellow daffodils and red tulips in full bloom. Fifteen minutes later, I pulled into the parking lot of the restaurant.

The cool, crisp March day was perfect for a hike. I reminded myself to put on a happy face as I tried to keep up with Charles's long stride. I had to admit his warm strong hand felt good wrapped around my fingers as we walked around the park. Charles pointed out the red bud trees and wild azaleas. The whole world was coming back to life, but I barely noticed.

"Look there's a waterfall," Charles pointed out.

"I'm not too good at this. I have limitations," I said as we climbed a hill before reaching a bridge over a small creek.

Sue's words rang again in my ears. Tell him right away. The sooner you tell him, the less you'll get hurt. After all, he seems like a nice guy and needs to know the truth. But the words stuck in my throat.

"See the rock outcropping up ahead?" Charles said. "Let's sit and rest a while before we turn back." The granite rocks were stacked at just the right height for sitting and, although cold through my jeans, a welcome respite for my out-of-shape body.

"Tell me more about your work." I had learned during our very enjoyable lunch that Charles had retired early from a career as an aerospace engineer.

"Well, I do research for government contracts. After my wife died I didn't want to just sit around. Now I'm thinking about starting my own company." I was impressed, but still cautious. I had been warned there weren't many eligible men with ambition. Or the good ones were already taken. Since I wasn't being entirely honest with him, he probably wasn't being honest with me either.

I glanced at Charles and liked what I saw. He was well built, suntanned and his baseball cap sat at a cocky angle on his head. He was just plain cute as he looked up into the cloudless blue sky. Maybe there was more to him than I was willing to admit.

"Do you want to go flying?" he asked.

"What? You're a pilot, too! What kind of planes do you fly?"

"Small light aircraft."

"Sure!" I said, throwing caution to the wind.

"I'll call and see if there is a plane available."

"Now? I didn't know you meant now!" I said in a shocked voice.

Charles looked amused, "Why not? It's a perfect day for flying."

* * *

From 1,000 feet in the air, my problems took on a different perspective. They seemed as small as the ant-sized cars, *Monopoly*-board houses and white steeple churches that dotted the ground below. The roar of the engine drowned out normal conversation. But an unexpected still small voice seemed to speak to me. Isn't this how an all-knowing God sees your life — viewing the big picture and not focusing on just your daily trials?

As I gazed over the cockpit and focused on the smoky horizon, I recalled teaching that truth to my class members last month. My hesitation and indecision disappeared. I would tell Charles about my disease and my need for an organ transplant, and leave his reaction and my future in God's hands.

"Wheels down! Request permission to land," Charles announced to the air traffic controller.

"That was fun — a great flight and landing," I commented as we walked hand in hand toward his car. "Thanks for taking me up. Let's get dessert — my treat. I have something to tell you."

* * *

Charles brags that at age sixty-five, he made two winning proposals.

After three weeks of dating, he proposed marriage and, after ten years of widowhood, I accepted. Then the United States Air Force agreed to fund his second proposal, giving him a contract to improve aircraft flying characteristics.

Two years after our marriage, I received a liver transplant. My adventurous life would not have been possible without a generous donor family and Charles' loving support. At age eighty, Charles continues to promote his patents and his ideas for aviation improvement.

— Frieda S. Dixon —

91

Flowers from Gary

Love is something eternal; the aspect may change,
but not the essence.
~Vincent van Gogh

y husband and I were relocating to a new town due to my work. Everything would be new to us since we had never been there before.

I went ahead to begin my new job and find us a place to live. My husband, Gary, stayed behind to pack up our possessions. He would join me in a month.

Two weeks later, two police officers arrived at my work. They told me my husband had passed away earlier that day. They had located me from some paperwork at the previous house. It was a blood clot to the lung, which killed him suddenly. I was devastated.

A few weeks later, I received a piece of mail claiming I had won a free bouquet of flowers at a local florist. I figured it was junk mail and set it aside since no one knew me, and I had not entered any contests.

A few days later, on the day my husband had been due to join me, I found the gift certificate again. Feeling low, I thought maybe some flowers would cheer me up.

When I arrived at the florist, they assured me that the gift certificate was indeed legitimate, and I had won the contest. She asked me what kind of flowers I wanted. Teary-eyed, I explained how I had lost my husband Gary not long ago, and I wanted something to cheer me up. The florist said, "Just a minute. I have something perfect for you."

A few minutes later, she came back with a beautiful arrangement of potted plants. She said I didn't need flowers that would die in a few days; I needed plants that would continue to live as I would. I was crying by now and thanked her very much. Then I asked if there was a way to see who had submitted my name in the contest.

"You don't know?" she said. "They were from Gary."

Ten years later, the plants are still thriving.

— Linda Eiffert —

92

With This Ring

The love game is never called off
on account of darkness.
~Tom Masson

It was a sunny afternoon in October, and we were sitting in our living room, chatting and sharing the newspaper. Gary glanced down at his hand and said, "I'm missing my wedding ring."

"It's got to be here somewhere. I'll help you look," I said.

We searched every inch of the house. We searched his truck and my car. We searched the garage, the workshop he had been building in our back yard, the front and back lawns, the flower beds, and the driveway.

No ring.

"When do you last remember seeing it?"

"I'm not sure. I'm worried it flew off my finger when I tossed an apple core out the truck window the other day."

My husband of almost thirty-seven years looked close to tears.

In May of that year, Gary had been diagnosed with diabetes, and one of his symptoms that our doctor chalked up to the diabetes was weight loss.

"That's normal," he said. "It's nothing to worry about."

Then one day in September, Gary choked on his supper.

The next day, he was fine. But it happened again. And again.

Our doctor arranged for a surgeon to perform an endoscopy in a nearby hospital, and after the procedure we went home to await results.

Neither of us mentioned the word "cancer," but it was definitely on my mind.

The follow-up appointment with the surgeon was good.

"Your esophagus was constricted, so I stretched it," he said. "It also has a lot of ulcers, so you need to take this prescription and eat only soft foods for a couple of weeks to let everything heal."

The "C" word was not uttered.

By mid-October, Gary was no better. Swallowing remained a struggle, and he lost more weight.

We went back to the surgeon, who said to give the diet and medication more time and let him know if things didn't improve.

After another week, Gary was unable to swallow any soft foods at all, and his daily weight loss continued.

He switched to soups, milkshakes and protein drinks, and took a short-term leave of absence from work.

And to top everything else off, he lost his wedding ring.

Gary and I had been childhood sweethearts and soulmates, and we married at the age of nineteen. Our simple white-gold wedding bands, engraved with our names and our wedding date, had been on our fingers since 1972, and now his was gone.

I made a mental note that if we didn't find his ring before Christmas, I would buy him a new one and have it engraved with the same words as the original one.

But that wasn't in our future.

Gary died on December 13, 2009, exactly one month after finally being diagnosed with stage IV esophageal cancer that metastasized into his chest cavity, liver, adrenal glands and lungs.

I thought I would never stop crying.

How could the man I had loved since childhood be dead at the age of fifty-six? How would I find the strength to continue living without him?

I had no answers.

Days and weeks drifted past. I arranged for someone to plow my driveway and mow my lawn. I learned how to do simple mainte-nance projects around the house and to call someone when I needed additional help.

I learned to navigate life as a woman alone, missing her soulmate, and to dance the dance of the "new normal" into which I had been unwillingly thrust.

But it was tough.

When Gary was in the hospital, I took him a spare laptop to use for e-mails. The morning he died, I brought it back home and tucked it away in a drawer.

A few months later, my son turned it on again. While browsing, he found a note that Gary had written to me shortly before his death.

"Honey, remember, I have just moved on ahead to get the water hooked up and your lawn swing set up, and I will be waiting for you. Just make sure you don't come too soon. I'll wait for as long as necessary until we are together again."

His note almost broke me.

The fall after Gary died, I flew to Alberta to spend a few weeks with my brother and sister in-law. I arrived back home shortly after my thirty-eighth wedding anniversary.

My son met me at the airport and drove me home. After he carried my bags in from the car, we sat in the family room to catch up.

"Mom," he said, "I have something to show you. I know that it's going to make you sad, but I think it's going to make you happy, too."

I had no idea what to expect.

"Okay, show me," I said, and he pulled Gary's wedding ring from his shirt pocket and handed it to me.

Of course, I cried.

"That's impossible. Where did you find it?"

"It's really weird, Mom," he said. "I was in the garage a few nights ago and saw something shiny on the floor, right in front of the overhead door. I figured it was a bottle cap or a quarter, so I went over to pick it up. When I did, I realized it was Dad's wedding band."

I shook my head.

"That doesn't make any sense," I said. "We've been in and out of that garage a million times this past year, and your dad and I searched it thoroughly last year when his ring first disappeared. How could it just show up now?"

"Mom," my son said, "it really was just sitting there, in the open, as if someone had carefully laid it on the floor for me to find."

That night, sleep eluded me.

Where had Gary's ring been for the last thirteen months? Why did it show up now?

I tried and tried to come up with a logical explanation for its reappearance, but I couldn't. After a few days, I decided to simply be thankful that it had been returned.

I took the ring to a jeweler and had it resized to fit me. Now I wear it to honor Gary's memory and the love we shared.

But I still don't know where it had been or how it found its way back to me.

Could it have been an anniversary present from Gary, a sign from him that love really is eternal? I am a skeptical person by nature, but I have no better explanation than that.

I recently wrote the following note to Gary: "Thanks for turning the water on, dear, and for setting up my swing. I'll be along to join you when it's time. And, oh yes, I'll be wearing your ring."

— Sylvia Morice —

93

Purim Power

There is no love without total faith.
~No'am Hamiddot

As much as I loved single life, watching all my friends get married, settle down, and start having babies was making me lonely. I grew up in a marriage-minded community, where we dated solely for marriage and tended to marry young. It was time for me to find the right man.

And so I prayed. I prayed that I would find my soul mate soon, and that I would be blessed with love, harmony and fulfillment.

On March 10, 2008, I prayed like I had never prayed before. It was the Jewish holiday of Purim, the most joyous day in the Jewish calendar, marked by festive celebration and partying. It's also known as an opportune time for prayer because those who pray on that day, taking time away from all the merriment, tend to see increased blessings as a result. I spent hours throughout that night pouring out my heart to G-d, asking Him for the one thing I wanted more than anything else — to find love.

Two weeks later, I met my future husband. We were married in September of that year, and have enjoyed nine blissful, meaningful and beautiful years together. While one never knows the reasons for what happens in life, I always gave a lot of the credit to my prayers on that day.

But I didn't realize just how important those prayers were until several years after our marriage.

One day, I shared my story with my students to encourage them to find some time for prayer on the holiday of Purim. They were visibly moved.

When I came home, I told my husband what I had taught that day, and I realized I had never actually shared with him how hard I had prayed that day and how soon after he had come into my life.

He looked at me and smiled.

"You don't even *know* how quickly your prayers were answered!" he told me. "Before we met, I was inundated with offers from matchmakers who wanted to set me up. I brushed everyone off, telling them I wasn't ready for marriage. I told my parents and my mentors the same thing. I needed some more time before I started dating, and they were very understanding. Then, one morning, I woke up and decided I was ready. It was inexplicable. Nothing had changed; there was no revolutionary incident. I just decided I was ready and started the ball rolling. And out of all the girls who had been suggested to me, I chose you to meet first."

Can you guess the date this "wake-up" occurred?

It was March 11, 2008.

— Devora Adams —

Love that Doesn't Die

94

Repairing Brokenness

Blessed are the hearts that can bend;
they shall never be broken.
~Albert Camus

n 2001, just a few months before 9/11, my future wife Lucy
went to New York with her mom. They saw several Broadway
shows and bought a snow globe filled with the city's top land-
marks and signs from the more popular Broadway shows. She
always enjoyed collecting snow globes from her travels.

Then five years ago, when we'd just gotten married and had
moved to a new house, Lucy left the snow globe on the garage floor
while searching for something in a trunk we had out there. She should
have put it back where it belonged, but she didn't. I saw it there the
next day. I was somewhat peeved that she'd left it there. I should've
picked it up and put it back in its proper place, but I didn't. I was
wrong for that.

That snow globe remained on the floor of the garage for several
days. Each of us saw it and had multiple opportunities to pick it up
and do the right thing, but both of us failed.

One night, I turned on the light in the garage, but the bulb blew.
It didn't faze me. I continued to do whatever it was I was doing. Several
seconds later, I accidentally kicked the snow globe over and it shattered
into seemingly a million pieces.

My heart started racing. I knew she'd be upset. I picked everything
up the best I could, discarded the glass, put the base in a box, and set

it aside. It was something special, so I vowed to get it repaired one day. In my heart and soul, I knew it could be fixed.

Less than a year later, Lucy and I were divorced. We argued, fought, and even suffered a devastating miscarriage. We were broken. She took her stuff, and I took mine. I also took the broken snow globe. I knew it could be fixed.

We didn't see each other for a year and half, although we texted from time to time. Sometimes it was nice; other times, not so much.

Before her, I was alone yet never felt lonely. When I lost her, I was a mess. I served in the U.S. Army for many years, including three yearlong tours of duty in Iraq. My body hurt. My mind hurt. My soul hurt. My heart hurt. I was broken from head to toe.

There were times I turned to extreme amounts of alcohol to escape the hurt. I only hurt more. On one occasion, I went with three of my best friends to the Georgia Dome in Atlanta to see our beloved Auburn Tigers play the Louisville Cardinals. I watched the first series of the game and then disappeared. I sat on the floor in a corner away from everyone and never watched another snap. I was so alone. I hurt so much.

Finally, in early December, I stopped in at my local VA hospital to ask for some help. I could've walked in to the mental health clinic and seen a doctor right then, but it wasn't urgent. I wasn't going to do anything stupid. I knew I could be fixed. I just didn't know how.

The first available appointment was the last slot of the day on Christmas Eve. I thought that was quite special. What a gift! I saw a doctor for my physical pain and a counselor for my mental pain. I was well on my way to repairing my own personal brokenness.

I needed to cut Lucy loose. I had to. I needed to move on. "If you love something, set it free," they say, and I did.

Besides an occasional text, we didn't communicate at all for the better part of a year… until we did.

She was going through her own hard times, trying to deal with her own brokenness. One day, she felt that she'd hit rock bottom. Her mom, sister, and daughter told her to talk to me, because "Jody was the only guy who really ever loved her."

So, she called me. I was shocked. She's not someone who likes talking on the phone. We talked for a while. She said she was in the area, so I asked her to stop by if she wanted. The funny thing is that we lived in a small town, so she was always "in the area."

We spent the rest of that day just hanging out in my back yard. I had a bountiful garden, so we picked fresh vegetables and ate them raw. I think we cooked something later that night.

From that night on, we saw each other frequently. We were just friends enjoying each other's company; we were trying to get to know each other better than before.

Inevitably, we started talking about a possible future but knew we had to fix some things. When I saw the writing on the wall that we indeed could be fixed, I sent the broken snow globe to a shop in Colorado to be repaired.

I'd hoped to get it back by Valentine's Day. I had a speech and a romantic presentation laid out for her. I wanted to use the snow globe as a symbol for our failed marriage and how we both contributed to it but also as a symbol of how something so special could be repaired. Unfortunately, the repairs on the globe took longer than expected so I didn't have it in time for Valentine's Day.

It turned out that we didn't need the snow globe to symbolize our brokenness or our repairs. We made a decision to give our relationship another go while the repairs were still taking place.

When I finally surprised her with the repaired snow globe, she was blown away. It looked brand new — better than ever. She had no idea that I had sent it off and had no idea that it could be salvaged. I did. I knew it could be fixed.

Upon further review, it wasn't perfect. The Statue of Liberty's torch had broken off, but that was okay. It wasn't perfect, but it was close enough.

We've been back together for more than two years. We've truly never been happier. We live in my family home, which sits on fifty-eight acres of land in the country near a river just two miles down the road from my mother. Her mother lives a whopping nine miles away. It's quiet, and we love it. My late father was born in our house. It's special.

We're in a good place, figuratively and literally.

Speaking of babies, we have our own. Her name is Abigail. She was born seven and a half weeks early, in the back of an ambulance on Friday the 13th. Just your typical birth, I guess. She's perfect in every way.

When something is special and you know it, you don't throw it away. You keep it. You hold onto it the best you can, and when the timing is right, you fix it.

—Jody Fuller—

Luke 16

And he began to say to them, "Today this scripture is
fulfilled in your hearing."
~Luke 4:21

A s I sat in the pew, listening to the pastor became increasingly difficult. I continued to push back scenes from that horrible day as I prayed for God to help me listen to the message.

It had only been a few weeks since the accident and, honestly, I was exhausted. I tried to focus, but flashes from that day kept pressing in, when Max, my husband of just two years, was killed in a car accident. I didn't understand why God had allowed it, but I knew He was still in control.

I continued to try to listen as I held my ten-month-old sleeping daughter, Breeanna, and prayed for peace from the terrible memories.

As I sat praying, those memories were replaced with a nudging to open my Bible to the sixteenth chapter of the book of Luke. I wasn't sure what I would find "new" in the book of Luke as I had read it many times.

Nevertheless, I decided there must be something that God wanted me to see at that moment so I flipped through the pages to the book of Luke.

I cried and laughed when in the right margin beside Luke 16, in my husband's handwriting were the words, "I Love You! Max."

— Lisa Jo Cox —

Did You Love Me?

The LORD is near to the brokenhearted
and saves the crushed in spirit.
~Psalm 34:18

 y soul ached. I stared blankly at the e-mail I had received telling me my husband had succumbed to ALS. It had been ten long months since his sudden departure a few weeks after our wedding. He couldn't put me through it, he said. He couldn't watch *me* watch *him* dwindle to nothingness.

The last time we spoke he told me that when the time came, I should go to our favorite beach and celebrate him.

The coolness of the California night hit me immediately as I pulled into the hotel. The sadness of his death coupled with the last ten grueling months weighed heavy on me. I slept deeply and woke at the crack of dawn with only one thought fueling me: "Get to the beach." I quickly dressed in my running clothes and jumped into my truck. I drove the few short miles to our favorite beach and parked, inhaling the delicious salt air and letting the gentle sound of the pounding waves soothe me.

What had bothered me during those ten months was simple: How had I married someone who could leave me so easily? Did he love me? Did I not know what love was? How could I be so blind? Why did God let this happen?

I felt used and foolish. Our courtship and wedding had been beautiful. Despite the fact that he was dying, we felt like we had it all. We truly felt God had a greater purpose for us and would see us through what was going to be a difficult time.

I remembered the laughter, the inside jokes, his love of Coca-Cola and the half empty Coke cans he would leave in the fridge. I thought about the way he would look at me and brag about me to anyone who would listen.

And then he was gone and I was alone, left to wonder what had just happened.

As I made my way from the cliff to the beach below, I was alone. The surfers were still up top staring at the waves. It was overcast and as I started to run I noticed how smooth and blank the wet sand was, the tide having just gone out. Suddenly I was sprinting, my heart beating hard and my breath catching in the cool morning air. I ran and ran until I couldn't hold back the tears any longer.

I stopped running and faced the ocean, shouting my anguish to the Lord.

"Why did this happen? I thought You had a purpose for us! Why did he leave? Did he ever love me?" I sat down in the still wet sand and sobbed.

And then I heard a voice. "Look at where you came from…"

I sniffed loudly and ran my arm under my runny nose. "Look at where I came from?" I answered angrily, "That's all I've been doing!"

The voice was still and small. "Look at where you came from…"

I sniffed again, got up, and dutifully looked at where I had come from on the beach and gasped, my hand flying to my mouth.

There was another set of shoe prints right next to mine in the wet sand. I looked around. Could I have missed seeing someone else on the beach? No, I was still alone.

Excitement rose in me, "Lord! Is it You?" I asked. "No, it can't be You. You'd be barefoot!" I exclaimed.

I bent over the prints and looked at the familiar running shoe tread of my husband's shoes in the sand next to mine, his stride longer than mine, but there! Once ALS had taken his hands, I had put those shoes on his feet so many times that I knew the tread like the back of my own hand.

I started to cry again, but this time they were tears of joy. My words were a jumble talking to him and to God.

"You did love me, you did, thank you," I sang out through the tears. "Thank you Lord for letting me know. Thank you for healing me. Thank you for this confirmation, and look Jon, your foot isn't dragging! It must feel so good for you to run! ALS can't touch you in Heaven!"

— Lily Blais —

97

Roses in Winter

Flowers grow out of dark moments.
~Corita Kent

I love to garden and have always enjoyed the beauty of roses in spring and summer. At my house, there is only room for a small rosebush, so I grow miniature roses.

The tradition began as I planted my flower garden in May 2004. My husband Gene surprised me with the gift of a miniature rosebush. He suggested we plant it in front of the house.

As each delicate bloom opened that summer, my husband seemed to delight in plucking one to give to me when he came home from work. He even began to take an interest in watering it as the summer went by. That spring of 2004, Gene had been especially happy due to having come through another cancer battle successfully that past winter. We were both delighted when the doctor said they had gotten all the cancer and there would be no need for further surgery or treatments.

The following March, our hopes would be quickly dashed when more cancer was discovered in a routine check-up. More surgery followed in April of that year, and this time the cancer spread quite quickly. As if to punctuate the losing battle that spring, my beautiful, miniature rosebush died. I was really not interested in gardening anyway. It was hard to think of anything except the cancer battle.

Gene struggled on, trying his best to be optimistic. For Mother's Day, he bought me another miniature rosebush to replace the one that had died. All through the summer, the bush remained green but without any sign of a rose. It was late in the month of October before the first rose blossoms appeared.

By Thanksgiving, Gene's cancer had spread and was out of control. He rapidly began to decline, and he could no longer work or leave his bed.

Early December remained mild, and that beautiful little bush just kept growing and blooming. On December 9, Gene entered the hospital for what would be the last time. Through those dark days, the little, blooming rosebush gave me comfort as I returned home each evening from the hospital. On the day before my beloved died, the weather turned cold and dark, and the roses began to die. How my heart grieved that next evening as I returned home from the hospital after Gene's death. The roses were dead and lifeless, too. It only seemed to drive home the thought that I now must face a life without my love.

On the day of my husband's funeral, we had the first snowstorm of the season. It was icy, and snow was coming down so hard that only the hardiest of souls could attend the funeral. The forty or so people who did attend remarked how even the graveside services in the snowstorm seemed as if God was surrounding us.

We were amazingly comfortable and warm as we gathered under the tent beside the grave. No one hurried away after the internment. Instead, we all stood around for about thirty minutes hugging and sharing stories, and all the mourners were given a rose in memory of my beloved.

Later that evening, after all the guests and friends had left my home following the funeral dinner, I stood for a time looking out the window at the snow that covered my little flower garden. Gently pressing a rose from the funeral to my cheek, the tears began to flow. The weight of grief felt as if it would swallow me up, and I knew that winter had truly arrived.

Winter in my garden and winter in my new stage of life… I was now a widow, and there would be no more roses of affection from Gene. I felt hopelessly frozen in that spot at the window, watching the last rays of daylight fade away. The last rays of a memory of life with my beloved had been laid to rest in that snow-covered grave.

As I stood praying and trying to gain control of my emotions, the outdoor security light came on suddenly. There, in my little front garden, a miniature rose peeked through the snowdrift, looking as alive as if it were June and not December. One last rose of summer that I like to think God allowed Gene to give me.

Today, entering the fifteenth year of my widowhood, that miniature rosebush still cheers me up each day when I come home all summer long. This past fall was once again a very difficult time, but amazingly, on the anniversary of my husband's death, the rosebush bloomed once again in a snowstorm.

— Christine Trollinger —

98

Love Again

There are things that we don't want to happen
but have to accept, things we don't want
to know but have to learn, and people
we can't live without but have to let go.
~Author Unknown

"I think Jay wants to ask you out," one of my co-workers told me as everyone else left the office for the day. "But he's a little nervous."

I was a little nervous too. Danny, my childhood sweetheart, father of our now twelve-year-old son, and love of twenty years, had been dead two years — long enough for me to have grieved and moved forward — but I couldn't entertain the thought of a new man.

I knew Jay. We shared a few cases together. He was a mental health social worker; I worked in child and adult protection. So occasionally our paths crossed.

Danny and I had vowed to love each other and stay true to each other forever. Our hopes and dreams had been wrapped up in each other and in our child. He would often say, "I have hope, you have faith."

And it was true. He had high hopes that anything and everything would turn out okay. In turn, my faith, in him and in God, was so strong I thought nothing could stand in our way.

When you're young, death is a safe wisp of smoke in the distance. Barely thought about. Barely a reality. You believe you're invincible and that somehow you are immune to that depth of pain and loss.

But in the middle of a cool, quiet September night, one phone call changed all of that.

"It's Danny," I heard a family friend telling my mother on another telephone extension at home. "He died in a car wreck."

He said more, but those were the last words I remember.

I should have done something. Gotten out of bed, driven to the crash scene, called his mother, run around the house clawing into my face with my fingernails, pounded my head against the wall, stabbed my heart with an ice pick... but I didn't. I just lay there in the bed in dark silence, hot tears sliding from my eyes.

What kept me going was our ten-year-old son Travis. He was the reason I got up in the morning, put on a smile when I didn't feel like smiling, thought ahead instead of behind, found a way to push through each day, week, and month. I wouldn't let death cheat him out of a healthy, vibrant, whole mother.

"It's okay," he would tell me if he caught me crying. "It'll be all right."

Work and motherhood helped ease the pain of losing Danny. In the two years following his death, little by little I rebounded. I learned to laugh again, play again, have fun and make plans.

A few guys asked me out, but I turned them down. I wanted to move on, but it just didn't feel right. It had nothing to do with grief. It had more to do with feeling like I would betray Danny if I dated someone.

When my best friend Jolene heard that Jay was interested in me, she said, "Don't be afraid to give him a chance, Tammy. Danny would want you to love again."

Her words clicked into place in my heart like the final piece of a jigsaw puzzle.

She was right. Danny would not want me to waste the prime of my life missing him and pining for him. He would want me to have someone to love and share my life with, and be a part of Travis' life too.

When Jay called, I was alone in the office. Jay sounded bright and sunny, so cheerful after a long day at work.

We made small talk about cases, he asked me how my day had

gone, and then finally he asked me if I wanted to go to dinner Friday night.

"Yes," I told him. "I'd like that." I knew Danny would want me to have a chance at love and happiness again.

As I drove home after work, I began to have second thoughts about saying yes to Jay, and for some reason the tears came. I began to talk to Danny in my heart. I needed to make a stop on the way home — a client's house. The family lived up a rocky dirt hollow and across a rickety wooden bridge. I loved driving in the countryside, so it was a nice drive. But all the way there, I had second thoughts.

What if it was a mistake? What about the vows I made to Danny? Would he really want me to date someone else? I didn't know what to do. Should I call Jay back and break the date, or keep it and take one more step into the future? I just needed a sign from Danny. I asked him to show me a sign that it was okay.

That's when it happened. As I was driving up the hollow toward my client's home. A flock of a thousand or more butterflies floated from the bushes at the side of the road and across my windshield, so thick I couldn't see through them and had to stop the car.

I felt rather than heard Danny's soft, calm voice saying, "It's okay, Tammy. Go ahead. Love again."

Somehow. Somehow he sent those butterflies to me as a sign that it was okay to move forward and open my heart to romance, companionship, and love again.

— Tammy Ruggles —

99

Closing Caption

We loved with a love that was more than love.
~Edgar Allan Poe

We sat at the kitchen table, huddled around my ancient laptop, watching snapshots of Rickey's life as they transferred over from the digital camera and appeared on the screen. The process was painstakingly slow. I waited impatiently, my nephew David by my side, just as he had been since his uncle Rickey — my husband of sixteen years — had passed away forty-eight hours earlier.

I glanced at the download status bar at the bottom of the screen: 2% remaining.

"We're almost done, kiddo," I said, yawning loudly. Though we were both exhausted in every manner imaginable, neither of us would get any rest until we had finished compiling and editing the tribute video for Rickey's visitation the following day.

David gave two thumbs-up, sighed and stretched. I removed my glasses, wiping them clean with my shirt. I rubbed my bloodshot eyes and tried to recall what day it was. I'd been so busy getting everything in order for Rickey's funeral. When was the last time I'd slept? Or eaten? Or even showered?

The laptop dinged, snapping me back to the task at hand. I opened the movie-making program and began importing over 200 photos. David watched over my shoulder, and we noticed that several of the thumbnail images had come across with a banner beneath them that said simply "digital camera" while the rest remained captionless.

With the download now complete, David and I had to sort through hundreds of images from Rickey's life, string them together like pieces of a puzzle, and set them to music. We scoured the image gallery in search of the perfect picture to use for the closing. When we reached the final page, there it was: a portrait of Rickey in his ball cap and jacket, smiling with his glass of sweet tea. The photo was taken a couple years prior at Cracker Barrel, one of Rickey's favorite restaurants, when our then five-year-old great-niece Trystan had swiped the camera and taken a handful of random pictures. As I opened my mouth to tell David we'd found the picture, he stood up suddenly and started gesturing excitedly, pointing toward that very photograph.

"Yep, that's the one we're gonna use for the finale," I said, sharing his enthusiasm, happy that he seemed to be thinking along the same lines.

"No, Aunt Mandi, look!" he said with such urgency that it almost frightened me. He reached up, his hand trembling, and pointed directly beneath the image of Rickey and his sweet tea. My mouth dropped open; I couldn't believe my eyes. I squeezed my eyes shut quickly a few times, and then opened them. Once again, I was sure I was dreaming. There, in big bold letters beneath the image, was a caption that read: "I love you."

"Oh, David, tell me you see it, too!" I said excitedly, even though he had been the one to point it out initially. I double-clicked the thumbnail so we could see the actual picture, praying silently the words weren't some computer glitch that would vanish into thin air. When the photo expanded to full size, both of us stared in awe and amazement at the bright white words "I love you" that were emblazoned across the picture.

David hugged me so tightly that I thought I might faint as tears spilled down both our cheeks. Then he smiled slightly and shook his head.

"Uncle Rickey loved you so much; he wanted to make sure you never forget. He still loves you even now. He always will," David said.

I tried to speak, but for the first time in my thirty-six years, I had no words that could express everything in my heart — the joy, sorrow, thankfulness, excitement, awe and pure exhilaration that filled me as I realized that just because our life together had come to an end didn't mean that our love ever would.

I grabbed my cell phone from my back pocket and quickly snapped a shot of the screen filled with my special message, just in case anyone wanted proof or thought I was hallucinating in my moment of mourning. I posted the picture on social media, eager to share our love story with everyone.

***

Just over two years later, I was going through an especially difficult time emotionally and missing Rickey more than I ever thought possible. I thought of my "I love you" moment and selfishly longed for another. I was at such a low point, so lost in my grief and heartache that I could barely function from one day to the next.

One of the few things that kept me going was my parents' upcoming fortieth wedding anniversary. My sister Rachel and I had decided to make a slideshow celebrating Mom and Dad. We included a variety of images, from black-and-white childhood photos of our parents to group pictures that expanded as our family grew. Rachel and I couldn't decide, however, whether to include any photos with Rickey. He had been a part of our family for close to two decades, and everyone grieved for him a great deal. We didn't want to bring down the mood of what should have been an occasion to celebrate. After much debate, we went ahead and added pictures of Rickey, feeling that not doing so would be like trying to erase a huge part of our family album.

Rachel and I gathered at my kitchen table much like David and I had done, transferring files into the movie-making program. As my favorite picture of Rickey and me filled the screen, this time it was I who pointed excitedly at the screen.

"Rachel, do you see it?" I whispered, again unable to trust my own eyes. She nodded rapidly, and then pointed at the bottom of the image where "I will always love you" was written in white type. I wept tears of joy as I snapped another photo of a message from my sweet Rickey.

I thought back over the life we had built, the love and laughter we had shared, and I finally understood how unbelievably blessed I had been.

—Mandi Smith—

100

A Song from Beyond

Music is well said to be the speech of angels.
~Thomas Carlyle

"We're really living it up here," my husband used to say with a large, satisfied smile on his face. Julie had the good fortune of being able to retire from his podiatry practice at age sixty-two, and soon after we moved into a new townhouse in southern Florida. Everything about the community was inviting, and Julie loved the warm weather. He was simply happy to sit at the large bay window by our kitchen table, surveying the cherry blossom tree. But with his kindness, positive nature, and sweet laughter, he soon drew a large group of friends to him, who joined us in the pool, at card games, and during occasional day trips.

Being alone with my husband was my favorite part of retirement. We both felt we were in the prime of our lives. We shared a new grandchild, trips to the beach, and a love of nature and music. Before we went to bed, we sometimes lifted the lid of the music box Julie had given me to hear Debussy's "Clair de Lune." The gift symbolized not only our mutual love for music, but our deep love for one another.

Neither of us realized that our wonderful life would change drastically for the worse three-and-a-half years later. The first sign of a problem was when Julie was unable to swallow a carrot he had just chewed. He succeeded in dislodging what was left of the carrot and wasn't worried at all. I urged him to see a doctor, but it took three-and-a-half months of persuading for him to see a gastroenterologist. His diagnosis — stage III esophageal cancer that had spread to his stomach — was devastating.

Having had so many in my family die — including my mother and grandmother — before I reached age eleven, I became almost obsessed with the question: "What happens after we die?" I hoped that we were allowed somehow to continue on. Believing this would help me to make sense of my early losses. It also gave me hope that Julie and I would not be parted permanently.

Years earlier, I had suggested that my husband and I make a pact. I told Julie that if he died before me, he should send me a sign that he was okay. Of course, if I predeceased him, I would provide the same courtesy, although I'm not quite sure it was a courtesy he wanted! Nonetheless, mostly to humor me, Julie agreed.

But now that the possibility of an early death was more of a reality, I only spoke about life and my husband getting well. Julie chose the traditional chemotherapy route, designed to destroy the cancer and save his life. When I read about the curative value of drinking freshly made juice several times a day, I kept my husband on a steady juicing regimen, seldom leaving his side.

Within a year and a half, Julie had improved to the point where the doctors could no longer detect cancer. I threw him a "return to wellness" party in our condominium clubhouse. Julie still looked gaunt, but he was alive. I cried through much of the celebration as friends and family surrounded us with their love and good wishes.

In time, Julie's hair, which had fallen out, began to grow in — endearingly curly this time. His body filled out, and he even felt well enough to take a cruise. One evening on the ship, my husband, who had resumed his love for eating, began to choke on his food. Once again, he was unable to swallow. Immediately after we returned home, his physicians prepared to surgically implant a feeding tube. I remained full of hope despite some nagging doubts. Julie also agreed that it didn't matter what concessions he had to make. The important thing was life itself.

When the surgeons opened my husband to insert the tube, there, in places the CT scans and MRIs had been unable to detect, hid an insidious colony of cancer. The surgeons quickly sewed up my husband. The doctors would try to make him comfortable, but there was nothing they could do to keep him alive.

For the first several weeks after his death, I was a sobbing mess. I often let out a primitive howl that sounded like a wounded animal; my hurt was so deep.

I knew I had to do something to get myself back on my feet, so I pushed myself to attend a bereavement group. The pain I felt was still needle-sharp, but at least I had begun to get my sobbing under control.

Several weeks later, upon arriving home from a meeting, I was greeted by the sound of "Clair de Lune" coming from the music box Julie had given me. I ran into the bedroom and looked at my dresser to see if I had left the lid partially open. The top of the music box — the part that released the musical mechanism when open — was shut tightly. There was no rational reason for the music to be playing!

As I remembered my pact with my husband, my eyes began to tear. My husband had indeed found a way to let me know he was okay. Tears fell as I first looked down at the music box and then up to the ceiling. "Thank you for waving hello," I said.

In case I had further doubt that Julie was sending a sign, the fire alarm in my home went off twice the following week. A friend of mine who was an electrician was unable to find a short in the wire. I could almost hear the sweet sound of my husband's laughter from the other side. I thanked him again for coming, but this time I told him he needed to return to where he belonged — to move forward on the path he had let me know really does exist.

I managed my way through my grieving after that and even did new things. This once-shy woman went on to teach English abroad and become the leader of a large bereavement group. I still miss Julie and feel sad that he died young, but I am proud of the independent life I made for myself. I'm ninety now, and when my own time comes, I hope to leave this world with grace, comforted by the knowledge that Julie and I will be reunited.

— Mary Bader Schwager —

101

Messages in His Books

A great soul serves everyone all the time. A great soul
never dies. It brings us together again and again.
~Maya Angelou

My husband bought books like some women buy shoes. Long before I knew him, he had amassed a vast library of books — sales, marketing, consulting, leadership, biography, sports, religion, spirituality. And after we were married, he continued to buy them. Following seminars or outings at the mall, he'd come home with another shopping bag full of books. He'd cram the new books into the already packed ceiling-high shelves in his office, often wedging the books sideways above the upright ones.

"Even if you get just one idea from a whole book," he said, "it's worth it."

In one of those famous compromises of marriage, I learned to live with the growing collection of books, keeping my sniping comments down ("When will you ever read them all?") and occasionally dusting or straightening them.

After his passing, when I could finally stand to enter his office, I yielded to an insistent need to weed, straighten, and streamline everything. So, I tackled his bookshelves.

As I did, I discovered books behind books behind books and titles I'd never even seen in our many years together. To my surprise, a random title in marketing or sales or spirituality caught my eye, and then another and another. Instead of putting them in the box to give away, I started piling them up in a corner to read or at least skim.

I collected quite a pile, and one lunchtime I picked one to read. Opening it, I saw what I'd forgotten — his habit of marking up the pages. And I felt again my irritation at the excess. Not the occasional bracket or asterisk, but strings of exclamation points, stars, curlicues, arrows, and marginal notes: "Important!" "Take note!" He underlined entire paragraphs twice, three times, even four times, and with colored markers. I could hardly read the printed page through the notes.

The ink markings weren't enough. He also stuck Post-its on page after page. Often, there were so many Post-its that the book bulked to twice its thickness. He also dog-eared pages, a taboo for many of us.

In my own books, I cherished the unsullied page. Once in a while, I might draw a modest, light bracket at an especially gorgeous, evocative, or memorable phrase or sentence. Or I gently placed a Post-it next to a particularly meaningful passage. Whenever I saw a turned-down corner anywhere, even in a dentist office magazine, I unbent it.

But here, in my husband's books that went back twenty, thirty, sometimes forty years, I stared at the uncontrolled pen markings, some faded almost beyond legibility; the multiple Post-its straining the bindings; the turned-down corners about to flake with age. I sighed with annoyance at what I felt was desecration of the books.

Despite my disapproval, though, they pulled me in. I read one musty, marked-up book after another. And I saw something.

All those markings and wads of Post-its were his way of teaching himself. In his career, he was a superb seminar leader, trainer, teacher, and consultant for companies and individuals. That's how I'd met him. A friend whose business he'd miraculously gotten off the ground suggested I contact him. Our first meeting was a "conference" for his help with my writing and editing business.

Through the books and their ever-proliferating markings, I could trace his thinking, his development, his growth, his voracious zest for learning, his hunger for knowing and always improving. Only now, after his passing, did I understand him.

I kept reading, or rather mining, those books, his writing making me uncomfortable. He put dates down, too — of his readings, re-readings, and re-rereadings. To reinforce and cement the thoughts, at the bottoms of pages or ends of chapters, he summarized what he was reading. "I am worthy of it all." "I attract what I need." "Concentrate on what you want."

These messages leapt out at me. Many years old but ever new, they were messages I needed. To my shock, next to the dates, some of the Post-its had my name on them. He was thinking of me, my worries, my concerns, my needs, and wanted to give me the comfort and help he'd gotten from the books.

I wept.

Through those old books, the ceaseless markings, the blizzards of Post-its, and my name on so many, I feel my husband's presence. He is here. In his books, he continues to support me, guide me, encourage me, and love me.

— Noelle Sterne —

We are pleased to introduce you to the writers whose stories were compiled from our past books to create this new collection. These bios were the ones that ran when the stories were originally published. They were current as of the publication dates of those books.

Meet Our Contributors

Devora Adams is a writer and life coach who lives in New Jersey with her husband and four daughters. She is the author of *Amazing Women: Jewish Voices of Inspiration*, published by Menucha Publishers, as well as a proud contributor to the *Chicken Soup for the Soul* series. E-mail her at the_write_direction@yahoo.com.

Kristina J. Adams has bachelor's and master's degrees in Elementary Education and minored in English as a Second Language. Teaching sixth grade social studies in Middlebury, IN, she enjoys relating stories of growing up overseas when they connect to curriculum. She and her husband Ryan have two children, Mackenzie and Carter.

Elizabeth Atwater is a small town Southern gal whose love of reading as a young child turned into a love of writing at an early age. She is currently seeking an agent to help her get her books published. She can be contacted at eatwater@windstream.net.

Ardy Barclay received her Bachelor of Arts degree from the University of Western Ontario. She started her teaching career in 1970, specializing in Special Education. Retired in 2007, Ardy enjoys winters in Florida as well as fishing, reading, and spending time with her granddaughters.

Nancy Beaufait has lived in Michigan all her life, and loves her mitten state. She enjoys reading, knitting, and has always enjoyed writing. Nancy is looking forward to retiring soon from her nursing profession and living in their little cottage on the lake.

Richard Berg is an author, artist, and advocate. He is the Host-Producer for *For the Love of Words* TV series, Host of Brockton Library poetry series, Music Coordinator of Poetry and the Art of Words, performs original work as Edgar Allen Poe. His poetry and photography appears in publications and galleries. Rich is an advocate for Brain Injury Association and the Safe Roads Alliance in Massachusetts.

Rob Berry is a graduate of California State University, Bakersfield. He lives in Bakersfield with his wife and best friend, Amy.

Paula Bicknell began her writing career as a civilian contracted to write for the U.S. Air Force's newspaper and magazines. Later, she wrote for a daily California newspaper. Paula has seven children and enjoys farming with her family in Northern California. Visit her weekly blog at psbicknell.com.

Lily Blais works in risk analysis but writing is her passion. Her first novel is complete and she is currently submitting it to literary agencies. Time with family and friends means the world to her and she has just welcomed into the world her first grandchild.

S.L. Blake was born and raised in Northern California and now lives wherever the Army sends her active duty husband. She loves giraffes, chocolate, and reading. She spends her time writing novels and raising her two biggest fans.

Lil Blosfield is the Chief Financial Officer for Child and Adolescent Behavioral Health in Canton, OH. She loves writing and tries to capture her own photo album in words of many life experiences. Lil enjoys music and laughter or, in other words, karaoke! She adores time spent with friends and family. E-mail her at LBlosfield40@msn.com.

Michele Boom turned in her teacher chalkboard to be an at-home mom. While juggling two toddlers and a traveling husband, she began to write. Her work appears in regional magazines across the U.S. and Canada. She is also a contributor to *Chicken Soup for the Soul: Parenthood*. Visit her at mammatalk.blogspot.com.

Jill Burns lives in the mountains of West Virginia with her wonderful family. She's a retired piano teacher and performer. She enjoys writing, music, gardening, nature, and spending time with her grandchildren.

Eva Carter has a background in finance. She is a freelance photographer and a frequent contributor to the *Chicken Soup for the Soul* series. She and her husband live in Dallas, TX with their cat, Ollie.

Jennifer Chauhan is the Executive Director of Project Write Now (www.projectwritenow.org), an organization dedicated to fostering a love of writing in young people. She has an M.A. degree in English Education from Teacher's College, Columbia University. She lives on the Jersey Shore with her three children.

Jacqueline Chovan is a mother of three and a military wife currently residing in Germany and drawing inspiration for her first novel from the fairytale-like surroundings. This is the second time she has been published in the *Chicken Soup for the Soul* series. Aside from writing, she enjoys adventures and traveling with her family.

Jane Clark is an eighty-eight-year-old life coach. She enjoys reading, travel, yoga, meditation, ballet and socializing with her many friends and family members.

Joan Clayton retired in 1992 after thirty-one years as a teacher. She then began her second career as an inspirational author. Joan has been published in over 300 articles and has six books to her credit. She also served as the long-time Religion Columnist for the *Portales News-Tribune*, Portales, NM.

Courtney Conover is a mother, writer and certified yoga teacher who always believes in miracles. She and her husband, a former NFL offensive lineman, reside in Michigan with their two young children, and they always root for the Detroit Lions. Learn more at courtneyconover. com, Facebook, Instagram, and YouTube.

Lisa Jo Cox is the widowed mom of an amazing teenage daughter, Breeanna. She is working on a degree in Information Technology. She works for a preschool in Spottsville, KY. Lisa enjoys reading, writing, crocheting and would love to learn to knit. Please e-mail her Breezmom37@yahoo.com.

Betty Johnson Dalrymple is a freelance writer of inspirational devotions and stories. Her work has been published in *The Upper Room*, *Chicken Soup for the Soul* books, *Guideposts* books, and Jim Bell compilations. She loves spending time with her large family, golfing with friends, and knitting afghans for her ten grandchildren.

Born in Stockton, CA, **Margaret Markov Damon** began her acting career in 1969 and quickly moved from bit parts to starring roles in numerous films. She also did guest spots in many TV shows. Maggie is married to film producer Mark Damon. They have two adult children and live in Los Angeles.

Born in Chicago, **Mark Damon** began his Hollywood career as an actor, starring in dozens of films. When he moved on to producing, he revolutionized the way the industry funded film production costs, through his company Producer Sales Organization (PSO). Mark and Maggie Damon have two children and live in Los Angeles.

Katie Denisar hails from Galesburg, IL where she taught first grade for eight years before marrying her husband Bradley and joining the Army family. They have one daughter Laura, and since they married they have lived in the D.C. area, Anchorage, AK and currently reside in Honolulu, HI.

Frieda Dixon received her religious education degree from New Orleans Baptist Theological Seminary. She and her husband own an Atlanta-area aerospace engineering company. Frieda likes to swim and volunteer at her church. She is writing her memoir, of which this story is a part. E-mail her at friedas@bellsouth.net.

Hailing from Cleveland, OH, and a graduate of Syracuse University, **Joan Donnelly-Emery** is a freelance writer and avid gardener. She and her husband, Alan, just celebrated their twenty-fifth anniversary by viewing the Northern lights in Alta, Norway. They're enjoying life in Franklin, TN along with their Terrier, Dottie, and their pet birds.

Sarafina Drake is a determined writer and mother who refuses to cram her star-shaped spangly self into a beige round hole. She believes there are no limits to what you can do and the only boundaries to success that exist are the ones you create in your own mind. E-mail her at sarafinadrake@gmail.com.

Christina Dymock earned her Bachelor of Science Degree in

Mass Communications from the University of Utah. She has worked as an editor and taught Marketing at the local community college. She is currently learning to cross country ski.

Linda Eiffert is a retired mother of three and has two grandchildren. In her spare time she enjoys gardening, all types of crafts, including rehabbing old and used furniture for interior decorating.

Terri Elders, LCSW, lives near Colville, WA. Her stories have appeared in many anthologies, including a dozen *Chicken Soup for the Soul* books. She is a public member of the Washington State Medical Quality Assurance Commission. In 2006, she received the UCLA Alumni Association Community Service Award. She blogs at atouchoftarragon.blogspot.com.

Tanya Estes is a writer, blogger, photographer and mother. She graduated from The University of Texas with a Bachelor of Fine Arts in Art History and a Master of Science in Library and Information Science. After many years as a librarian, she decided to write in the hopes of one day leaving a literary legacy for her son.

Susan Farr Fahncke has been published in over seventy books and is the author of *Angel's Legacy: How Cancer Changed a Princess into an Angel*. Her volunteer group, Angels2TheHeart, supports people battling cancer and other serious illnesses. Learn more or take an online writing workshop at 2TheHeart.com.

Valorie Fenton, aka Valorie J. Wells, Ph.D., is a clinical hypnotherapist in Kansas City. She and her husband Kenny enjoy traveling for his fine art landscape photography hobby. Valorie is proud of their eighty-year-old bungalow and cottage gardens, which are a certified urban wildlife habitat on the line between Kansas and Missouri.

Jill L. Ferguson is an award-winning writer and the author of thirteen books. She is the founder of Women's Wellness Weekends and Creating the Freelance Career. She is sad to report that Nacho, her beloved Heeler, died in August 2020, but he has since sent her Coconut, another Red Heeler, to live with and love.

Erin E. Forson has been an educator, social worker and librarian. She loves to read, write, spend time exploring the world with her family, and learn! She is currently working on an MBA so she can explore more opportunities in her world.

Jody Fuller is a comedian, speaker, writer and soldier with three combat tours in Iraq. He is also a lifetime stutterer. In 2018, *Alabama* magazine named Jody one of Alabama's top 40 men and women over 40 whose lives and careers are characterized by great levels of giving and achievement.

Heidi Gaul lives in Oregon's Willamette Valley with her husband and four-legged family. She loves travel, be it around the block or the globe. Active in Oregon Christian Writers, she is currently writing her fourth novel. Contact her through her website at www.HeidiGaul.com.

Dalia Gesser entertained audiences for twenty years with her delightfully original one-woman mime clown and mask theater shows. Since 2000 she has been bringing her theatre arts programs to children and adults. She lives north of Kingston, Ontario in beautiful lake country and can be reached at daliag@kingston.net.

Angelene Gorman was an elementary teacher for sixteen years and now owns a school photography company. She loves anything to do with the ocean, including boating, diving, fishing and collecting seashells.

Rebecca Gurnsey holds an A.A.S. degree in Business Technology and has worked many years in business, as well as teaching. She is now a full-time author and speaker. Rebecca has published five faith-based novels. Rebecca enjoys her children and grandchildren, as well as camping, traveling, and gardening. She resides in Texas.

Kenneth Heard is the Northeast Arkansas bureau reporter for the *Arkansas Democrat-Gazette*. He has also taught English and journalism at two universities, been a television reporter, a golf course greenskeeper, a cable television salesman, a repo man and a romantic dreamer.

Paula Perkins Hoffman is currently working on her bachelor's degree in secondary language arts education at Anderson University. She has been an Army wife for almost eight months now, but she feels like it's been longer. She hopes to one day pursue a master's degree in educational psychology.

Cindy Hudson is the author of *Book by Book: The Complete Guide* *to Creating Mother-Daughter Book Clubs*. She lives in Portland, OR with her husband and two daughters and enjoys writing about things that inspire her: family life, her community, reading, and family literacy. Learn more at CindyHudson.com.

Sharilynn Hunt is a retired medical social worker and founder of New Creation Realities Ministry, a teaching and prayer ministry. Her writings include a 31-day devotional, *Grace Overcomes Today*, and other inspirational nonfiction stories published in various compilations. Her four grandchildren fill her life with joy!

Marilyn June Janson received her Master of Science degree, cum laude, from Long Island University in 1980. She is the author of *Recipe for Rage*, a suspense novel, and two chapter books: *The Super Cool Kids Story Collection* and *Tommy Jenkins: First Teleported Kid*. Now, she is writing a YA novel. E-mail her at janlitserv@cox.net.

Bonita Jewel moved to India when she was sixteen and lived there for twelve years. After returning to California with her husband and three children, she earned an MFA in creative writing. A freelance writer and editor, Bonita blogs irregularly, drinks homemade chai, and loves it when rain graces the arid valley she calls home.

Kara Johnson is a freelance writer living in Boise, ID, with her husband Jim, and dog, Barkley. She is a mentor for high school and college girls, and enjoys reading, traveling, and all sorts of outdoor adventures.

Susan Maddy Jones is a former computer-science nerd, rewired for creativity and spending time in nature, not cubicles. She blogs about navigating life's ups and downs at www.SwimmingInTheMud. wordpress.com and about her awesome camping, hiking, and DIY adventures at www.TeardropAdventures.com. E-mail her at susan. jones326@gmail.com.

Sylvia J. King is a sixty-nine-year-old author enjoying retirement. Writing has been a lifelong love. She keeps herself busy by being the learning coach for five online, home-schooled children through the K12 program.

Vicki Kitchner is a retired educator who taught Exceptional Student Education for thirty years. She divides her time between North Carolina and Florida. She and her husband love to travel, hike, garden, and entertain friends and family.

Alice Klies is a past contributor to *Chicken Soup for the Soul: Just Us Girls*. She is a member of Word Weavers International. She is published in *Angels On Earth*, *The Wordsmith Journal*, and four anthologies: *God Still Meets Needs; Grandmother, Mother and Me; Grandfather, Father and Me* and *Friends of Inspire Faith*.

Elizabeth Stark Kline earned her B.A. degree with honors in English and history from Vanderbilt University in 1977. A medical biller by day, she continues to write fiction and enjoys metal detecting, crafting, and keeping up with her two kids, four cats and a dog named Linus.

April Knight is a frequent contibutor to *Chicken Soup for the Soul* books. She is also the author of several books about Native Americans, including *Crying Wind* and *My Searching Heart* and others written under her tribal name, Crying Wind.

Kathleen Kohler is a writer and speaker from the Pacific Northwest. Her articles, rooted in personal experience, appear in books and internationally in magazines. She and her husband have three children and seven grandchildren. She enjoys bird watching, gardening, traveling, painting, and of course dancing. Learn more at www.kathleenkohler.com.

Helen Krasner has a degree in psychology from the University of Edinburgh. Over the years she has had a number of different careers including being an occupational psychologist, helicopter instructor, and freelance writer. She lives in Derbyshire, in the middle of England, with her partner David and their five cats.

M.D. Krider is a stay-at-home mom of two girls. She likes to express her creativity through writing, watercolors, drawing, and jewelry making. Melissa is currently working on her first novel.

Cathi LaMarche is the author of the novel *While the Daffodils Danced* and has contributed to numerous anthologies. As a composition teacher, author, and writing coach, she spends most of her day reveling in the written word. She resides in Missouri with her husband, two children, and three dogs.

Janeen Lewis is a freelance writer living in central Kentucky with her husband and two children. She has previously been published in several newspapers, magazines and three *Chicken Soup for the Soul* anthologies. Please e-mail her at jlewis0402@netzero.net.

Queen Lori, aka Dancing Grammie, is ninety-one, a mother of seven, grandmother of twenty-two, and two-time contributor to the *Chicken Soup for the Soul* series. She began writing after being crowned queen of the 2016 Erma Bombeck Writers Workshop. Lori leads and tap dances with the Prime Life Follies. Follow her at DancingGrammie.com.

Jesse Malarsie is a stay-at-home mom with three young children and works as a child photographer in the Great Salt Lake City area. She also helps manage her husband's business endeavors and is a fan of traveling. Jesse likes to read, craft, be outdoors and is an avid NHL and college football fan.

Freelance writer **Chantal Meijer** lives in Terrace, BC with her husband Rick. They have four children and four grandchildren. Chantal's work has been widely published in magazines, newspapers and anthologies — including four *Chicken Soup for the Soul* editions. She is currently working on a memoir. E-mail her at meijer@telus.net.

Jamie Miles, a junior at Syracuse University, majors in magazine journalism in the S.I. Newhouse School of Public Communications. In the spring semester of 2009, Jamie studied abroad in Madrid, Spain and traveled throughout Europe. Jamie enjoys playing racquetball, spending time with her close friends and family, and going to the movies!

Patricia Miller earned a B.A. degree in Social Sciences from UWO, and a Recreation diploma from Centennial College, before studying Creative Writing at Durham College. Patricia is a Coordinator and mom who enjoys snowboarding. In 2012, she wrote her first novel, *The Mausoleum Road Affair*. E-mail her at patriciamillerwriting@gmail.com.

Bruce Mills is a civil engineer living in Boise, ID. Born in Michigan, he has also lived in Colorado, Utah, Washington, Idaho, and Ireland. Seeing new places is an obvious passion, along with howling out tunes with his guitar, hiking and spending time with family. E-mail Bruce at brucegmills@gmail.com.

Sylvia Morice writes fiction, creative nonfiction, essays and poetry. Her work has been published in Canadian literary journals and magazines and she has self-published several eBooks. Sylvia is retired and lives in Atlantic Canada.

Lava Mueller is grateful to be a frequent contributor to the *Chicken Soup for the Soul* series. She lives in Vermont with her very cute husband Andy and their two children, Sophie and Max. Lava is also a fiction writer and is working on a novel for young adults. E-mail her at lavamueller@yahoo.com.

Lynne Nichols is a retired elementary and middle school teacher. She divides her time between Taos, NM and Naples, FL. She enjoys reading, traveling, swimming, and spending time with her family and friends.

Emily Oman is currently working toward her Bachelor of Arts degree in English from Northeastern University in Boston. In addition to maintaining a 3.8 grade point average, she is also a stay-at-home mom to a twenty-month-old daughter and wife to her husband of seven years. She enjoys reading, drawing, hiking, and spending time outside.

Michelle Paris is a Maryland writer who is enjoying chapter two with her fiancé Kevin and their two cats. Her first full-length novel, *New Normal*, is loosely based on her own life as a young widow.

Jami Perona received her degree in Education from Pittsburg State University. She is currently an elementary teacher. Jami enjoys spending time outside with her family. She plans to keep writing and would like to have a book published. Check out her blog at jamidawnperona. blogspot.com.

Lori Chidori Phillips resides with her beloved mate of thirty-two years in Southern California where they enjoy spending time with their grown children and learning new things every day. She invites readers to correspond with her at hope037@hotmail.com.

LeDayne McLeese Polaski is the Program Coordinator of the Baptist Peace Fellowship of North America which works around the world for peace rooted in justice. She lives in Charlotte, NC, with her husband Tom and daughter Kate. E-mail her at ledayne@bpfna.org.

Marsha Porter has co-authored a movie guide and published numerous articles. She got her start in writing when the 500-word essay was the preferred punishment at her Catholic school.

Sandy A. Reid lives and teaches high school English in St. Louis, MO. Her greatest joy in life is her family, both nuclear and extended.

Tammy Ruggles is a freelance writer, artist, and filmmaker who lives in Kentucky. She is also a mother, grandmother, and retired social worker. Her first book, *Peace*, was published in 2005. Her screenplay, *The Legend of Hayswood Hospital*, was turned into a low-budget horror feature in 2010.

Karen Sargent is the author of *Waiting for Butterflies*, which was named the 2017 IAN Book of the Year and received the Foreword Reviews Gold for Christian fiction. After teaching high school and college English for twenty-five years, she retired to focus on writing. She is a frequent presenter at writers' workshops and conferences.

Mary Bader Schwager has worn many hats throughout her long life, including that of award-winning painter, art teacher, respiratory therapist, craftswoman, docent, and bereavement group leader. At age ninety, she is still designing necklaces. She thanks her daughter, Nancy K. S. Hochman, for her help with this essay.

Timothy A. Setterlund is an attorney practicing in Boca Raton, Fl. He welcomes the relief of literature from the constipated legalese he works with daily. He intends to continue, and write fiction as well. E-mail him at taslaw1@aol.com.

Deborah Shouse is a writer, speaker, editor and creativity catalyst. Her writing has appeared in *The Washington Post*, *The Christian Science Monitor*, *Reader's Digest*, *Newsweek*, *Woman's Day* and *Family Circle*. She wrote *Love in the Land of Dementia: Finding Hope in the Caregiver's Journey*. Read more at www.deborahshousewrites.wordpress.com.

Jen P. Simmons is a wife and a new mom who works full-time for an outdoor clothing company. Jen enjoys a good cuppa, being with family, writing short stories, gardening, the great outdoors, and triathlons. She hopes to write content that inspire others to embrace this life motto: live well, laugh often, and love much.

Connie Cameron Smith is an international speaker and has authored three books, eight stories in the *Chicken Soup for the Soul* series, and hundred of articles. She enjoys prison ministry and missionary work in Africa. Widowed in 2015, she is now married to Pastor Rocky, and happily learning to "love each other unconditionally." Learn more at www.conniecameron.com or e-mail her at conniecameron@sbcglobal.net.

Mandi Smith began writing at age six and has yet to put down her pen. She was married for sixteen years before being widowed in 2012. She has found love again and shares a home in North Texas with her boyfriend Lonnie, dogs Honeybun and Twinkie, and Bruce the cat. She works in telecommunications but dreams of becoming a writer.

Irene Spencer is a New York Times best-selling author of *Shattered Dreams: My Life as a Polygamist's Wife*. She was the second of ten wives, mother of fourteen of her late husband's fifty-eight children. To learn more and or to order a copy of her books visit www.IreneSpencerBooks.com.

Judee Stapp is a speaker for women's events and retreats and has written for the *Chicken Soup for the Soul* series and other publications. Through speaking and writing, her dream is to inspire people to recognize miracles in their own lives. She is a wife, mother, and grandmother. E-mail her at judeestapp@roadrunner.com or visit www.judeestapp.com.

Diane Stark is a wife, mother, and freelance writer. She is a frequent contributor to the *Chicken Soup for the Soul* series. She loves to write about the important things in life: her family and her faith. E-mail her at Dianestark19@yahoo.com.

Noelle Sterne (Ph.D.) has published over 600 essays, writing craft and spiritual articles, fiction, and poems. Her book, *Challenges in Writing Your Dissertation*, grew from her academic editing and coaching practice. Her book *Trust Your Life* helps readers reach lifelong dreams. Fulfilling her own, she is completing her third novel.

Mike Strand continued working for Andersen Windows another twenty-four years after his accident before retiring to fulfill his dream of acquiring a B.A. degree in English Literature, which he earned in 2014. He is a writer and a wedding officiant. He and his wife Linda live in Oakdale, MN.

Lynn Sunday is a writer and animal advocate who lives near San Francisco with her senior rescue dog. Twelve of Lynn's stories appear in eleven *Chicken Soup for the Soul* books and numerous other publications. E-mail her at sunday11@aol.com.

Ashley Thaba lives in Botswana, Africa. Her desire to be obedient to whatever God calls her to do has taken her on a journey of adventures across the world. She wrote an amazing book about the near-death experience of her son and his miraculous recovery. If you would like to read her book, e-mail her at ashleythaba@gmail.com.

Mark J. Thieman and his wife Theresa have been married for thirty-two years and have two grown children. Mark has worked as a computer automation engineer for thirty-six years. Mark is considering a second career in church ministry.

Jayne Thurber-Smith is an international award-winning freelance writer for various outlets including *Faith & Friends* magazine, *Sports Spectrum* and writersweekly.com. She loves tennis, volleyball and swimming, and leading her grandchildren on pony rides.

Christine Trollinger likes potlucks and bingo. Christine is a retired insurance agent who enjoys writing and reading, spending time with her children and grandchildren, and now great grandchildren. She has written many stories for the *Chicken Soup for the Soul* series over the last twenty years.

Since 1990, **Joseph Walker** has written a weekly newspaper column called "ValueSpeak." Some of his columns were published in three other *Chicken Soup for the Soul* books. His books include *Look What Love Has Done* and *Christmas on Mill Street*. Joseph and his wife, Anita, have five children and seven grandchildren.

Mary T. Whipple is a fantasy novelist and folklore enthusiast. Her debut novel, *A Venom Vice*, was released on July 1, 2017. When not reading or writing, Ms. Whipple can often be found playing video games with her husband while their puppy, kitten, and bearded dragon look on dolefully and beg for treats and tummy scratches.

Lettie Kirkpatrick Whisman is still enjoying marriage and texting Jim while also writing and speaking. Her newest book, *God's Extravagant Grace for Extraordinary Grief: Devotions from the Refiner's Fire*, offers encouragement to both those who are caregivers and those dealing with loss. E-mail her at Lettiejk@gmail.com.

Jennifer Wiche received several certificates and a degree from the University of the Fraser Valley from 2005 to 2010. Although she can no longer become a teacher, her life will be fulfilled with the love of her daughter Serenity and her husband Ray.

D.B. Zane is a teacher, writer and mother of three, and has been married for nearly thirty years. In addition to reading and writing, she enjoys knitting.

Phyllis W. Zeno has had stories in seven *Chicken Soup for the Soul* books. She was the founding editor of *AAA Going Places* for twenty years and editor/publisher of *Beach Talk Magazine* until that fateful day when she met Harvey Meltzer on Match.com. Both eighty-three years old, they were married August 22, 2009. They are still madly in love.

Meet Amy Newmark

Amy Newmark is the bestselling author, editor-in-chief, and publisher of the *Chicken Soup for the Soul* book series. Since 2008, she has published 191 new books, most of them national bestsellers in the U.S. and Canada, more than doubling the number of Chicken Soup for the Soul titles in print today. She is also the author of *Simply Happy*, a crash course in Chicken Soup for the Soul advice and wisdom that is filled with easy-to-implement, practical tips for enjoying a better life.

Amy is credited with revitalizing the Chicken Soup for the Soul brand, which has been a publishing industry phenomenon since the first book came out in 1993. By compiling inspirational and aspirational true stories curated from ordinary people who have had extraordinary experiences, Amy has kept the thirty-year-old Chicken Soup for the Soul brand fresh and relevant.

Amy graduated *magna cum laude* from Harvard University where she majored in Portuguese and minored in French. She then embarked on a three-decade career as a Wall Street analyst, a hedge fund manager, and a corporate executive in the technology field. She is a Chartered Financial Analyst.

Her return to literary pursuits was inevitable, as her honors thesis in college involved traveling throughout Brazil's impoverished northeast region, collecting stories from regular people. She is delighted to have come full circle in her writing career — from collecting stories "from the people" in Brazil as a twenty-year-old to, three decades later, collecting stories "from the people" for Chicken Soup for the Soul.

When Amy and her husband Bill, the CEO of Chicken Soup for the Soul, are not working, they are visiting their four grown children and their spouses, and their five grandchildren.

Follow Amy on Twitter @amynewmark. Listen to her free podcast — Chicken Soup for the Soul with Amy Newmark — on Apple, Google, or by using your favorite podcast app on your phone.

Thank You

We owe huge thanks to all our contributors and fans. Here at Chicken Soup for the Soul we want to thank our editor Kristiana Pastir for reviewing our library of previously published stories and presenting us with hundreds of love stories to choose from for this new collection. Publisher and Editor-in-Chief Amy Newmark made the final selection of the 101 that are included here, all personal favorites, and Associate Publisher D'ette Corona created the manuscript. None of these stories appeared in previous Chicken Soup for the Soul books about love, dating, or romance. They were compiled from our books on other topics.

The whole publishing team deserves a hand, including Senior Editor Barbara LoMonaco, Vice President of Marketing Maureen Peltier, Vice President of Production Victor Cataldo, and our graphic designer Daniel Zaccari, who turned our manuscript into this beautiful, entertaining book.

Sharing Happiness, Inspiration, and Hope

Real people sharing real stories, every day, all over the world. In 2007, *USA Today* named *Chicken Soup for the Soul* one of the five most memorable books in the last quarter-century. With over 110 million books sold to date in the U.S. and Canada alone, more than 300 titles in print, and translations into nearly fifty languages, "chicken soup for the soul®" is one of the world's best-known phrases.

Today, thirty years after we first began sharing happiness, inspiration and hope through our books, we continue to delight our readers with new titles, but have also evolved beyond the bookshelves with super premium pet food, television shows, a podcast, licensed products, and free movies and TV shows on our Crackle, Redbox, Popcornflix and Chicken Soup for the Soul streaming apps. We are busy "changing your life one story at a time®." Thanks for reading!

Share with Us

We all have had Chicken Soup for the Soul moments in our lives. If you would like to share your story or poem with millions of people around the world, go to chickensoup. com and click on Submit Your Story. You may be able to help another reader and become a published author at the same time. Some of our past contributors have launched writing and speaking careers from the publication of their stories in our books!

We only accept story submissions via our website. They are no longer accepted via mail or fax. Visit our website, www.chickensoup. com, and click on Submit Your Story for our writing guidelines and a list of topics we are working on.

To contact us regarding other matters, please send us an e-mail through webmaster@chickensoupforthesoul.com, or write us at:

Chicken Soup for the Soul
P.O. Box 700
Cos Cob, CT 06807-0700

One more note from your friends at Chicken Soup for the Soul: Occasionally, we receive an unsolicited book manuscript from one of our readers, and we would like to respectfully inform you that we do not accept unsolicited manuscripts, and we must discard the ones that appear.

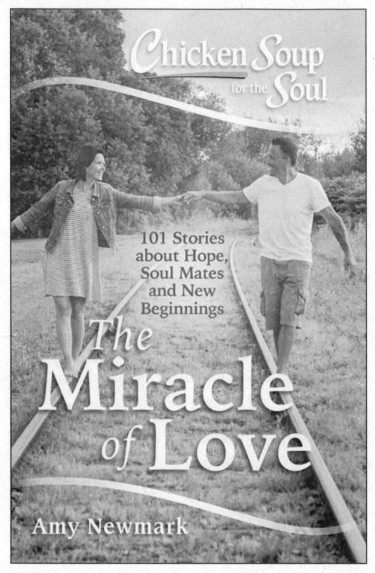

Chicken Soup for the Soul

101 Stories about Hope, Soul Mates and New Beginnings

The Miracle of Love

Amy Newmark

Paperback: 978-1-61159-980-0
eBook: 978-1-61159-280-1

More love and laughter

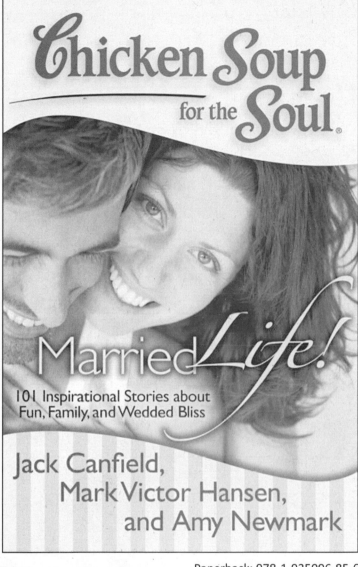

Chicken Soup for the Soul®

Married *Life!*

101 Inspirational Stories about
Fun, Family, and Wedded Bliss

Jack Canfield,
Mark Victor Hansen,
and Amy Newmark

Paperback: 978-1-935096-85-6
eBook: 978-1-61159-204-7

Fun and family

Changing lives one story at a time®
www.chickensoup.com